Life-Span Developmental Psychology: Introduction to Research Methods

Life-Span Developmental Psychology: Introduction to Research Methods

Paul B. Baltes

The Pennsylvania State University

Hayne W. Reese

West Virginia University

John R. Nesselroade

The Pennsylvania State University

LAWRENCE ERLBAUM ASSOCIATES, PUBLISHERS

Hillsdale, New Jersey

Hove and London

Lawrence Erlbaum Associates, Inc., Publishers
365 Broadway
Hillsdale, New Jersey 07642

Library of Congress Cataloging in Publication Data

Baltes, Paul B.
      Life-span developmental psychology.

      (Life-span human development series)
      Bibliography: p. 249
      Includes index.
      1. Developmental psychology.   2. Psychological research.   I. Reese,
Hayne Waring, 1931–   joint author.   II. Nesselroade, John R., joint
author.   III. Title.
BF713.B34   155   77-2342

This volume was originally published in 1977.

Isbn 0–8058–0235–5
Printed in the United States of America
10 9 8 7 6 5 4 3 2

Preface

This book is both more and less than a source of facts and information—a cookbook— about research design in developmental psychology and human development. More, because we go beyond a presentation of simple design methodology; we offer our version of what it means to do research with a developmental orientation, and we illustrate the need for a strong convergence between theory and methodology. Less, in part because the state of knowledge in developmental research design is incomplete. The eye and mind of a critical and creative reader will make this book work, though, since we believe we've identified the key questions and strategies of developmental researchers.

This text is introductory, although its content is usually not presented to lower-division students. At most institutions, the student audience for this book will comprise juniors, seniors, and beginning graduate students in the behavioral and social sciences (psychology, sociology, child development, human development, family studies, and so on). Occasionally, with appropriately selected audiences, the text may be used at the sophomore level. This is particularly true if the text is supplemented with other introductory materials.

The book is organized into five parts, each beginning with an overview of its contents. The initial two parts provide a general introduction, first of the developmental orientation in psychology (Part One), then of general issues in theory construction and research design (Part Two). Parts Three through Five reach the heart of the matter by presenting key methodological issues in developmental psychology. Part Three delineates the scope of developmental psychology in terms of research questions and research paradigms. Part Four deals with descriptive research strategies aimed at the identification of developmental change. Finally, Part Five presents methodology aimed at explaining developmental change; that is, it deals with the search for the origins and processes of change.

In this book, we focus on life-span developmental psychology, for we are committed to advancing that particular emphasis and therefore prefer to think and write in life-span terms. In fact, once in a while we allow ourselves to believe that the life-span developmental view can be considered at least the umbrella for any other more specialized developmental approach and perhaps even the only appropriate developmental orientation.

In our judgment, the focus on life-span developmental psychology has both costs and benefits. The theoretical and methodological benefits derive from the fact that a life-span approach is apt to dramatize key methodological issues of developmental research in an extreme and exemplary fashion—an effective feature from a didactic point of view. The major theoretical cost of a life-span orientation is its current strong focus on age development. We are, of course, aware that many developmentalists argue that the goal of developmental research should be the identification of key behavior-change processes rather than age changes and that they see the age variable as transient and therefore unproductive for theory construction. We will understand, therefore, if some readers wonder why much of our discussion centers around age development rather than behavior-change processes. We hope that such readers will be flexible enough to transfer our methodological perspectives to their own research questions.

This book—we still don't really know why—was a very difficult one for us to produce. If it were not for our sympathetic and supportive spouses (Margret Baltes, Nancy Reese, and Carolyn Nesselroade), cooperative and able editorial and secretarial helpers (Sally Barber, Diane Bernd, Kathie F. Droskinis, Barbara Gary, Margaret Swanson, and Ingrid Tarantelli), and competent editorial assistants (Steven Cornelius, Kathie F. Droskinis, Carol Ryff, and Alison Okada Wollitzer), the book would probably still be in its conception. We would also like to express our thanks to Nancy W. Denney, of the University of Kansas, and K. Warner Schaie, of the Pennsylvania State University, who provided many helpful comments and criticisms as editorial consultants for the original publisher, to Freda Rebelsky and Lynn Dorman, editors of the series in which this book originally appeared, and to the most able editorial staff of Brooks/Cole, the publisher of the original volume. At the same time, we are the ones responsible for any shortcomings that the full-term book may have. You, the reader, will determine whether or not the book will age gracefully.

Paul B. Baltes
Hayne W. Reese
John R. Nesselroade
November, 1987

Contents

Contents

Contents

Contents

Chapter 21   Heredity-Environment Research and Development   197

Chapter 22   Developmental Research on Learning: Group Designs   208

Chapter 23   Developmental Research on Learning: Single-Subject Designs   223

Part One

The Field of Developmental Psychology

Developmental psychology deals with behavioral changes within persons across the life span, and with differences between and similarities among persons in the nature of these changes. Its aim, however, is not only to *describe* these intraindividual changes and interindividual differences but also to *explain* how they come about and to find ways to *modify* them in an optimum way. In addition, developmental psychology recognizes that the individual is changing in a changing world, and that this changing context of development can affect the nature of individual change. Consequently, developmental psychology also deals with changes within and among biocultural ecologies and with the relationships of these changes to changes within and among individuals.

Chapter One

Why Developmental Psychology?

A Rationale for Developmental Sciences

What are the advantages to organizing and building knowledge about behavior around the concept of developmental psychology? The case for a developmental approach to the study of behavior is similar to the arguments developed in other sciences for using:

> knowledge about sociocultural history to better understand present political events;
> knowledge about paleontology to understand the nature of current world geography;
> knowledge about the length and frequency (life history) of cigarette smoking to predict the probability of adult lung cancer;
> knowledge about past stock market trends to predict next year's stock market situation and the value of a given portfolio;
> knowledge from archaeology to develop a fuller understanding of modern civilization; and
> knowledge about the summer climate in California to predict the quality and taste of California's fall wines.

The developmental psychologist, in a parallel fashion, is interested in questions centering around the description, explanation, and modification of processes that lead to a given outcome or sequence of outcomes. Examples of questions about the description, explanation, and modification of processes and outcomes are:

> Is cognitive behavior the same in various age groups, or does it change from infancy through childhood, adolescence, and adulthood?
> If there are stages of cognitive functioning, why do they follow one

another, and what mechanism explains the transition from one stage to another?

Are there sex differences in adult personality traits, and, if so, how do they come about?

Is schizophrenia in adulthood related to early life experiences, or does it develop instantaneously due to stress in adulthood?

What are the tasks that characterize adult development (for example, marriage, parenthood)? Is successful mastery of these tasks related to early life experiences, and how can a given life history be designed to maximize adult functioning?

How and when is achievement motivation formed? To what aspects of parenting behavior does it relate, and what do parents have to do in order to increase achievement motivation in their children?

In all of these examples, both from other developmental sciences and from developmental psychology, there are two primary characteristics: a focus on *change* and the study of *processes* leading to a specific outcome. Specifically, the sample questions presented suggest:

1. The phenomenon under study by a developmental scientist is not fixed and stable but subject to continuous and systematic change that needs description.
2. Because phenomena come about not instantaneously but as a result of processes, it is useful to know something about the present and the past when explaining the nature of a phenomenon, predicting its future status, and designing a context for optimization or modification.

Phenomena, then, are not fixed; they are changing. Furthermore, both the past and the present are a prologue to the future. Most scientists have acknowledged the usefulness of such a "historical," process-oriented developmental approach to the study of their subject matter. It is worthwhile to think a bit about other sciences that focus on change and time-related phenomena (history, archaeology, astronomy, and others).

All time- and history-oriented sciences share with developmental psychology a number of rationales and complexities of methodology. For example, when attempting to understand why some adult persons are extroverts and others introverts, a developmental psychologist may design a methodology to "retrospect" into the past in order to find key antecedents to the emergence of extroversion/introversion behavior. Such retrospective methodologies are not easily developed and validated. In our rapidly changing world, it is often possible only to approximate ideal methods, using so-called quasi-experimental (Campbell & Stanley, 1963, 1966) methodology. The same methodological complexity is confronted by the astronomer, the archaeologist, or the political historian, in at least equally dramatic fashion.

As will be seen later, it is occasionally desirable for the developmental psychologist to look to other "historical" disciplines for ideas about adequate research methodologies, since these disciplines are often more advanced. The development of sequential cross-sectional or longitudinal strategies, for example (see Chapter Fourteen), has a precursor in demography that goes back to the 18th century. Similarly, the term *development* has been widely discussed in the biological sciences, and the biologist's view of development has strongly influenced the meaning of this term in the behavioral sciences. As another example, the recently suggested use of path-analysis techniques (see Chapter Twenty-Four) as a way of testing hypotheses about long-term developmental chains has its roots in other "historical" disciplines such as epidemiology and sociology.

Describing, Explaining, and Optimizing Development

Before the methods of developmental psychology are described, the task of developmental research will be outlined. This exercise is aimed at helping the reader to focus on the questions developmental psychologists typically ask (Baltes, 1973).

Definitions of a concept or a discipline always reflect personal biases, and most researchers are somewhat reluctant to freeze a theoretical idea or orientation by specifically defining it. For the present purpose, a definition of developmental psychology is proposed that is methodology-oriented and that views developmental psychology less as an independent body of knowledge than as an orientation toward the way behavior is studied:

> Developmental psychology deals with the description, explanation, and modification (optimization) of intraindividual change in behavior across the life span, and with interindividual differences (and similarities) in intraindividual change.

*Intra*individual change is *within*-individual change; *inter*individual differences are *between*-individual differences. The focus of a developmental approach, then, is on examining within-person (intraindividual) variability or change and the extent to which such variability is not identical for all individuals. If intraindividual change is not identical for all individuals, it shows between-person (interindividual) differences. Although these terms may appear clumsy and confusing, their widespread use by behavioral scientists interested in methodology makes it desirable to include them here as key concepts.

The task of a developmental approach, however, does not stop with naturalistic description of the course of change. The aims of developmental psychology include the pursuit of knowledge about the determinants and mechanisms that help us understand the how and why of development: what causes the change? This aspect of knowledge-building is often called explicative, explanatory, or analytic, because its goal is to find causal-type relationships and thus to go beyond descriptive predictions of the nature of behavioral development. The decision as to where description ends, when explanation starts, and which form of explanation is acceptable to a given scientist will always be an arbitrary one. As a matter of fact, philosophers of science question the logical merit of such a distinction on the grounds that description and explanation go hand in hand and are intrinsically confounded. For didactic purposes, however, the distinction is useful because it helps us present a perspective on research strategies and particular emphases in theory-building.

The proposed definition of developmental psychology further states that developmental psychologists are interested not only in description and explication but also in modification and optimization of the course of development. This task requires that we discover which interventions or treatments are powerful change agents. A useful benefit of this aim is that knowledge that may be generated for its own sake may, by its application, serve society in its attempts to design an optimal context for living.

The simultaneous knowledge of what behavioral development looks like (description), where it comes from and why it comes about (explanation), and how it can be altered (modification) makes for a full-fledged body of knowledge. Accordingly, useful developmental methodology consists of methods that permit us to describe intraindividual (within-person) change sequences and interindividual (between-person) differences in these patterns of change, as well as assist us in our search for explanatory and modification principles.

Developmental psychology is a fairly recent scientific field. Therefore it is understandable that its methodology is often insufficiently formulated or inadequately adapted to the unique features of its basic approach. In fact, to give one example, many of the classic experimental designs (such as analysis of variance) have been developed within the framework of interindividual differences and not intraindividual variability. The best developmental designs, however, are the ones that yield descriptive and explanatory information about intraindividual change patterns.

Summary

A developmental approach, in any science, is based on the belief that knowing the past allows us to understand the present and to predict the future. In psychology, this belief leads to a developmental psychology that deals with the description, explanation, and modification (including optimization) of intraindividual change in behavior across the life span, and with interindividual differences in intraindividual change. For these purposes, methods are needed that permit description of intraindividual change and interindividual differences in the nature of intraindividual change, and that assist in the identification of causal mechanisms (explanation) and modification principles (optimization).

Chapter Two

An Illustration of the Developmental Approach: The Case of Auditory Sensitivity

The area of auditory sensitivity provides a good example to illustrate the goals of describing, explaining, and modifying a developmental phenomenon. This area of research has been well summarized by McFarland (1968), using data from a number of studies, including those by Glorig and Rosen and their colleagues. Figure 2-1 illustrates the key arguments.

Description

Auditory sensitivity, or acuity, has been measured in large samples covering a wide age range. When auditory acuity is plotted against pitch of tones, a fairly robust age-difference pattern can be seen. Specifically, Part A of Figure 2-1 shows the loudness (in decibels) required for a particular tone to be detected. In general, it takes more loudness for an older person to hear a particular tone than for a young adult to hear it. The louder a tone has to be in order to be heard, the less is the person's auditory sensitivity.

There is a definite age-related decrease in sensitivity, especially for the higher pitches (frequencies of 2000 cycles per second and higher); that is, as shown in Part A of the figure, auditory sensitivity seems to exhibit a definite developmental trend in that the loss is neatly correlated with tone pitch or frequency. (For a summary of design questions involving the distinction between age changes and age differences, see Chapters Thirteen and Fourteen.) Thus, auditory sensitivity is not fixed for a given person but changes with time. Moreover, as shown in Part B of the figure, there are interindividual differences in the developmental trends obtained. For example, women tend to show less of a decrement than men.

6

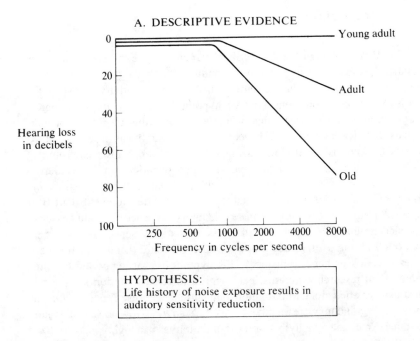

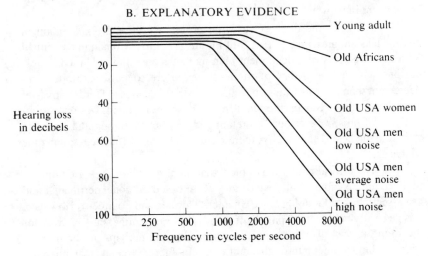

C. MODIFICATION/OPTIMIZATION OF SENSITIVITY LOSS
   1. Alleviation: hearing aids
   2. Prevention: control of noise history

Figure 2-1.   Descriptive and explanatory research on auditory sensitivity in adulthood. Based on data from McFarland (1968).

Explanation

Part A of Figure 2-1 describes average change in hearing acuity in adulthood. A series of studies has been conducted to shed light on the causes of this robust age-related change pattern in auditory sensitivity. Most of the studies were based on some kind of hypothesis about neurophysiological and/or environmental effects that accumulated over the life history of individuals. In this sense, most of the explanatory research was process oriented and focused on historical methods, looking into past organism-environment interactions in order to understand the decrement phenomenon in the elderly.

One class of hypotheses dealt with the relationship between the *life history of noise exposure* and the nature of auditory development. Part B of Figure 2-1 summarizes some of the explanatory evidence. The studies were designed around the hypothesis that loss in auditory sensitivity is largely controlled by the overall magnitude of noise exposure that a person experiences over his or her life history. This hypothesis was supported by three independent research programs, each with a different criterion sample that presumably varied along a continuum in magnitude of noise exposure. On one end of the continuum were members of an African tribe (low noise history), on the other American men living for most of their lives in a highly industrialized area (high noise history). American women (medium noise history) were somewhere in between.

The outcome of these research programs aimed at explanation of hearing loss are presented in Part B of Figure 2-1. First, women in the United States showed less of a decrement than men. Second, in the United States, persons with a life history of minimum exposure to noise exhibited less decrement than persons from urban and industrialized areas. Third, natives of an isolated tribe in Sudan (the Mabaans), whose environment was exceptionally free of noise, were found to retain auditory acuity throughout their life span into the 80s. (Incidentally, there were also no sex differences among the Mabaans.)

The critical reader may object that the three studies reported did not produce undebatable results, since they were based on nonexperimental and cross-sectional methodology (see Chapters Thirteen and Fourteen). However, it is generally held that the pattern of the results argues rather persuasively for the strong impact of noise exposure on the rate and perhaps on the form of auditory development through adulthood. In fact, it seems that no other explanatory research on this topic has provided us with an equally consistent outcome and equally strong relationships. Nevertheless, in principle the pursuit of explanations for developmental patterns never stops: researchers are currently seeking further explanations of the developmental relationship between noise and hearing sensitivity by searching for relationships of hearing sensitivity and noise to physiological mechanisms. They are also looking for additional developmental components that will more fully explain the phenomenon of auditory development.

In any case, the explanatory evidence available led McFarland (1968, p. 34) to formulate a developmental model of auditory sensitivity in adulthood. The model assigns fairly low importance to intrinsic physiological aging *per se*, and moderate importance to general life-history events associated with connective-tissue changes, vascular reactions, metabolism, nutrition, and stress. However, in line with the data summarized in Figure 2-1, the model assigns the major controlling power to the life history of exposure to noise. In this sense, then, the area of auditory sensitivity provides a good example of how descriptive developmental changes come to be explained in terms of age-correlated mechanisms without using age (or chronological time) *per se* as the final explanatory principle.

The explanatory analysis of observed age changes in terms of age-correlated mechanisms is a long and tedious task. The nature of the explanatory process differs along many dimensions of methods (such as experimental versus correlational, and laboratory versus naturalistic) and theoretical orientations (experiential versus genetic, learning versus maturational, behavioristic versus cognitive, organismic versus mechanistic). In fact, since strong disagreement about methods and theoretical emphasis is characteristic of developmental researchers, the presentation of developmental methodology is a complex project. Theory and method are closely related, and each is difficult to describe without the other; often what is sufficient explanation from one theoretical viewpoint is at best tentative description from another.

In this book, we emphasize the notion that a developmental approach to the study of behavior focuses on explanations or paradigms of research that are historical, not merely concurrent, in nature (Baltes, 1973)—on paradigms or theories that concentrate primarily on chains of events (antecedent-consequent relationships) as they lead to a given developmental product. The cumulative effect of noise input on auditory sensitivity is an example of such a historical paradigm. Explaining the cumulative linkage of causative chains making for developmental change is at the heart of developmental theory-building.

Modification-Optimization

Our illustration of the usefulness of a developmental approach can now be taken one step further to the task of modification and optimization. In many cases, the available explanatory evidence may not, for ethical or pragmatic reasons, permit the researcher to intervene effectively. Nevertheless, it seems fair to conclude that one of the strongest arguments for knowledge generation is that knowledge can be applied. Obviously, in some cases a developmentalist may judge the observed outcome to be acceptable or irreversible and thus decide not to interfere with the natural course of development.

When designing modification programs, one can distinguish between two classes of strategies. One is the a posteriori type, usually labeled *alleviative*. The second is aimed at altering the course of development in an a priori fashion and is labeled *preventive*.

In Part C of Figure 2-1, these two strategies of modification are summarized. In the case of auditory acuity, the classic technique of alleviation is to provide a hearing aid designed to amplify frequencies according to the specific losses in auditory sensitivity of the person involved. Alleviation is important because untreated loss in auditory sensitivity leads to other problems in interpersonal and cognitive functioning.

The remarkable strength of a developmental approach, however, lies in its potential for preventive action and optimization. Knowledge about the history of the dysfunctional behavior or problem permits interventions that direct development into more appropriate channels. For example, if loss in auditory sensitivity is seen as undesirable, noise reduction and the use of protective devices will be very effective and desirable interventions. Additional explanatory evidence on critical periods may help us further in designing optimal environments. For example, there is evidence that high noise levels damage the hearing of young adults more than that of older adults. The popularity of rock music among young adults may therefore be creating a serious problem.

Individual Development in a Changing World

Our illustration points to another core issue in developmental research—that of the relationship between individual and biocultural development (Baltes, Cornelius, & Nesselroade, in press; Riegel, 1976). This relationship is partially a reflection of the notion that developmental psychology deals not only with intraindividual change but also with interindividual differences, which can result from a host of factors, including biocultural, historical change. The relationship between individual and biocultural development becomes most apparent in the context of life-span developmental research, since the time period necessary for life-span development is obviously large compared with, for example, development in a restricted age range such as infancy or childhood.

Whereas it is a key assumption of developmental psychology that individuals are not fixed in their behavior, it is also necessary to realize that individuals do not develop in a fixed physical and social ecology; the world is also changing. The world changes both within a given cultural unit (intraculturally) and in distinct cultural settings (interculturally). It is reasonable to assume that any course of individual development varies over historical time periods, distinct cultural milieus, and biological generations.

Although there are no convincing data available to us, the area of auditory sensitivity can be used to illustrate the relationship between individual and historical development within a culture. In most Western societies, the average intensity of auditory stimulations has probably increased significantly over the last several decades. In addition, fads such as those for rock music, stock-car racing, or aviation have probably led to novel forms of auditory experiences. Consequently, the developmental pattern presented in Figure 2-1 for auditory sensitivity may very well be quite different (in level or shape) for generations to come, as it may be for members of different cultures. The differential age-related patterns for Americans and Africans shown in Figure 2-1 constitute one such case.

Historical time—consisting of myriad ecological conditions—thus defines the context for individual development. For the period 1970–1972, for example, Nesselroade and Baltes (1974) have shown that American adolescents (regardless of their specific chronological age) "develop" in the direction of less achievement orientation, less superego strength, and more independence. This pattern of adolescent development, however, may be typical only for the 1970–1972 period. Historical, time-related trends in childhood-socialization goals and styles are equally well documented in the literature and should be mirrored in the types of individual development exhibited by persons who are reared during distinct historical epochs. Furthermore, sociologists such as Keniston (1971) have argued that adolescence as a distinctive period of the human life span appeared only in the 20th century and that, especially in the past decades—with the ever-increasing speed of social change—a life stage called "youth" has emerged. As Neugarten and Datan (1973) noted, similar arguments can be made for novel forms of middle age, due to increases in life expectancy and changing rhythms of the work and family cycle.

Viewing a changing individual in a changing world has numerous implications for developmental psychology. For example, there is a need for methods that clearly identify within-individual (intraindividual) change as opposed to between-individual (interindividual) differences. Also, methods are needed to relate such within-individual trends to sociobiological, ecological change.

Max Weber, a noted German sociologist-philosopher-historian, reflected in the following manner on the essence of developmental sciences in general and their continuous need to adapt to a changing world:

> There are sciences which possess everlasting youth, and these are all historical developmental disciplines; all those disciplines which are faced with a continuous stream of new issues associated with eternal cultural change. Developmental sciences, therefore, have not only a built-in perva-

> sive transitoriness of constructs but also the inevitable task of developing per-
> petually novel systems and models [1968, p. 57; translation by the authors].

Indeed, a developmentalist must be aware not only of the changing nature of his developing individuals but also of the changing ecological conditions that link his search for knowledge intrinsically to patterns of historical and evolutionary change.

Core Requirements for Developmental Methodology

The preceding section, along with Chapter One, highlighted the basic rationale of a developmental approach to the study of behavior. This exercise allows us to compile a set of basic research questions with which a developmental methodology should be able to deal. These questions go beyond those that characterize the scientific method in general.

The following core requirements are derived from our proposed working definition of developmental psychology: developmental psychology deals with the description, explanation, and modification of intraindividual change and interindividual differences (and similarities) in intraindividual change across the life span.

1. As to the task of *description*, developmental-research methodology needs to focus on intraindividual change and interindividual differences therein. Such behavior change is not to be confused with time-specific interindividual differences and momentary behavior fluctuations.
2. As to the task of *explanation*, developmental-research methodology must be appropriate for historical analyses that will successively explain time or chronological age in terms of specific developmental antecedents and processes.
3. As to the task of *modification*, developmental-research methodology must be capable of examining the range of intraindividual variability both within and between individuals. The knowledge gained should help us better understand behavior and facilitate the planning of alleviation and optimization programs.
4. As to the *ecological* context for individual development, developmental-research methodology should be able to describe individual change in a changing biocultural ecology.

It will be useful to keep these core requirements in mind while reading the following chapters. The various chapters will amplify each of the issues mentioned and add a series of new ones. A sensitivity for what is unique to a developmental orientation and a developmental-research methodology, however, is critical and perhaps more important than an understanding of the numerous technical details contained in this book.

Methodological questions in developmental psychology are rampant and often badly conceptualized. The complexity of the historical study of behavioral development within a changing biocultural context calls for unique methodologies and a heightened sensitivity to the pitfalls, blind alleys, and frustrations produced by malignant data. Reflecting on the usefulness of history in the preface to *The Gulag Archipelago*, Solzhenitsyn (1973, p.x) quotes a Russian proverb that illustrates the conceptual and emotional dilemma of developmental researchers rather nicely: "Dwell on the past and you'll lose one eye—Forget the past and you'll lose both eyes." Indeed, developmental researchers are often put in a situation of conflict when they come to the task of implementing the goals of developmental research with complex and tedious methodologies. The belief in the long-range merits of the developmental approach is important when choosing not only what is practical but also what is right.

Summary

The developmental approach is well illustrated by research on developmental changes in auditory sensitivity, which seems to decline in old age, especially for the higher pitches. This descriptive fact is explained by research showing a relationship between hearing loss and a life history of exposure to noise. Modification in this case can be alleviative—the use of hearing aids—or it can be preventive—the reduction of noise levels or the use of protective devices during early segments of the life span.

The developmental research on auditory sensitivity also illustrates another facet of developmental psychology: relationships of intraindividual change and interindividual differences to the physical, social, cultural, and historical context of individual development—that is, the key concept of the changing individual in a changing world.

The core methodological requirements illustrated by the case of auditory sensitivity, and by the very definition of developmental psychology given in Chapter One, are methods that permit (1) distinguishing intraindividual change from interindividual differences, (2) identifying specific developmental antecedents and processes (beyond time or age) as explanatory variables, (3) developing effective programs for alleviation or prevention of dysfunctional developments and optimization of functional developments, and (4) describing individual change in a changing biocultural ecology.

Part Two

General Issues in Research Methodology

In Part One, developmental psychology was briefly defined to illustrate the unique features of a developmental approach to the study of behavior. The dominant focus of this approach is on describing, explaining, and modifying (optimizing) patterns of intraindividual change in behavior and interindividual differences in such change characteristics. A methodology for the study of behavioral development deals with the principles and strategies involved in the pursuit of knowledge about the ways individuals change with time.

Any methodology has at least two aspects. The first concerns issues of the empirical method in general. The nature of knowledge, the nature of the scientific method, and the strategies of theory construction and hypothesis testing are examples of such general issues of methodology. The second aspect of methodology is unique to the subject matter concerned. In our case, it is specific to developmental psychology. Examples of development-specific methodology are techniques developed to observe infant activity and social-interaction patterns in the elderly, or data-analysis models formulated to quantify and structure behavioral change along multiple dimensions. Comparing the use of cross-sectional designs with the use of longitudinal designs is another problem characteristic of development-specific methodology.

The chapters in Part Two provide an overview of general aspects of design methodology. Occasionally, we will show how issues of general methodology apply to the study of development, particularly when questions of measurement and the interplay between theory and methodology are discussed. The use of the term *development* is a good case in point. Various views of the term lead to distinct ways of operationalizing research questions, interpreting data, and building theories.

Chapter Three

The Nature of Theories and Models

Science and Knowledge

Science deals with knowledge—or, better, the pursuit of knowledge. *Knowledge* has several definitions in the dictionary, but all of these definitions refer to one or the other of two general meanings: (1) knowledge as information and (2) knowledge as understanding. *Knowledge* in its fullest sense means knowing what is true and knowing why it is true.

Not all knowledge is scientific, however, because science is not the only source of knowledge. Knowledge can be religious, common-sense, or literary and poetic, for example. Religious knowledge is "revealed"; common-sense knowledge is gained from everyday experience; and literary or poetic knowledge is insightful or intuitive. Scientific knowledge is obtained by the scientific method, which is discussed in Chapter Four.

All of these kinds of knowledge, including scientific knowledge, obviously refer to different kinds of understanding, but they also refer to different kinds of information—different meanings of the word *fact*. Clearly, some of the "facts" in religion are not "facts" in science. Note, however, that the converse is also true, in that religionists reject some of the "facts" accepted by scientists: divine creation versus evolution is an example.

It is important to realize that each kind of knowledge—religious, scientific, and so forth—has a sort of privileged status, in that the values and interpretations relevant for one kind are not applicable to any other kind. No one kind of knowledge is universally superior to any other kind; rather, each has value for its own purposes. The scientist should not *reject* other kinds of knowledge but should recognize that they are outside the domain of science. He or she should treat them as irrelevant to scientific purposes, not as wrong.

To summarize, *knowledge* refers to information, or facts, and to understanding of facts. Different kinds of knowledge are based on different sources of facts and different kinds of understanding. In science, a fact is obtained by the scientific method and understanding is obtained by theoretical methods. These methods are discussed in Chapter Four and need be characterized only superficially here as referring to research and the interpretation of research results. Both kinds of methods—research and interpretation—are intimately related to theories and models, as explained below.

The Domain of Behavioral Research

The domain of behavioral research is limited by two kinds of boundary conditions, one related to the definition of *behavior* and the other related to the definition of *research*. In the behavioral sciences, such as psychology, sociology, and cultural anthropology, the term *behavior* encompasses the activities of organisms, parts of organisms, and groups of organisms, including "observable overt responses, implicit 'mental' processes, physiological functions, etc." (Reese, 1970, p. 1). Behavior can be the activity of an individual organism, as in the subject matter of psychology; or the activity of a group of organisms acting as a group, as in the subject matter of sociology; or the activity of a tissue or organ, as in the subject matter of physiological psychology. In short, behavior refers to activities and processes, of whatever kind, performed by systems, however simple or complex.

The second kind of boundary condition is imposed by the definition of *research*. Broadly defined, the term means careful study. So defined, there are two kinds of research, one conducted in the library and the other conducted in the laboratory or in the natural environment. Library research is not the concern of this book (for a brief discussion, see Reese, 1970), and it is therefore possible here to give a more satisfactory definition of research as laboratory and field research: careful study through scientific methods (see Chapter Four). The immediately relevant consideration is that scientific methods involve observations of phenomena, and hence the domain of behavioral research encompasses observations of activities, provided that *activities* is given a broad meaning and provided that the observations are obtained in the particular way discussed in Chapter Four.

Theories and Models

Theories

In science, a theory is a set of statements including (1) laws and (2) definitions of terms.

The laws of science, or principles of science, are statements about relationships between variables. An example from physics is Boyle's Law: at constant temperatures the volume of a gas varies inversely with the pressure. An example from psychology is the Law of Least Effort: whenever either of two acts can be used to reach a goal, that act is chosen which requires the least effort.

A scientific law is a statement of fact; but, as we have seen, *fact* has several meanings, some of which may yield contradictory facts (as in the example of creation versus evolution). It follows that facts are not "out there" in the natural world but are, rather, what is known about the natural world. But knowing is a cognitive activity, and therefore facts are cognitions about the natural world, and laws are statements about these cognitions.

In other words, facts and laws are not naturally occurring events to be discovered, but rather constructions or inferences. They are abstractions imposed on nature by the observer rather than "discovered" in nature by him. Consequently, it should not be surprising that many "laws" that were once accepted have since been rejected. Boyle's Law, for example, is now known to be false at very high pressures, and the Law of Least Effort is often contradicted (presumably when the act requiring more effort leads to additional rewards). The laws of science at any one time, then, should be viewed as the best currently available abstractions about reality, and should be accepted tentatively until better abstractions come along.

Now, what are theories good for? The functions of scientific theories are (1) to organize or integrate knowledge and (2) to guide research designed to increase knowledge. Theories fulfill the organizational function by showing that some facts or laws (theorems) are deducible from other, more general laws (axioms), or by showing that all of the known facts and laws are interrelated to form a coherent pattern. Theories fulfill the research function by suggesting fruitful lines of further experimentation. A scientific theory is evaluated on the basis of how well it fulfills these two functions.

Models

It is important not to confuse theories with models and to understand their relationship. For example, any theory presupposes a more general model according to which its theoretical concepts are formulated (Reese & Overton, 1970).

A model is any device used to represent something other than itself. For example, straight lines and dots drawn on a blackboard can be used to represent straight lines and points in geometry, even though the straight line in geometry has length but no width and the point in geometry has neither length nor width. The blackboard model provides a means of visualizing these abstract geometrical concepts. Here, the model represents elements in a theory and their interrelationships. The irrelevant parts of the model—the width of the line and the dimensions of the dot—are supposed to be ignored. Geometry, as a mathematical system, is itself a model when it is used to represent reality.

A model is intended to be not a description of reality but only a *representation* of the features of reality that are essential for understanding a particular problem. For example, Figure 3-1 is a wiring diagram for a crystal

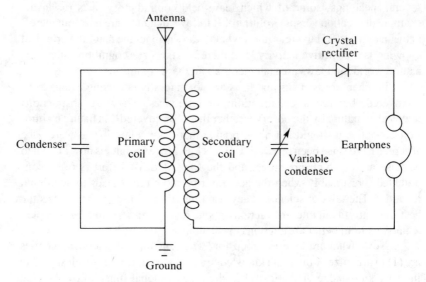

Figure 3-1. Illustration of a model: crystal receiving set.

receiving set, but no crystal receiving set ever had the physical appearance of this diagram. The wiring diagram is a model, representing the elements of this simple radio and their interrelationships. It would be entirely inappropriate to assert that this model (or any model) is wrong because it fails to provide a description of the thing modeled; it cannot be wrong as a description because it is not intended to be a description. Also, it cannot be wrong as a representation, because representations are metaphorical and not intended to be factually true. In certain circumstances it is appropriate to assert that the world is an oyster, as in the metaphor "The world is my oyster!" However, a model, like any metaphor, can be inept or useless; for example, for scientific purposes it is doubtful that the world can be usefully modeled by an oyster.

Models, then, are evaluated on the basis of their usefulness for some particular purpose. The wiring diagram is a useful model of the crystal receiving set; the blackboard model is a useful model of the geometric elements.

Levels of models. Models vary in scope or range of phenomena represented. The most specific models are scale models, which are used to represent a very limited domain. An example is a scale model of an airplane in

[handwritten margin note:] no model can be wrong as a description or representation only inept or useless

[handwritten margin note:] scale model useful if elements and relationships represented accurately

a wind tunnel, used to represent the flight of the actual airplane. In psychology, scale models such as flight simulators and car-driving simulators have been used in research. Such models are useful if the elements and relationships among the elements are represented accurately.

Other somewhat more general models are used to represent theories or parts of theories. An example is the model shown in Figure 3-2, used to represent the theoretical principles of the rectilinear propagation of light rays.

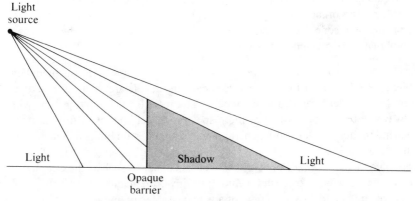

Light
source

Light   Shadow   Light

Opaque
barrier

Figure 3-2. Model representing the principles of the rectilinear properties of light rays.

As Toulmin (1962, p. 29) noted about this model, "We do not *find* light atomized into individual rays; we *represent* it as consisting of such rays." That is, again, the model is intended to be not a description of reality but only a metaphorical representation of reality. An example of this kind of model used in psychology is shown in Figure 3-3. This model represents the essential features of the Zeaman and House (1963) theory of attention as it affects discriminative learning. Note that this is a "stimulus-response" model; each element is a stimulus, a response, or a relationship between stimuli and responses. The relevance of this observation will be shown later.

There are still more general models, sometimes called *suppositions* or *paradigms* of science, or *principles* or *ideals* of nature. These models are intended to represent vast domains of phenomena, such as the whole of psychology. The "active" and "reactive" models of organisms are two examples. According to the reactive-organism model, on which most modern American psychology is based, the behavior of organisms can be represented by associations between stimulus and response elements in more or less complex combinations. The basic feature is an invariant relationship between input and output. According to the active-organism model, on which most modern European and Soviet psychology is based, the behavior of organisms is not a product of an invariant input-output relationship; rather, the input is transformed by the organism in essentially unpredictable ways to determine the output. (For a technical discussion of other differences between these models, see Overton & Reese, 1973; Reese & Overton, 1970.)

Finally, the most general models are intended, ideally, to encompass all phenomena. These models are called *world views, world hypotheses, paradigms, ontologies,* or *cosmologies.* Two examples from psychology are the mechanistic and organismic models. The mechanistic model represents the universe as a machine, with invariant input-output and other operating characteristics. The organismic model represents the universe as a developing organism, but it conceives of the organism as an organized whole rather than as a combination of elements such as cells.

Compatibility of models. Note that the Zeaman-House model in Figure 3-3 is related to the reactive-organism model, and that the reactive-organism model is related to the mechanistic model. Such relationships will always be found, because each more specific model is derived from a more general model, and the more general model exerts certain limits on features of the more specific models. That is, each more specific model is restricted in the possible meanings that can be given to basic concepts, such as the criteria for determining what is true (the meaning of *fact*), the nature of substance and change, and the form and content of adequate explanations.

For example, it would be inappropriate to simply introduce into the

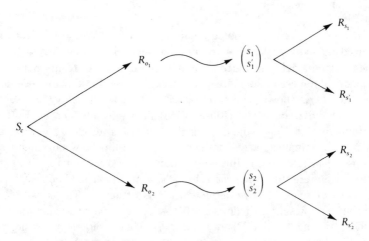

Figure 3-3. Model representing the Zeaman and House theory of attention. A complex multidimensional stimulus (S_c) arouses attention (R_{o1} or R_{o2}) to one or another dimension, which makes the values (S_1 and S'_1 or S_2 and S'_2) on the dimension available for responding ($R_{s_1}, R_{s'_1}, R_{s_2}, R_{s'_2}$).

Zeaman-House model (Figure 3-3) an ability of the organism to decide rationally which dimension to attend to. Attention to a particular dimension must be determined by the history of the organism—innate tropisms and learning—and not by rational activities, because this model is derived from the reactive-organism model. Rational activities would be capable of changing input-output relationships and hence would violate the reactive-organism requirement of invariant input-output relationships. (Such activities would, however, be consistent with the active-organism model.)

An important point to note in connection with rational activities and the reactive-organism model is that the existence of rational activities is not denied in the reactive-organism model. That is, this model does not assert that the human being is a robot; that would be description. Rather, it asserts only that the human being can be represented as a robot. The rational activities of the human being are not ignored, but they are assumed to be explainable in terms of invariant stimulus-response relationships. That is, in the reactive-organism model, such activities need to be explained; in the active-organism model, in contrast, such activities are used for explanation.

Any model, from the most specific to the most general, is used to aid understanding. It provides a way of looking at the universe, or a segment of it, that makes it more easily comprehensible. At the same time, however, the model may interfere with the comprehension of other viewpoints; since its view is biased, it often makes other views seem unreasonable or even subversive.

Thus, the positions of Piaget, Chomsky, and the Marxist psychologists—all derived from the active-organism model—are seen as dangerously loose and imprecise by American behaviorists, whose own position —derived from the reactive-organism model—is seen as a dangerous and sterile oversimplification of the other positions. The former cannot see the simplicities, according to the latter, and the latter cannot see the complexities, according to the former. Both approaches are only partially correct, in that the former group searches for complexities and the latter group searches for simplicities. Both can be scientific, but both are wrong when they believe that their own bias is the only correct position.

[handwritten margin note: Each model gives attention to a different element; neither is right or wrong]

The Interplay of Theory and Methodology

We have already noted that there is no one "scientific" world view. It is probably true that mechanism—the view of the world as analogous to a machine—is the most prevalent world view in psychology, and perhaps it is true that it is the world view most likely to be ascribed to science by the layman. Nevertheless, other world views not only are extant in science but also are useful and productive.

The criteria for determining the truth of statements are not entirely the same in different world views, and therefore these views will treat facts differently—especially facts labeled as circumstantial evidence or inference. Observations will tend to be understood or interpreted differently (Kuhn, T. S., 1962). However, the basic nature of the method by which observations are obtained will not differ (Overton & Reese, 1973); the basic principles of research remain the same no matter what the world view might be. By *basic principles* we mean the principles of control or description of the setting and of objectivity. Specifics of design can differ, and indeed in some ways they *must* differ.

For example, the components-of-variance model, which underlies measurement theory and the analysis of variance, is consistent with the mechanistic model, in which the components are additive (see, for example, Overton, 1973). In other world views, such as organicism, which is especially popular in the psychologies of development, cognition, and perception, the components are interactive. An example is the familiar principle of Gestalt psychology: the whole is different from the conjunction of the parts (or, more loosely, the whole is greater than the sum of the parts). Within such world views, the analysis of variance does not make sense, and hence it is not reasonable for their adherents to use designs obtained from the analysis-of-variance model.

Different world views have different implications in other areas in addition to that of design. In mechanistic systems, the basic "facts" are the data (observations); in organismic systems, the basic "facts" are inferences—facts that are demonstrated by data but not proved by data (Pepper, 1942). Also, the various world views differ in their attitude toward the influence of cognition in the transformation of experience into knowledge. From a mechanistic position, cognitive processes are derived from past experience, and therefore, ultimately, all knowledge derives from experience. From an organismic position, cognitive processes are emergent—that is, not predictable entirely from past experience—and therefore knowledge derives from the action of the person upon the experience (see Elkind, 1970; Reese & Overton, 1970); in organismic systems, cognition is often a key element, not "derived" but primary. An analogy is the position of Lloyd Morgan (1903) with respect to the perception of relationships. He believed that relationships among stimuli can be sensed, but can be *recognized* as relationships only through a mental act of "reflection." Thus, the *sensation* of relationships does not require any cognitive intervention, but the *knowledge* of relationships does.

World views also influence methodology and theory construction in other ways, some of which are seen in especially clear contrast in developmental psychology. These influences will be discussed in the rest of this chapter.

World Views in Developmental Psychology

The major world views in developmental psychology are mechanism and organicism (Overton & Reese, 1973; Reese & Overton, 1970). A materialist dialectic view has also been proposed (for example, Riegel, 1976) and will be discussed. Others have been described but are not currently popular and therefore are not discussed here.

Mechanism

The basic metaphor in the mechanistic world view is the machine. That is, the universe is represented as analogous to a machine. Different machines yield variants of the mechanistic model, but all share certain basic concepts.

The universe, like a machine, is composed of discrete parts operating in a space-time field. The parts are elementary particles in motion or at rest, depending on inertia of movement or rest. The parts are interrelated by forces. The parts and their relationships are the basic elements to which all more complex phenomena are reducible. Movement depends on the application of forces, which are therefore causal. The forces must be efficient or immediate—that is, not teleological and not arising from the nature or form of the machine itself.

Given a complete description of the state of the machine at a given time, *t,* and complete knowledge of the forces applied, complete prediction of any future state is possible, as is postdiction of any past state. (Heisenberg's principle of indeterminacy, according to Heisenberg and Niels Bohr, leads to rejection of this assertion; but Bunge [1963] pointed out that Heisenberg's principle only makes it impossible to test the assertion. According to Bunge, the principle of indeterminacy refers to epistemological indeterminacy—the impossibility of obtaining complete knowledge of the present state—and not to ontological indeterminacy—lack of causality or determinacy in nature.) Thus, substance is particles; change is in direction or speed of movement. Causes are immediate and antecedent-consequent. Therefore, such a universe should be expressible in quantitative terms and in functional equations.

In psychology, the mechanistic model is reflected by the reactive model of the human being. Thus, the human being, like the machine, is reactive to forces, and does not transform them except through mechanisms that are also reactive. For example, purpose cannot be a cause unless purpose has a concurrent status: the end (purpose) cannot determine the means unless the end is part of the antecedent to the means. In stimulus-response learning theory, the end is represented as an antecedent such as expectancy or, better, as a conditioned goal response (r_g). But then purpose is not a basic concept; rather, it is derived from antecedents. Also, the cognitive activities of willing, wishing, perceiving, thinking, and so on cannot be viewed as causal, because they must be derived from elements and forces. No free will is possible, although a belief in free will is possible. The model is deterministic.

A machine does not grow, although it can deteriorate. That is, a machine does not develop qualitatively; its structure cannot change except as a result of deterioration of its parts. However, the machine may be capable of performing different operations depending on the level of stimulation, kind of stimulation, or the machine's history. *History* in this sense means that the machine may have a part that does not function until after other parts have functioned. An example is the striking of a clock: the spring controlling the hour hand has operated for a certain length of time. Note, however, that this capacity was built into the machine.

In epistemology, mechanism is reflected by the philosophy of naïve realism: the world exists independently of the perceiver, and it is perceived approximately as it exists. The perceiver or knower sees or knows the world in a predetermined way. A copy theory of knowledge is required: the mind is a *tabula rasa* on which the external world impresses knowledge. The organism has no active role in the construction of reality. In psychology, the mechanistic model is reflected by stimulus-response behaviorism.

Organicism

The basic metaphor in organicism is the organic, or integrated, process; the organism is conceptualized as a process rather than as static and cellular.

In this model, the essence of substance is activity, or process, rather than substrate. Change is given, and the aim is to identify the rules of change or transition from one form into another, and to describe the system in which the changes occur. Thus, the process is the unit, but it is expressed in multiple forms. The present system is not static but changing, and its present state is explained by the rules of change, not by static rules. The whole is not a synthesis of its parts in this model; the whole is basic and is presupposed by its parts, to which it gives meaning. The parts cannot exist except in the whole.

According to Pepper, "The categories of organicism consist, on the one hand, in noting the steps involved in the organic process, and, on the other hand, in noting the principal features in the organic structure ultimately achieved or realized. The structure achieved or realized is always the ideal *aimed at* by the progressive steps of the process" (Pepper, 1942, p. 281; italics added). Thus, organicism includes final, or teleological, causes.

In Aristotle's system there were five kinds of causes: (1) The *material cause* of a phenomenon is the substance that constitutes it. It includes, in psychology, the genetic, maturational, and physiological substrate that is a necessary condition for behavior. Part of the material cause of human behavior is being human. (2) An *efficient cause* is an external agent or force, or independent variable, that regularly precedes and produces the phenomenon. (This is "cause" in Hume's sense, but with the notion of production added.) (3) A *formal cause* is the pattern, organization, or form of the phenomenon. (4) A *final cause* is the end or goal or ideal form toward which change is directed. It is teleological.

Material and formal causes are causes of *being;* efficient and final causes are causes of *becoming*. Thus, developmental psychologists will refer to efficient or final causes, or both, in explaining development. (5) The fifth cause in Aristotle's system is *incidental* or "chance" *cause*. It is the accidental coincidence of two lines of action that brings about a single novel result. This kind of cause is common in materialist dialectics, where conflicting causes have an emergent result or effect.

In organicism, emergence is a basic category, because since final and incidental causes are permissible prediction is impossible. Since qualitative differences in structure or form are possible, quantification is at best difficult. Change is qualitative rather than (or in addition to) quantitative.

In psychology, the organismic model is reflected by the active-organism model of the human being. According to this model, knowledge, or reality, is actively constructed by the knower. Experience becomes meaningful only after it has been transformed and incorporated into the structure of things already known. In epistemology, this position is called *constructivism*.

Dialectics

A good review of the principles of dialectics is contained in a collection of papers edited by Klaus Riegel in the periodical *Human Development* (1975; see also Datan & Reese, in press). For a critical discussion of the principles of dialectics, the reader is referred to Hook (1957; see also Baltes & Cornelius, in press).

Dialectics refers to the opposition of conflicting or contradictory principles and their resolution through emergent consequences. It implies a reciprocal interaction between the contradictions. In developmental psychology, an example of this reciprocal interaction inherent in dialectics is the contradiction between accommodation and assimilation in Piaget's theory: in accommodation, experience changes mental structures; in assimilation, mental structures transform experience. According to Karl Marx, "By acting on the external world and changing it, man at the same time changes his own nature." Human beings, through their activities and labor, transform their environment and create new conditions for individual development. Human beings create themselves by their own labor; by transforming nature, they transform themselves.

Knowledge, according to this view, is social—created by the activities of the society. But it is also individual, acquired by the individual through his own activities (as in Piaget's theory). Thus, there is a dialectic interaction between the individual's activities and society's activities, and the ✱ result of this interaction is the individual's knowledge—which may, however, change society's knowledge.

The basic laws of materialist dialectics are (1) the unity and struggle of opposites, (2) the transformation of quantitative into qualitative change, and (3) the negation of a negation (see Wozniak, 1975). To illustrate: (1) Opposites are characteristics of an object that are mutually exclusive but that presuppose each other. Accommodation versus assimilation is an example. (2) "When quantity is altered within certain limits, no transformation in the object as object is wrought; however, if quantitative change is of sufficient magnitude, then such change can pass into a change in quality, that is, the object may be effectively changed into another, into a new object" (Wozniak, 1975, p. 33). (3) The negation of a negation refers to "the replacement of the old by the new (negation) and the re-replacement of the new by the newer still (negation of the negation), which would reinstate aspects of the old but at a higher level than they existed in the old" (Wozniak, 1975, p. 34).

Note that these dialectical "laws" are actually analytical techniques—that is, ways of understanding relationships among events, particularly developmental events. What the basic metaphor of dialectics is is open to question. One may want to use the concept of contradiction for that purpose. In any case, the key ingredients to a dialectical position (Baltes & Cornelius, in press) include a focus on change, dynamic interaction, mutual causation, lack of complete determinacy, and a joint concern for both individual (ontogenetic) and historical (cultural-evolutionary) change processes.

Summary

Science deals with the pursuit of knowledge both as information and as understanding. Not all knowledge is scientific. In science, knowledge is obtained by the scientific method and understanding is obtained by theoretical methods. Within the framework of scientific knowledge, psychology deals with the domain of behavioral research. In the present book, both behavior and research are defined broadly. Behavior encompasses activities of organisms, however simple or complex. Research is defined as careful scientific study.

Scientific knowledge is constructed by the development of theories aimed at the integrative organization of information and at the guided search for increased information. Theories are sets of statements that include laws and definitions of terms.

In the process of theory construction, it is important to distinguish between models and theories. A model is structurally separate from a theory but functionally part of its axioms. In addition, a model is a device used to represent some phenomenon, which may be a theory. In this sense, a model is not evaluated on the basis of truth criteria (as is a theory) but on the basis of its usefulness for a particular purpose.

Models (like theories) vary in scope. Some models are very general; these are sometimes called suppositions or paradigms. It is important to view these general models not as theories but as axiomatic paradigms. For example, mechanistic and organismic models have been described as each having somewhat distinctive criteria for determining the truth of statements. Both models have restrictive and defining implications for the construction of theories and the conduct of research; neither, however, is true or false.

There are three major paradigms (world views) in developmental psychology: mechanism, organicism, and dialectics.

The basic metaphor in mechanism is the machine, which leads to a focus on quantitative reactive change, material and efficient cause, and predictability. Stimulus-response behaviorism is a reflection of the philosophy of mechanism. The basic metaphor in organicism is active process, not static and reactive principles. The primary focus of organicism in regard to causal principles is on formal and final cause and, in regard to the nature of change, on structural-qualitative, emerging properties. The basic metaphor for dialectics is subject to debate, but it is aligned with the concept of contradiction and associated dialectical laws. Its basic focus, however, appears to be on dynamic interaction, simultaneous mutual causation, joint concern for ontogenetic and historical change, and a lack of complete determinacy.

Chapter Four

The Nature of Scientific Methods

All persons—whether laymen or scientists—acquire knowledge about the world through experience with phenomena. However, the way the layman acquires the experience differs from the way the scientist acquires it. The phrase *the scientific method* is used fairly often to characterize the unique activities of scientists. However, textbooks usually assert that there is no such thing as *the* scientific method. Instead, these books point out, there are many scientific methods.

Scientific methods, however, have one feature in common. Any scientific method is based on the objective observation of phenomena under known conditions (see Bechtoldt, 1959). In the present context, the scientific method is based on the objective observation of *behavior* under known conditions. But the scientist does more than observe phenomena. He or she also tries to discover laws and to combine these laws into theories (Bergmann, 1957, p. 164). Thus, the scientific method includes obtaining observations in a particular way, generalizing from these observations to the general case, and integrating these generalizations. All three activities are examined in this chapter.

Scientific Understanding and Explanation

In science, "understanding" a phenomenon means being able to predict it or being able to explain it. That is, scientists are said to understand a fact or event if they were able to predict its occurrence, or if they can explain why it occurred. Prediction and explanation are essentially identical, except that prediction refers to events that have not yet occurred and explanation refers to events that have already occurred. The event to be explained can be an individual fact, or it can be a law (a generalized fact).

There are two types of explanation, *deductive* and *pattern*. Deductive explanation is obtained by the use of syllogistic reasoning; an event is explained if it can be shown to be deducible from the axioms of a theory. Pattern explanation is obtained by rational argument; the event is explained if it can be argued that the event is reasonable within a known pattern. That is, pattern explanation means showing that the event is consistent with a pattern or network of other events.

Analysis of Causal Relationships

According to logical-positivist philosophers of science, to ask for a cause is to ask for an explanation, and "to know laws is virtually the same thing as to know causes" (Bergmann, 1957, p. 61; also consult index of Feigl & Brodbeck, 1953). However, this refined concept of causality is not always appropriate in psychology, in which the concepts of cause and effect imply temporal sequence and regularity.

By *temporal sequence* is meant an antecedent-consequent sequence of independent and dependent variables, in which the first is identified as the cause and the second is identified as the effect. By *regularity* is meant that the consequent regularly follows the antecedent—same cause, same effect (a formulation that philosophers of science have argued against; see Feigl, 1953; Russell, 1953). According to Feigl, the notion of cause implies more than temporal sequence and regularity: namely, a variable that is subject to *active control,* or direct intervention; and the notion of effect implies lack of this attribute. "We can control the temperature or the concentrations at which some chemical process takes place and thereby influence the speed of the reaction. But we have no direct control over that speed by itself. Or, to take an example from social psychology, we can change the environment of a given individual, but have no direct access to his personality traits" (Feigl, 1953, p. 417).

On a practical level, then, the establishment of a cause is likely never to be absolute. A variety of rationales exist with Feigl's position (implying temporal sequence, regularity, and active control) representing an extreme set of conditions. In our view, the exercise of control or intervention on the independent variable is not a necessary condition for the demonstration of a cause-effect relationship. Co-variations that occur in nature may be observed without active control over the occurrence of either variable. However, without such active control, there is no way to make sure that the variables are cause and effect and are not both effects of some other, unobserved cause. For instance, there is a close correlation between chronological age and mental age, but it is obvious that growing older does not in itself cause intellectual improvement. There is a strong correlation between school attendance and achievement-test scores, but the learning of subject matter is the cause of high achievement-test scores, and school attendance is only accidentally correlated with these scores because it is correlated with the learning, which typically occurs primarily in school (at least for the subject matter covered by achievement tests).

The ambiguous nature of correlational data with respect to the identification of cause-effect relationships has led some psychologists to argue that only an experimental-manipulative approach can identify cause-effect relationships. In the experimental-manipulative approach, the researcher imposes some treatment or condition upon the subjects, and then observes how their behavior changes. Given appropriate control conditions, the treatment is identifiable as the cause, and the change in behavior is identifiable as the effect. Specifically, if changes in the behavior occur only when the researcher changes the independent variable, or treatment, then a cause-effect relationship has been demonstrated. Note that a correlation between the variables is still required: changes in the dependent variable are correlated with changes in the independent variable. The feature that leads to the causal inference, as opposed to the mere covariance inference, is that the researcher controls the independent variable and therefore knows what its characteristics are. He or she therefore knows, when the correlation is observed, that one or more of these characteristics is the causal agent.

In principle, a strictly correlational approach could justify causal inferences as adequately as the experimental-manipulative approach. The catch is that the justification requires that all of the irrelevant variables associated with the independent variable in nature—all of the possible variables that might cause changes in both the independent variable and the dependent variable and hence produce a noncausal correlation between them—must be not only known but also controlled. The control can be experimental or statistical. However, it seems doubtful, to put it mildly, that these requirements can be met in practice; not all of the irrelevant variables are known, and of those known not all can be controlled. Another rationale for using correlational data to infer cause-effect relationships is related to pattern deduction as a form of explanation. Pattern deduction, as mentioned earlier, involves reasoning that, the more "correlational" observations are collected, the more likely the observed covariations are to be the product of a cause-effect sequence. In this case, none of the separate observations is sufficient in itself. However, a pattern that emerges is more and more suggestive of a particular causal relationship. The use of pattern explanation is the rationale given by most researchers who favor correlational research such as factor analysis.

Proximal and Distal Causation

According to Bergmann, in a sense "any earlier state of a system may be said to be the cause of any later one" (1957, p. 127). In psychology, such a statement would be almost metaphysical, and it is convenient to distinguish between what are called *proximal,* or *immediate,* causes and *distal,* or *mediate,* causes. As we will show later (Chapter Eleven), the distinction between proximal and distal causes is important in defining the uniqueness of developmental-research paradigms.

The proximal, or immediate, cause produces its effect on the criterion variable directly; the distal, or mediate, cause produces its effect on the criterion variable by affecting other variables that include the immediate cause of effects on the criterion variable. The effect of the distal cause, in other words, is mediated by a proximal cause. For example, suppose that subjects in an experimental group are instructed to use visual imagery as a memory aid in a word-learning task, and subjects in a control group are not given this instruction. Suppose that the experimental group exhibits superior memory by outperforming the control group. It seems unreasonable to assert that the imagery instruction was the direct cause of the improvement in memory, because the instruction would surely have no effect if it were ignored by the subject. The instruction is the *distal* cause of the improvement; the proximal cause is inferred to be the imagery. Thus, the chain of proximal causes is: Imagery Instruction→ Imagery→ Improved Memory.

In the example, the distal cause—the instruction—is objectively observable; but the proximal cause—the imagery—is not objectively observable. The proximal-distal distinction is most useful when the proximal cause is unobservable and must be inferred, or when other mediating processes are a critical part of a theory.

Some psychologists—notably the operant group—are unwilling to postulate unobservable causes, such as imagery, and therefore do not make the proximal-distal distinction. The task they have set for themselves is to discover causes that are directly controllable; for example, for them the instruction is not necessarily the only cause of the change in performance, but if it is the only observable cause it is the only one that is interesting. Their research question is "What manipulatable variable is effective?" rather than "Why is it effective?" Their approach, in other words, is empirical rather than theoretical.

To summarize, the analysis of causal relationships is a complex task, and there is no single criterion for the establishment of causation. The strictest view is that it requires, in practice, an experimental-manipulative approach. Changes in the independent variable are interpreted as causally related to changes in the dependent variable. If the researcher is so inclined, and has a theory available, he or she can further interpret this cause as distal and a hypothetical cause as proximal. Researchers who use correlational analyses argue that a set of separate correlational studies can converge so as to make a case for an inference of causation. The rationale is similar to that of a pattern explanation.   pattern explanation

The Process of Designing Research

Ideally a research project is designed to provide an unambiguous answer to questions such as: What is the relationship between X and Y? Are changes in Y related to changes in X? For different levels of Z, does the relationship between X and Y vary? It is sometimes a relatively easy task and other times a difficult, even impossible task.

In developmental investigation the fundamental purpose of research design is the same, in principle, as in any other realm of empirical inquiry, although special emphases may be placed on this or that aspect (such as distal causation) of a given procedure. One has questions to ask of data but must engineer the gathering of data to reduce as much as possible any ambiguity in the nature of the relationships between the variables under investigation. Whether or not this goal can be achieved, and how well, depends upon a variety of issues, to be discussed in Chapters Five and Six. In general, there is no single research design that is universally best. Rather, an intricate relationship exists between the nature of the research question and the nature of that research design which will shed the most light on it.

Given that the research objective is to record and evaluate observations bearing on the relationships among variables, the researcher faces two primary kinds of considerations in planning a study. First is the issue of ①whether or not the relationship observed is accurately or validly identified and interpreted. Second is the matter of ②generalizing a relationship observed in one particular set of data to other potential data sets that might have been obtained but were not. Campbell and Stanley (1963) discussed both of these general research-design issues systematically under the topics *internal* and *external validity* of research design. They were instrumental in bringing to the attention of researchers the problems inherent in interpreting the outcomes of research projects, especially those done outside the laboratory setting. In Chapters Five and Six we present an examination of Campbell and Stanley's general notions about design validity and their implications.

Ethical Considerations

Science and Society

Because scientific inquiry is not a passive process but involves "constructing" new information about people's behavior for use by other people (usually but not always scientists) and manipulating events in search of explanations, it is important to recognize the societal and ethical context in which research proceeds.

For some time, the predominant view among scientists was that science is socially and morally neutral and that it is the social-political-economic structure of a society that determines how knowledge will be utilized (for example, Feigl, 1949). More recently, however, the view has become widely accepted that science also influences the social-political-economic structure of a society and that, therefore, the position of an ethically neutral science is invalid. Recognizing the intrinsic interaction between society and science has been made particularly explicit by Marxist psychologists and other dialectically oriented researchers (see Riegel, 1973a, for a review). In their view, science not only *should not* but in fact *cannot* be socially and morally neutral.

In addition to being responsive to formal, legislated rules (such as the right of privacy), researchers are regulated by informal rules of conduct suggested by professional organizations. For example, the American Psychological Association has published a booklet, *Ethical Standards for Research with Human Subjects*, which was developed by a committee on ethical standards in psychological research (American Psychological Association, 1973a). The following are the key ethical principles proposed by this committee and adopted by the Council of Representatives of the American Psychological Association:

1. In planning a study the investigator has the personal responsibility to make a careful evaluation of its ethical acceptability, taking into account these Principles for research with human beings. To the extent that this appraisal, weighing scientific and humane values, suggests a deviation from any Principle, the investigator incurs an increasingly serious obligation to seek ethical advice and to observe more stringent safeguards to protect the rights of the human research participant.

2. Responsibility for the establishment and maintenance of acceptable ethical practice in research always remains with the individual investigator. The investigator is also responsible for the ethical treatment of research participants by collaborators, assistants, students, and employees, all of whom, however, incur parallel obligations.

3. Ethical practice requires the investigator to inform the participant of all features of the research that reasonably might be expected to influence willingness to participate and to explain all other aspects of the research about which the participant inquires. Faiiure to make full disclosure gives added emphasis to the investigator's responsibility to protect the welfare and dignity of the research participant.

4. Openness and honesty are essential characteristics of the relationship between investigator and research participant. When the methodological requirements of a study necessitate concealment or deception, the investigator is required to ensure the participant's understanding of the reasons for this action and to restore the quality of the relationship with the investigator.

5. Ethical research practice requires the investigator to respect the individual's freedom to decline to participate in research or to discontinue participation at any time. The obligation to protect this freedom requires special vigilance when the investigator is in a position of power over the participant. The decision to limit this freedom increases the investigator's responsibility to protect the participant's dignity and welfare.

(margin annotations) clarify responsibilities of both parties — protect & inform about physical & mental harm — explain afterward and ensure no harmful consequences remain — confidentiality remove, correct undesirable consequences — special considerations for children and aged

6. Ethically acceptable research begins with the establishment of a clear and fair agreement between the investigator and the research participant that clarifies the responsibilities of each. The investigator has the obligation to honor all promises and commitments included in that agreement.

7. The ethical investigator protects participants from physical and mental discomfort, harm, and danger. If the risk of such consequences exists, the investigator is required to inform the participant of that fact, secure consent before proceeding, and take all possible measures to minimize distress. A research procedure may not be used if it is likely to cause serious and lasting harm to participants.

8. After the data are collected, ethical practice requires the investigator to provide the participant with a full clarification of the nature of the study and to remove any misconceptions that may have arisen. Where scientific or humane values justify delaying or withholding information, the investigator acquires a special responsibility to assure that there are no damaging consequences for the participant.

9. Where research procedures may result in undesirable consequences for the participant, the investigator has the responsibility to detect and remove or correct these consequences, including, where relevant, long-term aftereffects.

10. Information obtained about the research participants during the course of an investigation is confidential. When the possibility exists that others may obtain access to such information, ethical research practice requires that this possibility, together with the plans for protecting confidentiality, be explained to the participants as a part of the procedure for obtaining informed consent [pp. 1–2].*

The Application of Principles in Developmental Research

A scientist has a responsibility to generate new knowledge; but in doing so, as we have seen, the scientist also has a responsibility to society and the live participants—whether human or animal—involved in the research. Thus, the goal of a researcher cannot be the execution only of research with optimal internal and external validity (see Chapters Five and Six); the research must also involve ethically acceptable procedures. The principles presented above are general guidelines that need to be interpreted for application to any given research project. To ensure proper interpretation, one should read the entire booklet (American Psychological Association, 1973a), which includes interpretive supplements to the guidelines.

When the principles are applied to life-span developmental research, the researcher should consider special circumstances, such as dealing with very young or very old research participants. A representative set of standards for research with children, for example, is quoted by Reese and Lipsitt (1970, pp. 31-32). In child research the investigator is ethically bound to obtain not only the informed consent of the child's parent or other responsible agent but also, insofar as possible, the child's own consent. In obtaining the child's consent, the researcher may be unable to inform the child about the nature of

*From *Ethical Standards for Research with Human Subjects*, by the Committee on Ethical Standards in Psychological Research. Copyright 1973 by the American Psychological Association. Reprinted by permission.

the study in any meaningful way, but care should be taken to give the child a bona fide opportunity to refuse to participate or to refuse to continue, without any kind of censure or criticism if he or she chooses that option. Research projects involving aged persons that deal with situations of institutionalization, senility, or loss of consciousness during dying should follow comparable guidelines.

Decisions on questions of ethical appropriateness of a given research project are sometimes difficult, especially because they involve a conflict between alternatives that in themselves are ethically and societally positive (for example, the search for new knowledge versus the right of privacy). Since a single researcher may be overtaxed if asked to make an ethical judgment on his or her own research, the use of investigator-independent review processes is often critical for obtaining a satisfactory interpretative judgment. We concur in the belief that as a scientist one is easily biased toward the intrinsic advantages of searching for new knowledge. Therefore, we recommend that researchers actively seek out the counsel of their less-involved peers before they begin a concrete piece of research.

In order to facilitate such a review by peers, most research-oriented settings, such as universities, have begun to institute standing review committees charged with this task. Researchers are encouraged to use such review channels as fully as possible—recognizing that this process may not only lead to useful judgments on ethical standards but also serve an important educational function in maintaining a high level of ethical consciousness among the research community in general.

Summary

There are different kinds of knowledge and strategies of generating knowledge. The scientific method is the strategy of generating the type of knowledge that scientists find acceptable. It is based on the objective observation of phenomena under known conditions.

In science, understanding a phenomenon means being able to explain it. Prediction and explanation are essentially identical, except that prediction refers to events that have not yet occurred and explanation refers to events that have already occurred. A given theory is comprehensive if it deals with both prediction and explanation.

The search for explanation is often described as a search for causal relationships. There is a diversity of conceptions of cause; however, they always imply temporal sequence and regularity. In addition, it is often said that the notion of a cause also implies a variable (independent) that is subject to active control or direct intervention. Although the exercise of control over the "causing" variable is a desirable feature, it is not a necessary condition for the demonstration of cause-effect relationships. Employing the principle of pattern explanation, for example, makes it possible to use the results of a number of converging correlational studies for the purpose of causal analysis. Thus, both experimental-manipulative and correlational (see also Chapter Eight) approaches or designs are important in the process of generating knowledge.

For developmental researchers it is useful to recognize that the concept of causality is not a unitary and simple one. For example, the distinction between proximal (immediate) and distal (mediate) causes is helpful in identifying the uniqueness of developmental-research paradigms. Developmental research—due to its focus on historical relationships—is much concerned with *developmental* distal or mediate causes.

The process of designing research is aimed at examining the nature of relationships among variables for the purpose of generating scientific knowledge. The general strategy is to ask questions and to engineer the gathering of data in such a way that any ambiguity in the nature of the relationships between the variables is reduced as much as possible. In general, there is no single research design that is universally best. However, it is possible to evaluate research designs with regard to their quality or usefulness by considering the degree of their internal and external validity (see Chapters Five and Six).

When designing research, a scientist should not proceed with the sole goal of generating knowledge. Rather, it is important to see the scientific method and one's scientific behavior in the context of society at large. Society calls on scientists to select research questions that have not only theoretical but also social relevance and to conduct research with a high degree of moral and ethical responsibility.

In order to facilitate the goal that scientists consider questions both of theory and of ethics, scientific organizations such as the American Psychological Association have formulated key ethical principles that investigators are encouraged to apply when performing research. Decisions on the ethical appropriateness of a given piece or line of research are sometimes difficult, especially because they often involve a conflict between positive alternatives (such as the search for new knowledge versus the right of privacy). It is argued that the use of investigator-independent review processes by peers is necessary for a satisfactory interpretative judgment on the ethics of a particular piece of research.

Chapter Five

The Internal Validity of Research Designs

The Concept of Internal Validity

The concept of internal validity is related to the task of reaching unambiguous (valid) conclusions about the relationships among design variables. Imagine that before starting a research project you think ahead for a moment and ask yourself, "What is it that I would like to be able to conclude when I have finished gathering and analyzing my data?" Given that the objective of research is to record and evaluate observations bearing on the relationships among variables, the researcher faces two primary considerations in planning a study. The first, the one covered in the present chapter, is the issue of whether or not the relationship observed is accurately or validly identified or interpreted (internal validity). The second, to be discussed in Chapter Six (external validity), concerns the matter of generalizing from a relationship observed in one set of data to other potential data sets that might have been observed but were not. Questions of internal and external validity need to be considered conjointly when evaluating the overall merit of a given study.

If the project involves manipulating one or more independent variables and noting the effects of these manipulations on one or more dependent variables, one primary objective is to be able to attribute changes or differences observed in the dependent variable to the manipulations either produced or observed by the experimenter. To justify the conclusion that one set of events (intervention and manipulation) produced another set of events (changes or differences in the dependent variable or variables), the experimental procedures must be arranged to eliminate the possibility that some influence other than the observed or intended one is responsible for the differences or changes in the dependent variable. Campbell and Stanley (1963) have called this procedure eliminating plausible, rival explanations for the research findings.

The extent to which such alternative interpretations can be ruled out by the nature of the design in a given research study reflects directly the degree of *internal validity* of the research design. The greater the degree of internal validity built into a research design, the more confidence one may have that the specified manipulation or experimental condition was responsible for the observed effect. A design with a low degree of internal validity yields an outcome for which one or more events other than the specified manipulation or experimental condition may well be responsible. Such a design offers no conclusive means by which to identify any one of the possible influences as the causal agent.

Some potential rival explanations are obvious. They may be easy to eliminate or control for, or they may be difficult to deal with—as, for example, when one tries to conduct research outside the laboratory in naturalistic settings. Other potential alternative explanations are quite subtle, and the researcher must acquire substantial training and sophistication in a particular content area as well as in research design in order to ferret them out and eliminate them in designing the study.

It is not uncommon for students first grappling with the topic of research design to announce, as if by rote memory, that a good experimental design includes *a* control group. This statement is not necessarily wrong, but it may have a tendency to divert attention from more fundamental considerations. The primary concern of the control issue is to eliminate the explanations for one's findings that stand as alternatives to the explanation that the study is designed to examine. Controls are ways to eliminate, or at least to estimate the effect of, potential influences other than the intended manipulation. Controls may take a variety of forms, only one of which is the addition of one or more groups of subjects (control groups) to the design.

Campbell and Stanley (1963) have identified a number of general classes of effects that may operate to reduce the internal and external validity of experimental designs. Each of those that jeopardize internal validity may be interpreted as a potential rival explanation for an apparent relationship between two or more variables. It is these rival possibilities that must be controlled for in designing a study. In some cases, the necessary control may indeed be obtained by including a so-called control group. In other cases, however, no one control group suffices to enable the researcher to rule out alternative explanations for his findings—alternatives that may be every bit as reasonable as the particular one hypothesized.

Threats to Internal Validity

Underwood (1957) stated that good experimental design is mastered through practice and not simply through being told the potential problems for which one should be on the lookout. Certainly there is no substitute for immersing oneself in an area to learn it, but at the same time there may be some advantage to learning to recognize a tree before plunging headlong into a forest.

This section reviews the threats to internal validity identified by Campbell and Stanley (1963), giving some examples to illustrate how failure to control for them can lead to gross misinterpretation of the relationships among variables. Campbell and Stanley discuss eight distinct threats to the internal validity of research designs—influences that, quite independently of the target manipulation of the investigator, result in observed effects that may be erroneously attributed to the investigator's manipulations.

The eight threats to internal validity are listed in Table 5-1, and brief examples of appropriate controls are offered. In this chapter, we will define each of these threats without much concern for their specific relevance to developmental research. It will become clear, however, in later chapters (see also Schaie, 1976) that some of these threats to internal validity do not always play the role of error variables in developmental research.

History

During the period in which an experimental intervention or treatment is applied and allowed to influence another variable, all other activity does not cease. Over longer time periods, political and economic crises occur, weather changes, old friends are lost and new ones are found, and so on. Over shorter time periods, especially in an uninsulated environment, a variety of distracting events, such as loud noise and unexpected sights, may assault the subject's senses.

To the extent that the effects of influences such as these cannot be properly distinguished from the effects of the experimenter's deliberate manipulations, there exist plausible rival explanations for the outcome of the experiment, and the internal validity of the research design is weakened accordingly. Such uncontrolled environmental influences, which become confounded with the treatment of primary interest to the experimenter, are categorized by Campbell and Stanley as the *history* threat to internal validity.

Maturation

Somewhat in contrast to the externally originating influence of history as a threat to internal validity, *maturation* refers to changes within the individual that make the assessment of treatment effects problematic. Maturation effects are changes that would have occurred even if the experimenter's manipulation had not. But because they coincide with any effects of the treatment, maturation effects render an unambiguous conclusion impossible

Table 5-1. Threats to the internal validity of research designs and examples of general control techniques

Source of Threat	Strategy	Control Tactic
1. History	Distinguish between the effect of a particular event (A), such as application of a treatment, and the effect of any other events (B) that happen to coincide with the event of interest.	Obtain observations on an equivalent set of experimental units that has been exposed to event B but not event A, and compare with observations of those who experienced events A and B.
2. Maturation	Separate changes that were going to occur anyway from those that are attributable to an intervention or treatment.	Obtain observations that permit estimation of what the experimental units would be like if everything had been the same except that the treatment was not administered.
3. Testing	Determine the extent to which reactions to the measurement process interfere with the estimation of the effect of an intervention.	Compare an equivalent set of experimental subjects who have received the same testing experiences, including measurement, with the group that received the intervention.
4. Instrumentation	Discriminate between treatment effects and differences among comparison groups that are due to changes in the calibration of instruments used in the measurement process.	Maintain the measuring instruments in calibration with a standard.
5. Statistical-regression effects	Arrange to avoid them altogether, or to disentangle treatment effects from those expected on statistical grounds.	Instead of assigning treatment-level status to groups that are at the high or low end of a distribution, assign experimental units at random to comparison groups.

Table 5-1 (continued)

	Control	
Source of Threat	Strategy	Tactic
6. Selection	Distinguish between differences among comparison groups attributable to the intervention and those that existed prior to the treatment.	Use random assignment of experimental units to comparison groups.
7. Mortality	Discriminate between differences among comparison groups due to having received different treatments and those due to changes over time in the composition of the comparison group.	Statistically estimate the portion of any posttreatment group differences that can be attributed to differential loss of experimental units, and correct comparison values accordingly.
8. Compounded effects	Separate treatment-based differences among comparison groups from those attributable to interactive effects of two or more of the threats listed above.	Create experimental arrangements (such as random assignment of experimental units to groups) that preclude selection and other influences from interacting to confound the interpretation of treatment effects.

Note that alternative strategies and tactics for control are possible. Recommendations given are examples only.
Based on Campbell and Stanley (1963).

unless adequate control for the maturation threat to validity is designed into the research.

An example of how maturation effects can mislead is seen in this situation: after four or five days of putting up with cold symptoms, a person decides to take some medicine. The next day the symptoms have nearly disappeared; the person declares to his friends the fantastic therapeutic value of "Sneezeaway," happily ignorant of the fact that had he taken no medicine at all the symptoms would have abated, as the cold had simply run its course.

Testing

Considerable support now exists in the psychological literature for the conclusion that taking a test once will influence how a person scores on a second testing (Nesselroade & Baltes, 1974; Windle, 1954). To the extent that this phenomenon is reliable, it must be controlled for in research designs that involve repeated measurements; otherwise, what might be interpreted as an effect due to a particular treatment could as well be due to a *testing* effect.

Imagine, for example, a kind of psychological magician who, by using an ability measure that reliably produces testing effects, could repeatedly produce the following phenomenon. A group of naïve subjects would have the ability test administered to them. The magician would have the subjects eat a "brain pill" and then take the test a second time. The scores from the second testing would be significantly better than those from the first testing simply as a function of testing effects, but the magician could stage the demonstration so that the uncritical observer would believe that the pill was responsible.

Instrumentation

The observations obtained in research always involve some kind of instrument. The instrument may be a ruler, a voltmeter, a stop watch, or a more complicated piece of apparatus such as a polygraph; or the instrument may be a human who observes an event and makes a series of ratings to describe one or more of its aspects. When the mechanical or human instrument is used at two different points in time, it is possible that the measurements produced at time two are not directly comparable with those produced at time one. A piece of mechanical apparatus may get out of calibration through wear, humidity changes, or electrical fluctuations; a human observer may grow tired or change in a number of more or less subtle ways, even over a relatively brief period of time.

If changes occur in the measuring instrument and they coincide with the changes resulting from a treatment, how can the investigator decide between the two alternatives? Without proper controls for *instrumentation* effects, he cannot. Here is an example of an instrumentation effect in the case of a human observer. Ms. Smith, who operates a small nursery school, believes that youngsters are more troublesome in the afternoon than they are in the morning. She decides to keep records on the frequency of "annoying behaviors" she observes in her nursery school in order to test her hypothesis. But the fact that she finds the frequency of "annoying behaviors" higher in the afternoon than in the morning may well reflect her own fatigue and increasing irritability as the day wears on rather than any changes in the behavior of the youngsters.

Statistical Regression

As a threat to the internal validity of a research design, *statistical regression* can be subtle but nevertheless devastating. Effects that might be due to a planned treatment may also be attributed to statistical regression unless the latter possibility is ruled out by design. Statistical regression has been discussed extensively in the literature (Campbell & Stanley, 1963; Furby, 1973; Lord, 1963; Thorndike, 1942), and a variety of proposals have been made concerning how to interpret and how to control for the phenomenon.

Briefly, statistical regression means that individuals who obtain extreme (high or low) scores on a measure tend to obtain less extreme scores on a second testing. More precisely, if a group of individuals or other units is selected from a population on the basis of their extreme scores on a measure, the group's *mean* score, obtained at a different time with the same measure, or with a correlated measure obtained at the same or a different time, will tend to be closer to the population mean than is the mean of the scores on which the units were originally selected as extreme. We should be aware that, within the context of some of our prominent statistical models, with extreme-scoring groups we can be relatively sure of an "apparent effect," even in the absence of a deliberate treatment. Experiments must be planned so that these statistical-regression effects can be eliminated, or at least disentangled from the effects the experimenter has tried to bring about through manipulation of other variables.

Generally speaking, probably the clearest example of research that builds on a regression effect is the situation in which some characteristic is believed to require modification and specific treatment, and treatment is applied to those who seem to need it most, rather than to randomly constituted groups. For example, a spelling test is given to a class of third-graders and the ten worst spellers are given two weeks of supervised, intensive play with alphabet blocks. When the class retakes the spelling test, the mean score of the ten worst spellers is found to be nearer the total-class mean than it was on the initial test. Evidence for the effectiveness of supervised play with alphabet blocks? Hardly!

The increase in mean score for this group of youngsters was predictable from our knowledge of the statistical-regression phenomenon. One could also predict on the basis of statistical regression that, had the ten highest-scoring youngsters been given the block-play treatment, their second test-score mean would have been lower (nearer the overall mean) than their first one—data that could be interpreted as indicating that the treatment had detrimental effects. Thus, the very same treatment applied to differentially selected members of the same class of students could appear to be both facilitative and detrimental if regression effects were not controlled.

Selection

In designing an experiment, one makes explicit the nature of one or more comparisons, to be made subsequently, that will provide a basis for inferences about the differential effects of treatments. If two or more sets of subjects differ in ways other than in the nature of the treatments to which they are assigned, any differences observed after treatment may well be a function of differences that existed prior to the treatments and may be completely unrelated to the different treatments given.

Such *selection* effects are expected in naturally existing groups: the members must be like one another and different from members of other groups in order for them to be an existing group. One may grossly lump together those influences (often unidentified) that are responsible for the existence of a given group, as a class, and call them *selection factors*. To the extent that differences between groups on such factors are related to the dependent variable in a research design, they present an explanation competing with the experimental treatments.

Competing explanations are clearly undesirable from a design standpoint, since they create a situation in which inferences about the effects of experimental manipulations are always questionable. Selection effects may be such a culprit, particularly when two or more intact groups, such as classrooms or other "naturally" existing sets of persons or other experimental units, are given different treatments and then compared on some dependent variable.

Experimental Mortality

When the composition of comparison groups changes because subjects drop out—as a result of events such as illness, boredom, death, or mobility—the losses may not affect all comparison groups in the same way.

For example, the experimental group may be subjected to several "boring" training sessions and a control group not. The less conscientious members of the treatment group may refuse to continue the experiment, but no similar refusal will occur among control group members, since they have not been bored to the point of quitting. Now, suppose the treatment is designed to strengthen such characteristics as dependability and conscientiousness. A subsequent comparison of mean "conscientiousness" scores would favor the experimental group, not because the scores of experimental individuals increased but because the experimental-group members whose scores would have been low, and thus would have tended to hold down the mean value, are no longer involved in the experiment.

Compounded Effects

Campbell and Stanley discuss the possibility that two or more of the various threats to internal validity may combine to create outcomes that are not distinguishable from those presumed to be attributable to the experimenter's manipulation. Chief among these concerns are possible interactive effects involving *selection* and one or more of the other sources of invalidity. For example, *maturation* rates may differ for individuals who, by selection, are in separate, intact groups. If one such group is given a treatment and another is used as a control, the differential maturation rates may result in differences between the groups that cannot be disentangled from treatment effects.

The various threats to internal validity of research design can be largely avoided if one restricts the scope of his research to those problems that can be investigated in a controlled laboratory setting and uses random assignment of subjects to treatment and control conditions. The advantages of a laboratory context from the standpoint of internal validity must be weighed, however, against certain disadvantages associated with questions of external validity, to be discussed in the next chapter. The procedures, restrictions, and controls one decides are necessary in order to eliminate rival explanations may create a situation so artificial that one could never hope to observe it outside the laboratory walls.

For each threat to internal validity there may be a number of research designs that provide effective controls in the context of a given research problem. Campbell and Stanley, for example, distinguish between various kinds of designs and extensively discuss design features that provide controls for sources of invalidity. In principle, there are always two kinds of control arrangements possible (see also Chapter Twenty-Two); one is by *equation,* such as by random assignment, and the other is by *adjustment,* usually statistical. *Random assignment* of subjects to comparison groups, for instance, makes the groups randomly equivalent to each other with regard to events happening prior to the assignment to groups. From that point on, ideally, any ways in which the groups are systematically treated differently will be due to the planned interventions of the experimenter, and the differences between groups observed after intervention thus may be attributed to the manipulations of the experimenter.

The importance of becoming familiar with the eight threats to internal validity in their various manifestations cannot be overemphasized. Designing research studies and interpreting outcomes demands the ability to deduce logically whether or not a given design eliminates rival explanations of a given phenomenon.

Internal Validity and Developmental Research

Two related issues about internal validity are of particular significance to developmental researchers. One deals with the fact that much developmental research—because of its concern with so-called person variables, such as age—does not permit control by random assignment. The second involves the fact that some of the variables that Campbell and Stanley label as threats to internal validity can attain the status of independent variables in developmental work.

As to the question of general level of internal validity in developmental research, one need only take a cursory look at the literature to see that developmental research does not consist solely of well-executed, internally valid studies. First, much research is done in more or less natural settings without random assignment of subjects to treatment conditions. For example, comparisons may be made between adults who were reared in the absence of a father and adults who were reared in intact families. Moreover, many of the design variables in developmental work (age, sex, social class) are not amenable to strict experimentation—for instance, by means of random assignment. Therefore, it is often necessary to use strategies that permit statistical (a posteriori) rather than experimental (a priori) design control.

Second, some of the "threat" variables summarized by Campbell and Stanley are obviously not design threats for developmental researchers, but rather are their primary target variables—their bread-and-butter variables. Consider, for example, history and maturation. In line with the developmental focus on historical paradigms (see Chapter Eleven) and long-term antecedents, it is the antecedents and processes associated with history and maturation that are the origins (sources) of developmental change and differences. Any of the design threats listed by Campbell and Stanley, which typically have the status of control variables, can become the target of inquiry—that is, take on the status of independent or dependent (rather than control) variables.

Although this situation leads to some unique characteristics for developmental designs (see Part Four), it is not particularly surprising; neither does it negate the earlier discussion of the need to rule out alternative explanations. Developmentalists who focus on particular history or maturation processes, for example, must either assess or control for those effects of history or maturation that they exclude from their theoretical definition of history or maturation.

Summary

The major purpose of a research design is to provide data that will yield as unambiguous an answer as possible to a given research question. The researcher must be careful to minimize the number of plausible interpretations for any observed event, in order to be able validly to attribute observed effects to a particular treatment or cause. There may be a number of possible sources of plausible alternative explanations for a research finding, but these can be eliminated or minimized by proper design features.

Internal validity permits the researcher to reach unambiguous conclusions about the relationships among design variables. Eight threats to internal validity are: history, maturation, testing, instrumentation, statistical regression, selection, experimental mortality, and compounded effects. The task of designing internally valid research focuses on providing for conditions by which the alternative explanations (due to the various sources of invalidity) can be ruled out.

The value of any given empirical study is to a large degree defined by its internal validity. In developmental research, many design variables (age and sex, for example) are not directly manipulable. Therefore, control must often be exercised on an a posteriori rather than an a priori basis. Moreover, some of the conventional "threats" to internal validity, such as history and maturation, may have the status of experimental variables in developmental research. Even then, however, controls for unwanted or unintended effects of history and maturation need to be included in the research design.

Chapter Six

The External Validity of Research Designs

The Concept of External Validity

In Chapter Five, the question posed was, "What would I like to be able to conclude when I have finished gathering and analyzing my data?" Relevant to this question, the concept of *internal validity* of design was introduced and developed to clarify the notion of interpreting relationships among variables. A second major consideration pertinent to this question is how widely applicable a given research finding is. This problem relates to the concept of *external validity*. External validity, then, concerns generalizing from a relationship observed in one set of data to other potential data sets that might have been observed but were not.

The particular set of observations made in a research study is nearly always only a subset of a larger domain of potential observations that, hypothetically at least, might have been included but were not. Moreover, a further aspect of developmental thinking is that the domain of possible observations is undergoing changes. Because in any single research study only a relatively small number of the possible observations are likely to be made, the degree to which they are representative of the larger domain and its changing nature should be a matter of some concern. After all, it is for a "parent" domain of observations, rather than for the particular sample examined, that we intend our scientific laws to hold. (In the language of statistics, a parent population is not a population of parents but the population from which observations are sampled in a particular study.)

Campbell and Stanley (1963) used the concept of external validity to focus on the issue of generalizing from sample to domain. They phrased the issue of external validity of research design in terms of the question: "To what populations, settings, treatment variables, and measurement variables can what has been observed be generalized?'' Research designs with a high degree of external validity permit wide generalization. As is the case with internal validity, the question of external validity should be considered at the time of designing the research, rather than only after the data collection and analyses have been completed.

One shortcoming of much current behavioral research is that the issue of external validity is often either not addressed at all or, in the discussion of findings, dismissed with a perfunctory statement such as ''One must be careful in generalizing these findings beyond the present study.'' Some caution is, of course, always desirable in interpreting research outcomes, and therefore it is not particularly to the investigators' credit that they can do no more than offer a qualification that is already understood. In our view, the relative neglect of questions of external validity in psychological research (compared with questions of internal validity) needs to be corrected (see also Hultsch & Hickey, 1976). Both types of design validity are important and need to go hand in hand.

Dimensions of External Validity

To design a high degree of external validity into a research study, the best way known is to specify as explicitly as possible the potential domain of observations to which one would like to generalize and then to obtain a representative sample from it. One point to which the Campbell and Stanley definition of external validity leads is that the sampling involved in designing an externally valid study requires the investigator to consider explicitly at least four different dimensions: (1) *organisms* or *experimental units*, (2) *settings*, (3) *treatment variables*, and (4) *measurement variables*. Each of these dimensions will now be discussed in more detail. (Another dimension of external validity often considered is *time*. Since time is salient to all research on behavioral development, it will be considered in later chapters. In many ways, the role of time in the discussion of external validity is similar to the role of history and maturation in considerations of internal validity. Time, rather than being a dimension of control in external validity, is the target dimension of developmental research.)

Experimental Units

At one time or another, most of us have heard critical statements such as ''Psychology is the study of college sophomores'' or ''Psychologists should spend less time studying white rats and more time studying people.'' Statements of this type are a direct if somewhat inelegant way of questioning the external validity of behavioral research. Unfortunately, such criticisms are not altogether unjustified, even though most of the effort devoted to clarifying issues of sampling has been focused on the dimension of organism or experimental-unit sampling. In the actual design and conduct of research, the experimental subjects are frequently obtained essentially on a "catch as catch can" basis rather than through some sampling scheme explicitly designed to yield observations from the population to which one would like to generalize (see also Chapters Fifteen and Sixteen).

Settings

The *setting* of a study is the second dimension related to the generalization of findings. As noted in Chapter Five, many variables other than those manipulated or measured may be involved in a given relationship; the researcher may be totally unaware of some of these. Different settings may call into play unique configurations of unmeasured variables and produce setting-specific findings as the setting is varied. Antecedent-consequent relationships that can be demonstrated with a high degree of replicability in the antiseptic, soundproof, constant-temperature environment of the laboratory may dissolve in a noisy classroom or in the unique climate of a mental-health clinic. Or, conversely, important and apparently lawful (systematic) aspects of interpersonal behavior between husband and wife observed in the home may evaporate when scrutinized in the clinic or laboratory.

Treatment Variables

The choice of *treatment variables* that will fit a given antecedent-consequent relationship is the third dimension along which the issue of generalization r st be considered. For example, Hoyer, Labouvie, and Baltes (1973) demonstrated that the speed with which older adults respond to items on ability tests could be greatly increased by rewarding the participants with a particular brand of trading stamps. Would money or simple verbal praise have worked as well, or even better? Would a different brand of trading stamps have been as effective? Obviously, not all possibilities can be examined in a single study; but for that very reason the generalization issue should be dealt with in designing the study rather than after the study is completed. To the extent that one can specify potential treatment combinations in advance, investigators can choose among them to best satisfy their external-validity requirements.

Measurement Variables

The fourth dimension along which generalization must be considered is *measurement variables*. Suppose a researcher finds that, when subjects are asked to perform a series of simple arithmetic calculations with accuracy scores to be announced in front of the group, their scores rise on the Taylor Manifest Anxiety Scale. Would the same effect be found if a different measure of anxiety were used? Meeting a rabid dog in the street may accelerate your heart rate, but will it also elevate your blood pressure? Training may increase the frequency of a given response, but does it also affect amplitude of the response?

Discussing accident rates of older drivers, Kalish (1975) pointed out that the choice of measure influences one's conclusions about a phenomenon. For example, older drivers' accident rate is very high if the rate is based on accidents per miles driven. If, however, the rate is based on accidents per 1000 drivers within an age group, the elderly have a very low rate. Questions such as these point out the need to appropriately generalize to a set of measurement variables—an issue of importance here and also in a subsequent discussion of measurement *per se* (Chapter Seven).

External Validity and Theory

Our explicit recognition of four different aspects of external validity should help to emphasize a point that many writers have discussed but that seems to elude a number of students: that the issue of generalization is not restricted to inferences made from a sample of persons to a population of persons but, rather, applies to inferences made from a sample of observations to a population of potential observations. Each observation represents a unique combination of person, setting, treatment, and measurement variables. As developmentalists, we may also wish to specify that this unique combination occurs at a specific point in time—thereby recognizing another dimension affecting generalization, the dimension of time.

In this summarizing section on the concept of external validity, it is also important for us to emphasize that the concept of external validity is not a fixed one. First, the issues and concepts that were systematically addressed by Campbell and Stanley have been further developed and evaluated. Cook and Campbell (1975), for example, in addition to further clarifying the concepts of internal and external design validity, defined two additional concepts of design validity. The first is *statistical-conclusion validity*—validity of the conclusions made about cause-effect relationships on the basis of statistical evidence. The second is *construct validity*—validity of the labeling of cause-effect operations in the terms relevant to a theoretical position. For reasons of parsimony, this book is restricted largely to the work of Campbell and Stanley and its implications for developmental research.

Second, the definition of external validity varies with metamodel or world-view considerations. Hultsch and Hickey (1976) present an excellent discussion of this issue. The relationship between paradigms of research and the concept of external validity is similar to the one discussed earlier in the context of development. The concept of external validity is different depending on whether a mechanistic, organismic, or dialectical paradigm is used.

For the most part, Campbell and Stanley's (1963) exposition is developed within a mechanistic mode, and we need to keep in mind that alternative approaches to the concept of external validity are possible. Thus, the discussion presented by Campbell and Stanley treats external validity largely as a question of quantitative generalization. Were one to accept an organismic or dialectic perspective, the concept of external validity would not only be one of quantitative variation (across settings, time, and so on) but would involve structural-qualitative issues as well. Thus, in a dialectical framework, it would be assumed that the "basic" structural nature of a behavioral law under consideration could vary along dimensions of external validity. For example, studying people at different times, and therefore at different ages and developmental levels, could mean studying behaviors that are governed by qualitatively different principles, as evidenced, for example, in organismic models of development. Accordingly, it could be more useful to focus on differential laws than to focus on variation around a single relationship, as Campbell and Stanley did.

Threats to External Validity

Four general threats to external validity of a design have been identified by Campbell and Stanley (1963); they are summarized in Table 6-1 and briefly discussed below. The preceding discussion on dimensions of external validity represents a general framework within which the following specific illustrations can be understood.

The Reactive or Interaction Effects of Testing

If, in the conduct of an experiment, an event (call it A) that in any way mediates the relationships between independent and dependent variables occurs prior to the designated manipulation, then the apparent effect of the independent variable cannot be expected to occur in situations where event A has not preceded the manipulation. Generalizing about the relationship observed between independent and dependent variables from the experimental situation to those situations in which event A does not precede the experimental manipulation obviously involves some risk—risk created by the limited external validity of the experimental design.

Campbell and Stanley discussed how the actual measurement of subjects prior to introducing a treatment may act like event A above and predispose the subjects to react differently from the way they would have had

Table 6-1.   Threats to the external validity of research designs

Source of Threat	Example of How Threat May Restrict Generalization
1. Reactive or interaction effect of testing	Taking a pretest alters the effect of an intervention. Unpretested experimental units do not respond to treatment in the same way pretested ones do.
2. Interactions with treatment variables	Uncontrolled threats to internal validity combine with the treatment to produce a result that the treatment by itself does not produce.
3. Reactive effects of experimental arrangements	Treatment manipulation shown to be effective when applied in an institutional or clinical setting does not have the same effect in a field setting.
4. Multiple-treatment interference	The effect of several treatments applied concurrently or sequentially is not clearly decomposable into discrete contributions from each treatment.

Based on Campbell and Stanley (1963).

they not been measured prior to the introduction of the treatment. For example, suppose a new diet pill is to be tested, and members of the experimental group are all present at a weigh-in prior to the beginning of the program. At the weigh-in, perhaps inspired by the actual weighing or by the accompanying conversation, the subjects become quite weight conscious and become unusually conscientious about taking the diet pills and avoiding between-meal snacks. At the end of a month, the experimental subjects may show a highly significant weight loss. But could the apparent effect of the diet pills be generalized to persons who might buy them at the store and start taking them without first going through a group weigh-in? Without the weigh-in, the pills might be considerably less effective—a result signaling a lack of external validity of the original design.

Interactions with the Treatment Variable

In some cases, an influence identified in Chapter Five as a potential threat to the internal validity of a research design may combine with the influence of the treatment to produce an outcome that could not be produced by the treatment itself. When this interaction of variables occurs, one cannot clearly disentangle the treatment effect from the combined effect of treatment and some other influence, and thus cannot generalize to uninvestigated situations.

For example, consider a case in which selection, usually considered a threat to the internal validity of a research design, interacts with a treatment to produce an outcome. Imagine a situation in which a treatment to help people stop smoking is to be applied to a group of subjects. Now suppose that signs advertising the research project and soliciting volunteers to serve as subjects are placed only in locations where people are not permitted to smoke. It might be that the people who would be in such places, who would read the signs, and who would volunteer for the experiment are only light or moderate smokers to begin with. Very heavy smokers might avoid places where they cannot smoke. Thus, the subjects involved in this experiment would consist only of light and moderate smokers, and no heavy smokers would be included. If the treatment appeared to be effective—say, after two, three, or more weeks—one still would not be able to conclude that the treatment would be effective with any group of smokers. Only a selected group was studied, and therefore one is unable to generalize about the effectiveness of the treatment to the general population of smokers; one can generalize only to the light to moderate smokers.

Another example of such interactions is between history effects and a treatment. Imagine that the day a new soft drink is put on the market to measure consumer reaction happens to be extremely hot and humid. People might react in a very positive way to this soft drink partly as a function of the weather on the particular occasion when they were trying the drink for the first time. The question is, what would happen on a day of average heat and humidity? The reaction might not be so favorable—in which case generalizing from the reaction of consumers on that particular hot and humid day to other days would not be accurate. The external validity of this experiment would be in jeopardy.

Reactive Effects of Experimental Arrangements

In many situations, conditions such as the physical surroundings in which the experiment is conducted may produce effects that will not be separable from the intended effect of the treatment. In such a case one may form an erroneous picture of the effect of the treatment. One does not know what outcome may occur if the treatment, *per se,* is applied in a somewhat different context or setting.

For example, just knowing that an experiment of some type is taking place may cause the subjects to react differently to the treatment. If a treatment of some kind is tested in an experimental context and a given effect is observed, does this mean that a similar effect will be observed in a real-life kind of setting? "Deep Dimple" toothpaste may prove to be very effective in reducing cavities in a controlled experiment, but when it goes on the market and is purchased by the average person the user may not brush so strenuously as the subjects in the experiment did, and thus the apparent effect of "Deep Dimple" toothpaste will be lost.

It is easy to think of many situations in which the effect of some treatment ascertained under somewhat contrived conditions is unlikely to be repeated outside the experimental context. When an effect is observed in a highly controlled setting, it is at best risky to generalize from that observation to what one might observe in a real-life context. Such reactive arrangements may very seriously hamper our ability to generalize and thus may jeopardize the external validity of a design.

Multiple-Treatment Interference

Multiple-treatment interference involves a situation in which the simultaneous application of multiple treatments produces unknown or unwanted patterns of effects.

As a common, everyday example, suppose you plan to develop a program to assist frail individuals to gain weight. You might carefully prescribe various kinds of menus for them to follow, such as three meals a day, snacks between meals, dietary supplements, and so on. Suppose the individuals gain weight. Is the weight gain due to the regularity of meals, the snacks, or the dietary supplements? Such multiple treatments may produce the desired effect, but how can one tell just which particular aspect of the multiple treatment is the effective one? Perhaps all are effective but only when administered in combination. In any case, the design is bad because it does not permit the researcher to state explicitly what the effective agent is. If one is not sure whether a particular aspect of a global treatment is effective by itself or must be administered in concert with others, one's ability to generalize about the effects of any one aspect is clearly limited.

In a slightly more formal context, suppose you are interested in comparing four different ways of memorizing poems. Method B may appear to work best, but perhaps the supporting data were gathered in such a way that all subjects tried all methods one after the other. If so, maybe method B works best only because it follows method A; if it were tried before method A it would not be so effective as, say, method A. Designs in which the same subjects are given multiple treatments clearly run the risk of multiple-treatment interference as a threat to their external validity.

External Validity: Evaluative Perspectives

Each of the four threats to the external validity of a research design discussed above and summarized in Table 6-1 should be carefully considered by the reader. It is apparent that, even though a given study may exhibit a high degree of internal validity, it may yield conclusions that are of little use because of dubious external validity.

The researcher must carefully weigh alternatives between the two types of validity, because one is often purchased only at the expense of the other. Achieving a high degree of control over factors that would otherwise jeopardize the internal validity of a study may push the researcher toward working in a laboratory setting that, in turn, may threaten the external validity of the study. Alternatively, designing a study involving a wide range of treatments and settings may make it difficult, if not impossible, to achieve strict experimental controls over unknown or unnamed factors that might influence the variables under study.

For some kinds of treatments—for example, a particular type of antitoxin that will always be administered in an institutional setting and only by trained personnel—the effects can be validly ascertained through research conducted in a single type of setting. However, other types of treatments —such as a particular training regimen for teaching children to read—are expected to be used in a variety of settings, such as private or public classrooms, large and small schools, and so forth. For such treatments, the effects may be validly ascertained only through research conducted in the full range of relevant settings.

The control of threats to the external validity of a research design is at least as important as the control of threats to its internal validity and perhaps more so. For example, to ask whether the same outcome would be observed if the experiment were done again under highly similar circumstances is to raise the venerable question of *replicability,* which is a special type of external validity or generalizability. In this sense, the concept of external validity is particularly important for a relatively young discipline such as developmental psychology.

For the developmentalist especially, the domain of potential observations to which one may wish to generalize on the basis of a sample is not static (Bronfenbrenner, 1976; Hultsch & Hickey, 1976). As the organism ages, the stimuli to which it is sensitive change, and the responses it may make differ—in some cases markedly. Furthermore, the final intent of developmental research is, of course, the description and explanation of "naturally" occurring behavioral changes. The dimensions of experimental units, settings, treatments, and measurement variables can be taken by the developmentalist as a challenge to explore systematically the linkages among home, institution, culture, and behavior, all in a developmental context.

As Campbell and Stanley pointed out, the range of accurate generalizations cannot be unequivocally demonstrated; but as developmental researchers we must take an aggressive lead in extending the limits of our empirical research toward the unknowable boundaries of the domain of generalizability—not by accident but by design. This is particularly important because for the developmentalist external validity is often a matter not only of quantitative variation but also of structural-qualitative variation. Variation of time, for example, can alter the developmental level of subjects. Such structural differences suggest that it might be useful to represent in some situations generalization in terms of differential laws rather than simple quantitative variation around a single behavioral law.

Summary

The major purpose of a research design is to provide data that will answer a given research question as unambiguously as possible. The researcher must be careful to minimize the number of plausible interpretations of the event observed, so that he or she can validly attribute observed effects to a particular treatment or cause. At the same time, however, a given project should be designed to provide the soundest basis on which to make the desired generalizations to the larger set of observations that is represented only by sample in the research.

The concept of external validity is used to evaluate the level to which findings may be generalized. Four general dimensions of external validity are: experimental units, settings, treatments, and measurement variables. Four specific threats to external validity are: reactive or interaction effects of testing, interactions with treatment variables, reactive effects of experimental arrangements, and multiple-treatment interference. The concept of external validity also varies depending on one's world view. In developmental psychology, there are researchers who view external validity as involving not only a dimension of quantitative variation. Following an organismic paradigm, they emphasize qualitative-structural issues as well.

Internal and external validity are somewhat incompatible, in the sense that a high level of one kind of validity may be purchased at the expense of the other kind. However, in order for knowledge to have applicability, it must have generalizability. Therefore, researchers need to pay equal attention to internal and external validity, preferably by continually examining the overall "validity balance" of a research program and by considering both internal and external validity throughout the conduct of a study.

Chapter Seven

Measurement

The Nature of Measurement

Investigations of behavioral change and development rely heavily upon the quantification or measurement of both those variables in which developmental changes occur (consequent or dependent variables) and those variables that may be responsible for the changes (antecedent or independent variables). In fact, it is in the assessment of changes in behavior that some of the most troublesome and difficult issues related to measurement in the behavioral sciences have been identified, as discussed in Chapter Twelve. To facilitate the presentation of certain issues related to the measurement of change, some elementary measurement concepts will be presented for consideration and review in this chapter.

Measurement is one of the cornerstones of empirical inquiry in any scientific discipline. It directly represents how we have elected to define salient concepts. Without some means of quantifying important aspects of our observations, the study of development would never progress much beyond the accumulation of ream upon ream of verbal descriptions and untestable assertions. The capability of using numbers, as a kind of accurate, efficient shorthand, to describe pertinent events provides advantages that we often take for granted but without which utter chaos would reign (Nunnally, 1967). Meaningful numbers enable us to describe and summarize by computing averages, ranges, and other simple indexes, which we may then easily and accurately communicate to others. Numbers (measurements) also provide raw material for the mathematical and statistical-analysis machinery we use to construct the nature of relationships among variables.

Imagine, for example, that someone dares you to spend the next hour of your existence without using numbers for any purpose related to quantification of events. To accept that challenge is to violate the conditions immediately, because *one hour* of time was specified. Time is an example of an attribute we are constantly measuring. Suppose we overlook that, however, and you agree not to quantify events in any other way for an hour. Imagine that you continue reading. You may not count the number of pages or words read. If you stop reading and go for a walk, you may not count steps, blocks, or miles. Nor, we might add, would there be any grade-point average for you to worry about. You may not watch or take part in most kinds of athletic contests, and you may not give a stranger directions such as "go three blocks north, turn left, and the Dew Drop Inn is on your right, three-quarters of a mile farther." You may not buy or sell anything, and so on.

The examples given are all relatively simple ones, but the point should be exceedingly clear. Evidence of the usefulness of quantification and measurement is everywhere about us, and it is no less indispensable in research than in day-to-day existence. Whenever we conceptualize in terms of numbers (time, distance, rate, and so forth), we are quantifying concepts. We concern ourselves with both the appropriateness and the accuracy of the measurement processes we develop. Let's now consider more carefully just what is involved in measurement and some of the more familiar kinds of measurement issues.

What Is Measurement?

Our discussion of measurement will be a rather conventional one, emphasizing some concepts and principles that have been useful to psychologists for several years. These concepts, however, are highly relevant to those concerns that occupy the developmentalist in understanding systematic behavioral change.

When one measures, he or she is assigning numbers to objects or events according to a set of rules (Nunnally, 1967; Torgerson, 1958). The numbers assigned are intended to convey information about quantity —sometimes about quality—of attributes, and the rules by which they are assigned may be simple or very complex. Such a definition of measurement is quite simplified, admittedly, but it serves our purpose here. More sophisticated discussions, directly pertinent to the behavioral sciences, are available elsewhere (for example, Lord & Novick, 1968; Krantz, Luce, Suppes, & Tversky, 1971).

Nunnally (1967) pointed out that measuring makes explicit a process of abstracting out of the object or event a particular attribute or dimension to which the assigned numbers apply. A developmentalist, for example, might measure the height of an infant, the weight of an adolescent, or the IQ of a senior citizen. The developmentalist might also measure the duration of interaction sequences between infant and mother, the level of aggression of the adolescent, or the reaction time of the senior citizen. In each case, it is not the organism *per se* that is being measured but some particular characteristic or attribute associated with that organism.

Making available a set of measurement rules or procedures for some phenomenon of interest has many positive aspects. For example, measurement offers a way to "capture" for further study those characteristics of persons or events among which we seek to establish lawful relationships. It forces the investigator to specify quite explicitly just what the focus of inquiry is, thus providing a basis for communicating the concept to others so that they too may evaluate its usefulness.

Of course, a measurement procedure must meet certain requirements to be generally useful and acceptable. Although producing a good measuring procedure or device is not an easy task, it is often taken lightly, not only by students but by established researchers as well. This is unfortunate, because poor measures will almost invariably result in poor research outcomes, even though the research problem is theoretically well conceived. In subsequent sections we will consider selected cases in which the measurement process sometimes goes awry.

How Is Measurement Done?

Attributes such as height, length of hair, and so on can be measured directly in terms of physical distance, and the rules for assigning numbers to represent the amount of the attribute are relatively simple.

To measure height, for example, a standard unit such as the inch or the centimeter is selected, and this unit is placed end to end, with no overlapping and no gaps, as many times as are needed to traverse the length of the body. The number of times the unit is used is counted, and that count is the height measurement for a given individual. Obviously, it is more practical to hook a number of inch units together permanently (as in a yardstick or tape measure) and to subdivide the inch into smaller units such as an eighth, a sixteenth, or a thirty-second in order to obtain greater precision, but the essential process is as described above. Weight is another attribute of objects that can be measured by rather simple rules. A standard unit such as the ounce, pound, or gram is selected, and the number of these units required to balance the object being weighed on a scale is the number assigned to that object as its weight measurement.

Other attributes such as psychological characteristics, however, are more abstract, and the measurement rules are less obvious. Concepts such as dependency, hostility, ego strength, and extroversion are studied and speculated about in relation to a major portion of the life span, but the proper measurement of these concepts is a considerably more technical enterprise than is the measurement of obvious physical characteristics such as height and weight. Similarly, important concepts such as attachment not only are abstract but may be defined in terms of combinations of organisms, such as mother and child, thus further complicating the process of measurement.

Focusing on the measurement of psychological traits, one may decide, for example, that the way to measure the level of extroversion is to count the number of "yes" responses made to a series of 30 questions about activity preferences. Such decisions should be (but unfortunately are not always) accompanied by an explicit rationale about the nature of the underlying attribute (extroversion), the nature of the set of items to which individuals respond, and the nature of the relationship between items and attributes. Specification of these kinds of properties is necessary within a formal measurement framework (Nunnally, 1967); the specification is needed to justify the inference that a given measurement procedure reflects a particular attribute. Considerable effort has been devoted to a rigorous study of the formal aspects of measurement. On the positive side, some very elaborate measurement theories and models have been developed (Lord & Novick, 1968), but we have also been made aware of a number of reasons why one should exercise some caution and skepticism in measuring quite abstract psychological concepts.

Although a distinction was made above, between the measurement properties of physical and psychological attributes, the general utility of this distinction is limited. For example, some important physically based attributes, such as beauty and physical attractiveness, are not straightforwardly measurable; for this reason a simple distinction between physical and psychological attributes may not be particularly useful.

Measurement Levels

Often there are alternatives, each having different properties, available to the researcher in designing a measurement procedure. Discussions of measurement, especially those offered within the context of the social and behavioral sciences, typically recognize one important set of properties by distinguishing among *levels* of measurement or, alternatively, *scales* of measurement. The distinctions rest upon the specification of characteristics of the procedure and of the resulting numbers or measurements that are generated by it. Several levels of measurement have been defined by a variety of writers, but here we will be concerned only with some of the most common ones.

From a strict mathematical perspective, level of scale has implications for what operations are permissible to perform on the numbers generated by the measurement procedure during the process of data analysis. Some social and behavioral scientists tend to adhere strongly to the notion that only permissible manipulations yield interpretable outcomes and should be used in analyzing data. Others have been somewhat more pragmatic and have performed those operations that seem to lead to worthwhile empirical relationships, evaluating the reasonableness of their data manipulations in that light. To further clarify the idea of permissible data operations, let's next consider the recognized primary levels of measurement and see just how they differ from one another.

Measurement rules, and the resulting measurements, differ in such characteristics as:

1. Whether or not the numbers assigned to individuals or objects reflect an accurate ordering of the individuals or objects with respect to the amounts of the attribute each possesses;
2. Whether or not the differences between the numbers assigned to three or more individuals or other objects accurately reflect the relative differences in the amounts of the attribute possessed by those individuals or objects; and
3. Whether or not the number zero is assignable in such a way that it actually signifies that the object scored as zero possesses *no* amount of the attribute being measured.

The three characteristics just listed provide the basis for distinguishing among *ordinal, equal-interval,* and *ratio* scales of measurement. Many researchers recognize a fourth major level of measurement, *nominal,* which will be presented later in this chapter.

Ordinal measurement.   An ordinal scale or measurement device is one that yields numbers or values reflecting characteristic (1) but not (2) and (3). We often use the term *rank* or *rank order* to characterize the results of ordinal-level measurement.

Four people, for example, may be measured on the attribute height by standing them back to back, two at a time, until the ordering of tallest, next tallest, and so forth down to shortest is achieved. Alternatively, one might label the individuals first, second, third, and fourth in height. Measuring height in this manner does not lead to a precise specification such as the familiar feet-and-inches value, but some useful information is obtained nonetheless. For example, if a basketball coach desperate for players wanted to interview the three tallest men in each class, their teachers could easily select them by using ordinal level measurement, without resorting to the tape measure. But remember that, if all that is known about the three men is that they are the tallest in their class, they might all be over seven feet or under five feet. There might be a one-inch or a one-foot difference between any two of them.

An important point to remember is that, whereas the attribute height is relatively easy to measure, many characteristics are not so accessible; yet being able to measure them, if only at an ordinal level, is scientifically important. It may be that interesting psychological concepts such as intelligence, anxiety, and dominance can be measured only at an ordinal level, given current measurement theory and practice.

Equal-interval measurement.   If one's procedure satisfies both characteristic (1) and characteristic (2), then measurement may be claimed to be at the equal-interval (sometimes referred to simply as interval) level.

In practical terms, the interval scale not only provides an ordering of objects from most to least, as does the ordinal scale, but it also renders interpretable differences between the scores or values assigned to individuals. If X possesses two units more of an attribute than Y does, and Y possesses four units more of the attribute than Z does, then it can be concluded not only that X possesses six units more than does Z but also that the difference between Y and Z in amount of attribute possessed is twice as great as the difference between X and Y. If the intervals or units were not equal all along the scale, such conclusions would not be valid.

An ordinary mercury thermometer calibrated to give Fahrenheit temperature readings provides equal-interval measurements of the attribute temperature. If Monday is two degrees warmer than Tuesday, and Tuesday is four degrees warmer than Wednesday, one can conclude that the temperature drop from Tuesday to Wednesday was twice as great as the drop from Monday to Tuesday. Obviously, one can do somewhat fancier calculations with numbers derived by equal-interval measurement than with those derived by only ordinal-level measurement. The equal-interval scale conveys ordinal information, but the converse is not necessarily true.

Ratio measurement.   Some measurement procedures satisfy all three of the characteristics listed on page 62. Measurement at that level is called ratio measurement. In common-sense terms, a ratio scale is an equal-interval scale with a meaningful zero point. Prime examples are distances measured by a tape measure, or weights measured by a balance scale using a set of standard weight units. Although one does not expect to see a person who scores zero on height, zero can nevertheless be identified in a meaningful way as the beginning of the tape measure or as the weight measured on the balance scale with nothing in the pan.

The significance of the label *ratio* is that one can form meaningful ratios of scale values or measurements. For example, if we carefully measure with a tape measure the standing heights of two persons and find that one person is 76 inches and the other 38 inches, it is permissible to divide 76 by 38 (thus forming a ratio) and to conclude thereby that the first person is twice as tall as the second. To help fix this concept in your mind, contrast the ratio-measurement case with the temperature example of equal-interval measurement used above. If the temperature is 76 degrees on Monday and 38 on

Tuesday, we cannot conclude that Monday was twice as warm as Tuesday, because zero on the Fahrenheit scale does not mean *no* temperature; it is simply an arbitrary location on the scale. We will return to this last point below.

Nominal scales.   Sometimes an attribute is conceptualized in such a way that notions of quantity are not immediately apparent. In these cases of nominal measurement, the task is one of classifying objects into mutually exclusive categories. Whether this procedure is called measurement or not depends on one's assumption about this process. If one assumes that classification into qualitatively distinct categories requires an underlying "latent" dimension of quantity, then nominal categorization can be considered measurement.

Examples of nominal variables are sex (male, female), religion (Protestant, Catholic, Jewish, Buddhist), and marital status (single, married, divorced, widowed). One may use a number code for the alternatives and assign all single individuals a 0, all married individuals a 1, and so on. Such cases are referred to as *nominal scales* or *categories*. Researchers disagree on whether or not nominal scales represent a crude form of measurement. The important point here is that such variables are of interest to developmentalists at times (see, for example, Wohlwill, 1973), and that there do exist a variety of statistical tools, some quite powerful, for exploring relationships in categorical data sets (for example, Smith, 1976).

Table 7-1 dramatizes once more the differences among measurement

Table 7-1.   Distances traveled by cars A, B, and C as they might be expressed based upon different levels of measurement

Level of Measurement (Scale)	*Examples of Information Provided*
Ratio	A traveled 100 miles, B 200 miles, and C 300 miles. C traveled three times as far as A.
Interval	B drove 100 miles farther than A, and C drove 100 miles farther than B. The distance by which C exceeded A was twice as great as the distance by which C exceeded B.
Ordinal	C drove farthest, B next farthest, and A drove the least distance. C drove farther than B; B drove farther than A.
Nominal*	A drove to Richmond; B drove to Washington; C drove to New York.

*The nominal case is included in this table even though there is some question among researchers about its appropriateness as a level of measurement.

levels and their implications. Notice how the information available from the measurement process decreases from the top to the bottom of the table. Clearly, for the developmentalist, who is interested in both absolute status and changes on attributes, appropriateness of measurement level is a pertinent topic. Procedures for measuring very abstract characteristics such as extroversion, anxiety, and hostility are often not precisely classifiable as to their level of measurement. But, as we mentioned above, concern with measurement has led specialists to search in many directions for both procedures and criteria by which to evaluate the merits of specific measurement procedures.

Many of our important statistical-analysis techniques and routines are predicated upon certain expectations about the quality of the data to be analyzed. The level of measurement is one aspect. Below, two additional areas of concern in measurement—*reliability* and *validity*—will be discussed. Both terms actually identify a series of concepts that have received considerable attention and have prompted endless, and at times lively, debate.

The Concept of Reliability

Reliability, a venerable concept in empirical science, is employed both to describe features of observation and measurement and to characterize the nature of substantive phenomena. In the behavioral sciences, empirically oriented researchers have thought a great deal about how to define and assess reliability and how to improve their observation and measurement procedures in light of these considerations. Several aspects of the reliability concept have been recognized, and our objective here is to single out and discuss some of the more salient ones.

In very broad terms, reliability of measurement refers to the consistency or repeatability of measurements of the same phenomenon. Anastasi (1968) argued that, at least in the domain of psychological measurement, consistency is the essence of reliability. In measuring, one would like, of course, to be sure that numerical values have been assigned to events in the most accurate, precise, and consistent way. There are various obstacles to this unattainable ideal, however, and those obstacles constitute sources of so-called measurement error. Since errors invariably distort and obscure lawful relationships, researchers often focus their efforts to refine a measure directly on ways of reducing errors of measurement. Any reduction in the influence of error sources thus attained increases the reliability of the measure.

In the context of psychological measurement, writers such as Anastasi (1968) and Nunnally (1967, 1970) have explicitly listed various influences that lower the reliability of a measurement instrument in particular circumstances. Nunnally (1970), for example, included poorly standardized instructions, test-scoring errors, and errors due to influences such as measurement subjectivity, the testing environment, guessing, content sampling, fluctuations in the individual, and instability of scores. Although the potential impact of each error source is different in different situations, the list dramatizes the multitude of ways in which irrelevant effects can get involved in the measurement process.

The following example illustrates more explicitly how sources of various errors get involved in measurement. One common operational definition of the reliability of a given measure is the degree of correlation between alternative forms of the measure. Assuming that it is possible to have alternative forms of a measure, any two forms, if administered to the same people at the *same* time, would still fail to correlate perfectly due to differences in the nature of the items or content sampled—one of the sources of unreliability mentioned above. If the parallel forms were administered at *different* times to the same individuals, they would fail to correlate perfectly not only because of content differences but also because of various changes in the individuals over time. If one parallel form were administered by person A in setting X and the other form by person B in setting Y, and each was then scored by still a different person, even more sources of unreliability would be introduced.

Sources of unwanted or irrelevant variability in scores may be due to the researcher, to the instrument, or to the experimental subject. They are the reason why several definitions of reliability and their accompanying estimation procedures have been formulated by psychometricians. Thorough discussions by Anastasi (1968), Cattell (1964), Cronbach, Gleser, Nanda, and Rajaratnam (1972), and Nunnally (1967, 1970), to mention a few, explore issues related to defining and estimating measurement reliability. We cannot mention all of them here but, in line with a helpful discussion by Selltiz, Wrightsman, and Cook (1976), we will focus briefly on three major aspects of reliability: *equivalence, homogeneity,* and *stability.*

Equivalence

The equivalence aspect of reliability hinges on the degree of agreement between two or more measures administered nearly concurrently. The accuracy with which a given measure reflects the score one would have achieved on a somewhat different sampling of the same content material is an important characteristic to know about many measurement procedures. With precautions, one can engineer a measurement situation to control for many sources of unreliability and obtain, from the correlation of putatively equivalent measurement devices, an indication of how reliably the underlying phenomenon can be measured in the sense of how comparable scores would be if other forms of the measure had been used.

Homogeneity

As an alternative to correlating one measure with another, methods have been developed for assessing reliability on the basis of how well the different items in a measure seem to reflect the attribute one is trying to measure. A common-sense statement of the rationale is: "If a set of items are measuring a common something, in addition to whatever they may be measuring individually, they ought to intercorrelate with one another more or less substantially." Because of the emphasis on internal relationships, the term *internal consistency* is often used to characterize the homogeneity aspect of reliability. Nunnally (1967), in a very readable discussion, develops the internal-consistency notion of reliability in terms of the correlation between the one actual test and a hypothetical alternative form.

Stability

Stability, and its complement, lability, are of such pertinence to developmentalists that they will be given a lengthier discussion than other reliability aspects. A distinction must be carefully made and maintained between the repeatability of the measurement (reliability) and the repeatability of the phenomenon being measured (stability). If one particular event is observed by two independent observers (and the observers might be ultra-complex, sensitive pieces of apparatus), and they assign the same measurement (number or score), then a basis exists for arguing that the measurement is reliable (consistent scores were assigned). The scores obtained at some later time, however, may indicate that the phenomenon being measured has changed. The question is, did the amount of the attribute actually change, or is the apparent change simply due to some peculiarity of the measurement process? The correlation between measurements on occasion 1 and measurements on occasion 2 reflects both changes in the attribute being measured and unreliability of the measurement instrument, and it is these two sources of variance that one should try to disentangle.

For example, two independent assays of a small amount of blood extracted from a reluctant subject may be in close agreement on that person's blood-sugar level. If another two independent assays are made three hours later, and no food is consumed by the subject during that interval, they may again be in close agreement on blood-sugar level. We would not, in general, expect the first pair of measurements to agree with the pair made three hours later, because blood-sugar level changes over intervals of time. In that case, the measurements from one time to another are not repeated, but lack of repetition does not reflect negatively on the measurement procedures *per se*. Rather, it indicates something about the temporal stability of the phenomenon being observed. Therefore, it is important to distinguish conceptually between reliability (referring to an aspect of the measurement procedure) and stability (referring to an attribute of the phenomenon to be measured). In practice, however, both are sources of variance in observed measurement, and the conceptual distinction is often not easy to maintain.

As alluded to above, the assessment of reliability and stability may be accomplished in a variety of ways. Not all ways of estimating reliability are appropriate for all measurement problems (Anastasi, 1968; Nunnally, 1967). This book only outlines selected important issues, and the reader is strongly encouraged to become more broadly acquainted with issues and proposals through discussions such as that of Cronbach et al. (1972) on the theory of generalizability. Cronbach and his colleagues further broaden the reliability concept to embrace diverse aspects of reliability, such as when different tests, raters, occasions, and so forth are involved.

The Concept of Validity

The issue of validity of measurement traditionally has been focused on the question "What is being measured?" Or, perhaps more popularly, "What are these measurements good for?" In principle, a measure can be good for different purposes. Therefore, we would like to point out that a measure has many validities. Nunnally (1967), for example, insisted that a measure should be validated for each use to which it is put.

The notion of research-design validity (Chapters Five and Six) is related to the concept of measurement validity in the sense that, in each case, inferences about relationships among variables are being made, and it is desirable that they be sound ones. Recall, however, that internal and external validity of design refer to the validity of causal attributions *vis-à-vis* one's experimental arrangements, and to the generality of one's research findings. Measurement validity is usually restricted to the relationship between a measure and the attribute it is purported to indicate.

Over the years, a number of kinds of validity have been identified. The value of some of them has been questioned, but we shall briefly summarize the main ones here in order to draw attention to how broad and important the validity issue is (see also American Psychological Association, 1973b).

Face Validity

Face validity means that the device, test, or procedure seems to measure what it is purported to measure. A series of arithmetic problems, for example, would lack face validity as a test of vocabulary; but a series of words to be defined would have face validity as a test of vocabulary. However, a series of words to be defined may actually be a very poor vocabulary test if, for example, all of the words are rare, or all are very common.

One reason a test needs face validity is that face validity will get the subjects to cooperate and take the test seriously; but face validity by itself is a weak concept on which to base a measurement procedure. Moreover, in some situations it is important that the purpose of a measurement process not be obvious in order to minimize distortion of responses. In the case of an unobtrusive measure (Webb, Campbell, Schwartz, & Sechrest, 1966), for instance, the subjects do not even know that measurement is taking place, but the validity issue still must be dealt with by the researcher.

Content Validity

Content validity means that the measurement device includes a representative sample of items from the content domain of interest. For example, a vocabulary test would have content validity if the words in the test were a representative sample of all the words in the language. Content validity is often claimed for a test, but the claim is seldom justified because there is usually no way to tell how representative the items are. In the vocabulary test, representativeness could be assessed, and content validity could be claimed; but in an arithmetic achievement test, different experts might not agree upon a definition of the universe of possible items, and therefore it would not be possible to justify a claim of content validity.

Empirical Validity

There are two major kinds of empirical validity: *predictive* and *concurrent*. Predictive validity refers to the extent to which the scores on one measure can be used to predict scores on another measure. It is assessed by correlating the two sets of scores. A test may have many kinds of predictive validity; that is, it may be highly valid as a predictor of performance in some situations, moderately valid for others, and without validity for still others.

Concurrent validity differs from predictive validity only in the time when the predicted scores are obtained. In concurrent validity the tests are given simultaneously, and in predictive validity the predicted test is given after the predictor.

Construct Validity

Construct validity means that the test is valid as a predictor of performance in situations that are related by theory to performance on the test. For example, on the basis of a theory it is predicted that a relationship exists between some variable and some criterion, such as between intelligence and speed of learning. Suppose that a test is made up intended to measure intelligence. If scores on the test predict speed of learning, then the test has construct validity as an intelligence test. This kind of validity is empirical, but, unlike predictive and concurrent validity, it is based on a prediction derived from a theory.

Campbell and Fiske (1959) clarified several aspects of measurement validity by focusing simultaneously upon *convergent* and *discriminant* validity, multiple measures of constructs, and sources of variance in test scores. They advocated that measures of psychological constructs be validated in an experimental scheme designed to include at least two different methods of measuring at least two different attributes. Empirical evidence favorable to the measures' construct validity include, among other outcomes, correlational patterns showing relatively high correlations among different measures of the same construct (convergent validity) and relatively low correlations among measures of different constructs (discriminant validity).

Perspectives on Validity and Reliability

The examples above give some idea of the scope of the validity issue. A measure may be quite reliable but useless. No matter how well a test measures whatever it measures, it is often not useful for theory-construction purposes unless it measures what it is supposed to measure. This is the problem of validity. To say that a test is valid as a measure of some particular characteristic means that the test actually measures that characteristic. A reliable test can be invalid, but a valid test cannot be unreliable. Even if the characteristic being measured is a labile one, a valid measure will be reliable if one uses an appropriate procedure for assessing reliability, such as the correlation of equivalent forms administered at the same time.

Reliability and validity are periodically looked at anew. Problems with some of the current concepts are pointed out, and alternative concepts are proposed (for example, Cattell, 1964; Cronbach et al., 1972). In the *theory of generalizability*, Cronbach and his colleagues suggested that the distinction between the concepts of validity and reliability becomes much less marked when one focuses on the following notion. When a measurement process is undertaken, what is desired—but unattainable—is an "average" based on a whole set of scores that might have been obtained but were not. A potential set of scores—which could include those obtained from various persons at several different times of day by several different testers—defines a universe of observations. The theory of generalizability deals with the issue of generalizing from one observation or a small set of observations to some defined universe of observations. The universe of generalization is defined by one's interests and intentions. Depending upon what universe one wishes to generalize to from a particular set of observations, the question being asked may be traditionally called one of either reliability or validity.

Clearly, the generalizability notion here is the same, in an abstract sense, as that of external validity of research design discussed in Chapter Six and is also directly related to the presentation of a basic data matrix for descriptive developmental research (Chapter Twelve). But the universe of generalization of pertinence to research design (and not measurement alone) is defined to include aspects of both independent and dependent, or cause and effect, variables and their interrelationships—a distinction not ordinarily made in dealing with measurement issues *per se*.

Measurement of Behavior

General Criteria

The area of application of measurement principles for psychologists is, of course, behavior. Psychologists have organized behavior in a variety of ways for the purpose of systematizing observation and measurement. As discussed in Chapter Three, the behaviors of interest to the developmentalist may range all the way from very specific muscular contractions to broad response classes conceptualized as descriptive concepts, behavioral dispositions, or traits. Behaviors may be dichotomized as *private* versus *public* (observable), or they may be categorized according to the *medium* through which they are observed or inferred (for example, ratings by others, questionnaire responses, performance measures), as Cattell (1957) has proposed. Still other classifications of behavior are based on the *method of constructing* the measurement device (ability tests, personality tests) or on *substantive areas* such as cognition or motivation.

To discuss these designations of behavior in relation to both their common and their unique measurement features would require a prohibitive amount of space, but we would like to explore in a little more detail some of the aspects of measuring behavior. To do this we have focused on behavioral indexes traditionally used in learning research that tend to be rather clearly observable, easily defined, and usable as measured across broad portions of the life span. This choice is determined by convenience rather than by any wish to downgrade the more abstract foci of measurement. For most of the concepts used in characterizing behavioral measures, such as amplitude, speed, and frequency, there are counterparts in the measurement of more abstract kinds of behavior.

Behavioral Indexes

After defining or specifying the behavior to be studied, the researcher usually needs to select a measure or index of the behavior. The indexes most often encountered are *amplitude, magnitude, latency, speed, frequency,* and various *ratio measures*. Each of these is discussed below in some detail.

Amplitude and magnitude.   Amplitude and magnitude are usually used synonymously to refer to the strength of a response. Most often, they refer to force, but they can also refer to the amount of excursion or distance traversed, electrical resistance, volume, and so forth (Spence, K. W., 1956, p. 72). For example, the amplitude of an eyeblink response has been defined as the degree of closure of the eyelid; the amplitude of the galvanic skin response is the electrical resistance across the palm; and the amplitude of the salivary response is the volume of the saliva secreted (for example, in Pavlov's [1927] classical appetitive-conditioning work with dogs, and Krasnogorski's [1907] similar work with children).

Thus, in the definition of amplitude and magnitude, "strength" can refer to any one of several parameters in addition to force. "Intensity" or "vigor" may be better words to use than "strength" in characterizing the meaning of amplitude and magnitude, but strength, intensity, and vigor can also refer to the other response indexes. The problem is more apparent than real, however, because although all response indexes can be characterized as indexes of strength, intensity, or vigor, the index used in any specific application is not defined as the strength, intensity, or vigor of the response but as the force, distance, electrical resistance, volume, or some other selected parameter of the response. The problem arises, in other words, only in general discussions of the concepts of amplitude and magnitude, and not in actual usage of these concepts. (An analogous problem is encountered in discussions of the concept of physical development; see Meredith, 1957.) Thus, the reader of a research report will know exactly what parameter was assessed by the investigator's usage of the terms amplitude and magnitude, and the different usages can be kept separate in a review of research reports, if the reviewer is careful.

Latency and speed.   The latency of a response is the amount of time required for the response to begin to occur or to be completed. The time required to complete the response is sometimes divided into component latencies—one, the time required for it to begin to occur, and the other, the rest of the time required. The first component is usually called the *starting time*, or *starting latency*, and the other is called the *running* or *movement time*. The reason for analyzing these components separately is that they often have different functional relationships to the variables being investigated or manipulated (see, for example, Ryan, 1970, pp. 143-145).

When latency refers to the amount of time required to traverse a standard distance—whether the distance is the length of a straight-alley maze or the excursion of the eyelid in an eyeblink—it should be apparent that the reciprocal of latency is interpretable as the amount of distance traversed in a standard amount of time. Latency is time per unit of distance, and the reciprocal of latency is distance per unit of time. Hence, the reciprocal of latency is speed of responding.

Frequency.   Frequency is the number of times a response occurs while it is under observation. The referent, or source, of the measure can be either an individual subject or a group of subjects. That is, the frequency of a response can be the number of times it is emitted by a given subject, or the number of subjects who emit the response. Thus, in reporting frequencies, the investigator must specify whether the referent is the individual or the group.

Ratio measures.   Frequency can be transformed into several ratio indexes. The most common ratio measures are (1) proportion and percentage and (2) rate.

Proportion and *percentage* refer to the number of times a response occurs relative to the maximum possible number of times it can occur. The terms can refer to the relative frequency of the response in a group of subjects, or to the relative frequency of the response in a single subject. For example, "65% response" could mean that 65% of the group gave the response and 35% did not, or it could mean that the subject gave the response on 65% of the occasions on which he could respond and did not give the response on the other 35% of these occasions.

Rate refers to the number of times a response occurs relative to a unit of time. The duration of the selected unit of time is arbitrary, and it may depend on convenience or ease of interpretation.

Behavioral indexes and measurements.   Note that the behavioral indexes selected, although they are common and convenient measures, do not automatically lead to useful measurement.

The fact that behavioral indexes have a high degree of intuitive face validity does not mean that they are powerful in research and theory. What is necessary, then, for each of the indexes selected, is an examination of their measurement properties in terms of level of measurement, reliability, and validity, as outlined above. For the most part, the specific indexes presented are rather useful in terms of level of measurement. However, the fact that level of measurement is rather advanced does not imply that they are equally powerful in terms of reliability and validity.

Summary

Measurement is fundamental to the study of developmental change. Without the capability of assigning meaningful quantitative values (numbers) to events, the systematic development of an empirically based body of knowledge would be impossible. Numbers provide the raw material for a variety of mathematical and statistical analyses that enable researchers to specify the nature of relationships among variables. Measurement can be done at various levels of sophistication and accuracy. Three general aspects of measurement are: level of measurement, reliability, and validity.

The level of measurement (for example, nominal, ordinal, interval, ratio) determines to some extent the kinds of statistical analyses that may be performed subsequently. Reliability and validity are directly involved in evaluating the goodness or appropriateness of measurement procedures in the area of behavioral change and development. Reliability is a property of the measurement instrument; basically, it refers to its accuracy or precision. Reliability needs to be distinguished conceptually from stability, which is a property of the phenomenon to be measured. Validity is a property involving the relationship of a measure to the phenomenon to be measured. A number of validity concepts (face, content, predictive, concurrent, construct) have been proposed.

The concepts of validity and reliability have periodically undergone reexamination, and changes in their use and meaning have been suggested. Although considerable ambiguity and uneasiness regarding the concepts remain, they continue to be important to social and behavioral scientists as criteria for discussing and evaluating measurement instruments and procedures.

For application to the study of behavior, a wide array of measurement instruments have been developed. These measurement instruments can be classified along a number of dimensions (for example, private versus public behaviors, domains of behaviors, mode of observation). Behavioral indexes used in learning research include amplitude and magnitude, latency and speed, frequency, and ratio measures. These behavioral indexes are examples of convenient measurement. However, to assess their usefulness in concrete research, one needs to examine them for their measurement properties in terms of level of measurement, reliability, and validity.

Chapter Eight

Data Analysis and Interpretation

For the psychologist, the objective of data analysis is to ascertain the existence and nature of relationships among variables (see Chapters Five through Seven). Generally, the focus is on parsimony, precision, and level of certainty. This chapter deals with aspects of data analysis and interpretation. However, since this book's central theme is conceptions and design, questions of statistics are kept to a minimum. Our coverage here must therefore be restricted in scope, a constraint that prevents our doing justice to a number of both obvious and subtle issues. Fortunately, these issues are fully covered in the abundant books on statistics and data analysis, from primers to advanced texts.

Data-analysis procedures are classifiable in a number of different schemes, usually dichotomous, which dramatize several aspects having considerable relevance for developmental researchers. Like other generalizations, these classifications are convenient, but they do not necessarily represent mutually exclusive and exhaustive alternatives. Four of the applicable classifications will be briefly discussed to provide a sampling of general data-analytic issues.

Theory-Data Analysis Congruence

A first observation on data analysis is that it is not independent of a theoretical context. As discussed in Chapter Three, the nature of one's world view interacts with one's formulation of theories. Similarly, the nature of one's theories and one's knowledge of analytic techniques influences one's choice of a specific form of data analysis. Specifically, one can distinguish between two kinds of situations involving theory-data analysis congruence. The first deals with the fact that theories develop and exhibit different degrees of explicitness at different points in time. The second involves the relationship between theory and data analysis at a more abstract level of theory-building —that is, at the level of world views.

Let's look first at the relationship between theory and data analysis from the perspective of the continuing development of a given theory. For example, sometimes a researcher's data collection is guided by more or less explicit notions of the nature of the empirical world that are deducible from theoretical statements and propositions. The analysis task is then the rather straightforward one of examining the level of congruence between what the theory predicts and what the data actually reveal. Such a situation is sometimes labeled *hypothesis-testing*.

By way of contrast, data are often gathered and analyzed without the benefit of a clearly articulated theoretical framework. The purpose is to generate tentative ideas and hypotheses that might subsequently be more formally organized and tested. This situation is sometimes labeled *exploratory research*. Both hypothesis-testing and exploratory research play an important role in the development of a knowledge base, but they may involve different forms of data analysis and occur at somewhat different stages in the process of knowledge generation.

At a higher level of abstraction, the question of theory-data analysis convergence arises because researchers have differing world views. Organicists (see Chapter Three), due to their focus on structure, tend to look for relationships involving patterns of variables. Mechanists, in contrast, due to their concern with specific antecedent-consequent relationships, tend to look for relationships among single variables.

The general implication of questions regarding the congruence between theory and data analysis is that researchers need to be concerned with maximizing the appropriateness of specific forms of data analysis *vis-à-vis* their research questions. We believe that the fit between theory and data analysis can be optimized if researchers are aware of diverse and multiple forms of data manipulation.

Correlational versus Experimental Data

Despite some appeals to the contrary, a major distinction is made between so-called correlational and experimental research (for example, Cronbach, 1957, 1975). In *correlational* research, relationships among variables are studied without direct manipulation by the experimenter of independent variables or control of temporal sequences of events. Instead, the data collected and analyzed represent relationships as they exist in nature. In *experimental* research, circumstances are contrived so that the experimenter can arrange for certain events (interventions or manipulations) to happen so that their relationship to other events can be observed and studied. In Chapter Four, we discussed some implications of this distinction for the process of scientific inquiry regarding causation.

Experimental Data

In experimental research, the purpose of statistical analysis is to determine whether the treatment given had any real effect—that is, to determine whether the treatment functioned as a cause. The *causal inference* is typically justified for two reasons: (1) manipulative control of the independent variable (treatment) by the experimenter and (2) a brief time difference between the treatment and its outcome. A conclusion is reached about the magnitude of an effect, and the likelihood that it is a reliable phenomenon, by means of the formal procedures called *statistical inference*.

The usual procedure is to test a *null hypothesis*. The null hypothesis states that the treatments do not have different effects. The statistical analysis yields a computed value of probability that the null hypothesis is true. If this probability is large, the researcher infers that the null hypothesis may be true; and if the probability is small, he or she infers that the null hypothesis is false. In the latter case the null hypothesis is rejected as a representation of nature, and the investigator concludes that the treatment was responsible for the difference. The validity of such a conclusion rests, of course, on the internal validity of the research design.

Correlational Data

Correlational data are analyzed to detect the presence of relationships as they exist in nature. For example, one may analyze measurements of mothers and their children on a variable such as dominance to ascertain whether or not there is a tendency for dominant mothers to have dominant children. An implied null hypothesis of "no correlation between the dominance scores of mothers and their children" in the population of observations from which the sample was drawn can be statistically tested by the methods of statistical inference.

Correlational analyses do not lend themselves to immediate inferences about specific causation. A statistically significant relationship between scores cannot be interpreted as evidence that dominant mothers tend to produce dominant children and submissive mothers tend to produce submissive children. It may be that children are dominant or submissive for other reasons, and that they influence the dominance levels of their mothers. Furthermore, it may be that the influence is mutual between mother and child, or that some additional agent, such as the father, influences the dominance level of both mother and child. Note that causation always exists somewhere in correlational outcomes. The question is where and in which direction.

Many procedures for data analysis, such as regression analysis, tests of mean differences, and so forth can be defined as special cases of a general data-analysis model and may be applied to both experimental and correlational data. The interpretations of results, however, which must take into account the issues of internal validity of design, are clearly not the same. Because the process of theory construction often involves successive applications of both experimental and correlational designs, and because many relationships of interest cannot be studied in an experimental setting for ethical and other reasons, social and behavioral scientists have tried to formalize procedures for testing ideas about causal relationships by means of correlational data. This is particularly true for development research, where many of the important variables can often be studied only by so-called quasi-experimental designs.

Inferential versus Descriptive Data Analysis

Statistical Inference

Reference was made above, in the discussion of correlational versus experimental research, to the use of statistical-inference procedures. Procedures of statistical inference constitute a very important component of the developmentalist's research tools, and we will highlight some of them here. Although the domain of statistical inference is a broad topic, deserving the coverage of an entire book, essentially it concerns the orderly use of information based on a limited set of observations to make inferences about a larger set of observations.

Statisticians typically distinguish between a *sample* of observations and a *population* of observations of which the sample is more or less representative. A researcher is justified in inferring that what he or she has observed in a sample of observations is true of the population of observations from which the sample was drawn, provided that the sample was drawn *at random* from the population.

Random sampling is accomplished by following a particular procedure (see Blalock & Blalock, 1968, for review); a random sample may or may not be representative of the population. A random sample is one for which every member of the population had an equal chance of being selected, and for which the selection of any one member of the population had no influence on the likelihood of selection of any other member. For evidence of whether the sample is *representative*, one would compare the demographic or performance characteristics of the sample with the known demographic or performance characteristics of the population. To determine whether the sample is *random*, one would look at the method used to obtain the sample.

In a study of parent-child relationships, for example, although selection of the children could be random, the selection of their parents would not be random, because, once the sample of children is selected, their parents have a 100% chance of being selected and all other parents have a 0% chance of being selected. However, even though the sample of parents is not random, the sample of parent-child *sets* (families) is random because the selection of the children is random.

By utilizing concepts such as random sampling in conjunction with mathematical and statistical representations of what the population of observations is assumed to be like, researchers can then further elaborate on their notions about the population by using information obtained from the sample of observations. These inferences about the nature of the population may be used practically to decide among treatment programs, and they may be used theoretically to evaluate the consistency and validity of empirical relationships deduced from theory.

Much research is aimed at providing a basis for inferences about the nature of the population. But, as noted above, inferences may be made either from experimental data or from correlational data, and therefore the experimental-correlational distinction is not interchangeable with the inference-description distinction.

Descriptive Data Analysis

Less glamorous, perhaps, but no less important than inferential data analysis are the activities associated with descriptive data analysis.

Researchers may simply have a set of data at hand about which they would like to make descriptive summary statements—means, variances, and so on—and thereby characterize the nature of the data with an economy of expression. Such information about the performance of large numbers of otherwise unselected persons can be very useful to others who may wish to use that measure. Formal inferential procedures would not be used, although of course there is always the possibility that what is found for the particular collection of data may hold for some larger set of data.

Univariate versus Multivariate Data Analysis

Investigators may elect to focus on relationships among particular measured and manipulated variables, or they may study relationships defined by patterns among several measured variables. Often, which alternative a given investigator chooses seems more a matter of general scientific orientation than of conscious reflection stimulated by the particular research question. For example, a world view emphasizing structure and structural change (Chapter Three; Lerner, 1976) would lead to an emphasis on patterns of variables rather than on variable-specific relationships.

There is some consensus among writers (for example, Marriott, 1974) that the term *univariate statistics* should be used to designate concepts and procedures for analyzing a distribution of scores representing a single dependent variable, and that the term *multivariate statistics* should be used in those cases in which the joint distribution of two or more dependent variables is being examined. To be more concrete, analysis of the effects of early versus late toilet training, sex, and birth order on altruism scores would be a univariate analysis even though three "predictor" variables (toilet training, sex, birth order) are involved, because only one dependent variable (altruism score) is being studied. Quite in contrast, if one wished to consider the effects only of early versus late toilet training on both altruism and impulsivity scores jointly, multivariate statistics would be called for.

Univariate Analysis

1 dv = univariate

In situations in which the concept of interest to an investigator can be reflected by one measurement variable, a univariate design and (depending upon the question) some form of univariate data analysis are appropriate. One may wish to compare, for instance, the means of several treatment groups on a particular variable, or test to see whether a given sample of observations has been drawn from a normally distributed population.

Univariate statistical analyses are straightforward, well-known procedures, many of which are learned by students in their initial statistics course. Developmentalists, however, must be prepared to critically evaluate the appropriateness of a univariate approach in light of their research needs, since, in line with the earlier discussion of external validity, generalizations of outcomes to other measures are based on quite meager evidence (one variable).

Multivariate Analysis

≥ 2 dv = multivariate

As we noted earlier, multivariate approaches provide the researcher with the alternative of focusing upon several variables and their interrelationships rather than on single variables. In so doing, they permit operational definition of concepts in terms of a network of interrelationships. Many multivariate-analysis techniques become practical to use only with the availability of high-speed, large-capacity electronic data-processing equipment.

Among the more prominent multivariate-analysis procedures are *multivariate analysis of variance*, a tool for testing whether or not means of several groups differ from one another with respect to several variables considered simultaneously; *factor analysis*, a procedure for systematic examination of the structure of the covariations among sets of variables; and *discriminant-function analysis*, a technique used to separate two or more distributions by constructing a multivariate composite score. Another set of multivariate techniques of potential interest involves *multidimensional scaling* and *profile analysis*.

All multivariate techniques, although they are used for quite different purposes, exploit the information contained in the joint distributions of the measures (see Amick & Walberg, 1975; Cattell, 1966; McCall, 1970, for reviews). Much of the experimental tradition in developmental research reflects the univariate approach, but awareness of the mechanics and potential applicability of multivariate procedures is increasing (for example, Baltes & Nesselroade, 1973; Bentler, 1973; Cattell, 1970; Coan, 1966; Emmerich, 1968; Nesselroade, 1970; Wohlwill, 1973).

Summary

The purpose of data analysis is to summarize relationships among variables, focusing on parsimony, precision, and level of certainty. The choice of a particular strategy for data analysis depends primarily on the nature of the relevant theory, its state of development, the kind of observations and inferences sought, and the nature of pertinent assumptions.

One classification attribute of data-analysis procedures is the distinction between the analysis of correlational data and the analysis of experimental data. This distinction has implications for interpretation, causal inference, and internal versus external validity. A second distinction is between inferential and descriptive data analysis. Descriptive data analysis deals with the representation of a given set (sample) of observations. Inferential data analysis is, in addition, aimed at generalizing from a sample to a population of observations. A third distinction is between univariate and multivariate statistics.

No one of the various forms of data analysis (such as correlational versus experimental, univariate versus multivariate) is superior to any other. Each can be useful in specific instances. It is highly desirable for a researcher to be as familiar as possible with many schemes of data analysis, to permit selection of the specific form of data analysis that accords best with the research question, and, consequently, to enhance theory-data analysis congruence.

Part Three

Objectives and Issues of Developmental Research in Psychology

Part One of this book presented a first view of the unique characteristics of developmental research; Part Two provided an overview of general issues in theory construction and research design. It is our intent in Part Three to apply the general principles outlined in Parts One and Two to the study of behavioral development. Part Three is seen as an effort at integration.

Life-span developmental psychology includes diverse approaches associated with different world views or models of development. These models influence the selection of research priorities and strategies, but there are similarities in the methodological issues that arise—many of which also arise in research covering shorter segments of the life span. Some of the salient methodological problems that need to be effectively dealt with refer to the biocultural context of change; the causal variables that are correlated with the index variable, age; the continuity of change; the time requirement for studying an individual's life span; varying attrition effects; and the equivalence of measures.

Interindividual differences in behavior at any one age (except for differences resulting from concurrent and/or hereditary determinants) must result from earlier interindividual differences in intraindividual change, a lack of interindividual stability. Attempts to define life-span development with reference to invariant, irreversible change sequences have not become widely popular. A more flexible definition, more suitable for a life-span approach, refers to any age-related change that is not random, short-term, or momentary.

Three prototypical paradigms for developmental research are univariate, multivariate, and developmental-multivariate. In each paradigm, consequent (dependent) variables are related to antecedent (independent) variables, considering these variables singly (univariate) or in multiple sets (multivariate), and defining the antecedent variables as concurrent (proximal) or historical (distal). The historical paradigms are often more useful for developmental research. They have implications both for the theoretical construction of behavior-change processes and for application to the prevention of dysfunctions and the optimization of development.

Time is not a causal variable, but it provides a useful index for the ordering of events. Since life-span developmentalists are interested in change with age, they usually use time-ordered research designs. Time-ordered research designs can be categorized (with other designs) in a three-dimensional matrix of (1) persons, (2) tests or variables, and (3) time or occasion of measurement. This three-dimensional matrix is used to illustrate a variety of alternative analytic schemes for data analysis. In order to implement effective developmental research, the researcher should be aware of the various foci (average, variability, structure, trend) and strategies of data analysis (univariate-multivariate, experimental-correlational, hypothesis testing-exploratory, and descriptive-inferential) that can be derived from the data matrix presented (see also Chapter Eight).

Another implication of the three-dimensional data matrix is that the measurement of change is critical for developmental research. Change with time is most obviously measured by the difference between scores obtained at two times of measurement. However, difference scores have many technical flaws and require the application of various controls and adjustments. Moreover, a focus on difference scores distracts from the goal of representation of change. More appropriate is the application of various techniques for representing multiple-occasion data, by means of mathematical functions, for example.

Chapter Nine

The Scope of Developmental Psychology

A Definition of Developmental Psychology

Part One of this book provided a brief overview of the task of developmental psychology: *the description, explanation, and modification (optimization) of intraindividual change in behavior and interindividual differences in such change across the life span*. The preliminary conclusion of this introductory discourse was that developmental-research methodology should provide us with strategies that (1) focus on intraindividual change and regularities in change patterns, (2) are capable of identifying explanatory variable relationships of the historical type, (3) are sensitive to the production of knowledge about the range of intraindividual change patterns and the timing and form of possible intervention, and (4) view individual development in a changing biocultural ecology.

The purpose of this chapter is to expand on the prototypical issues identified in Part One, to put them into historical context, and to specify the types of research paradigms that are useful in studying developmental change. Our hope is that this can be done effectively now that Part Two has provided a general knowledge base on theory construction and design methodology.

Individual Development and Comparative Psychology

Development refers to change with time, either (1) with age or (2) with biocultural evolution. Change with age is *ontogenetic*, and change with evolution is *evolutionary*. Ontogenetic and evolutionary change are not easy to disentangle, since they are part of a dynamic system of interacting influences on behavioral development (Baltes, Cornelius, & Nesselroade, in press).

Traditionally, the major focus of developmental psychology has been on the study of ontogenetic change, whereas evolutionary change has been approximated by studying a posteriori differences among selected existing species or, occasionally, cultures at various levels of civilization. One major school of thought in developmental psychology has argued that ontogenetic developmental psychology should be conceived and studied in the framework of comparative psychology and, therefore, should compare and integrate analyses of ontogenetic and evolutionary change in cultures, generations, and species. This school of thought is known as comparative developmental psychology (Werner, 1948; Yerkes, 1913).

A focus on comparative developmental psychology has three implications (Baltes & Goulet, 1970). First, it exposes the narrowness of developmental research concentrated on one small aspect of individual change, such as individual development in middle-class America during the late 20th century, or individual development in infancy or childhood during this same historical period. Second, a focus on comparative developmental psychology implies that multiple dynamics are involved in the production of ontogenetic and evolutionary changes. Third, a comparative developmental approach is occasionally methodologically useful in providing naturalistic quasi-experiments that facilitate the explication of individual development in one's own cultural context (Eckensberger, 1973).

Individual Development and Age

The primary emphasis of this book is on methodologies for the study of individual development, although, as we stated before, emphasis is also given to individual development in a changing biocultural ecology. Development, in the sense of ontogenesis, may imply more than change in behavior with age, stage, or other variables indexing a sequence (see Chapter Twelve for a discussion of alternative sequence indexes). According to Nagel, the term *development* often connotes "the notion of a system possessing a definite structure and a definite set of pre-existing capacities; and the notion of a sequential set of changes in the system, yielding relatively permanent but novel increments not only in its structure but in its modes of operation as well" (Nagel, 1957, p. 17).

The two views of development that currently dominate the field can be characterized as (1) the stimulus-response behaviorist view of development as change in behavior with age and (2) the structuralist view of development as change in structures with age. The difference has direct implications for which type of descriptive and explicative research is seen as appropriate for the investigation of developmental phenomena. For example, which kind(s) of behavioral change is denoted as developmental change is an often-debated issue. It is important, however, to note again that developmental research is not synonymous with the study of age changes. Age changes are only a special case of a general class of ontogenetic behavior-change processes (Baltes & Willis, 1977; Hultsch & Plemons, in press; Lerner & Ryff, in press).

Description of Life-Span Development

The last decade has seen a growing interest in life-span developmental psychology. Developmental psychology is now studied over the entire life span, but usually not by any one researcher. Most researchers in developmental psychology deal with small segments of the life span—infancy, childhood, adolescence, adulthood, and old age—which most psychologists agree are related but functionally separate. Other researchers do cover larger segments of the life span but limit their work in another way—focusing on one psychological process, such as learning, memory, or intelligence.

In fact, most current researchers deal with one process in one small age segment, such as learning in infancy (or even learning in neonates). The focus of this book, however, is on methodology that is apt to produce models and theories approaching the scope of a life-span developmental psychology (Baltes & Schaie, 1973; Bühler, 1933; Elder, 1975; Goulet & Baltes, 1970; Huston-Stein & Baltes, 1976; Lerner & Ryff, in press; Nesselroade & Reese, 1973; Pressey & Kuhlen, 1957). Developing a theory that encompasses all ontogenetic changes throughout the life span, or studying the generalizability of behavioral laws across persons of all ages and extended time relationships, is certainly not an easy task. The basic approach is, nevertheless, methodologically and theoretically worthy. Furthermore, developmental-research methods, whether applied to restricted age segments or not, exhibit many similarities.

Explication of Life-Span Development

The relationships among development, time, and age become less simple as soon as the task shifts from description to explication. As stated earlier, the initial major variable in any developmental discipline is time; but in developmental psychology (and probably in other developmental disciplines) time is considered to be not a causal variable but rather an index variable. Initially, then, the developmental psychologist looks for relationships of the form

$$B = f(A).$$

To state this paradigm in words, behavior change (B) is related to (is a function of) age (A). However, the statement of such a relationship is not an assertion that time or age *causes* the behavior change. Instead, in subsequent explanatory research, one looks for causes correlated with age—that is, causes indexed by age. These causes are usually assumed to be related to developmental processes such as (1) maturation, (2) learning, and (3) the interaction between maturation and learning; or, in terms of antecedent systems, the causes are assumed to be related to (1) hereditary variables, (2) environmental variables, including past and present environments, and (3) the interaction between hereditary and environmental variables.

The strategy of successive explanation of age changes is perhaps best illustrated by showing how the core paradigm, $B = f(A)$, is expanded to include additional time-related parameters. Longstreth (1968) proposed, for example, a division of developmental antecedents into three categories: heredity (H), past environment (E_{pa}), and present environment (E_{pr}). Accordingly, an expanded paradigm (within an additive and mechanistic framework) would read:

$$B_A = f(H, E_{pa}, E_{pr}),$$

indicating that behavior change with age (B_A) or an age function is fully monitored by antecedents and processes associated with present and past organism-environment transactions. Examples of explanatory developmental research are heredity-environment research and research on the form and sequence of experiential processes that define age-change functions. The explanatory, analytic stance treats age as part of the dependent variable (Wohlwill, 1970a, b; 1973).

There are many examples of treating age and the age function (age-related behavior) as dependent variables. These include attempts to develop new concepts of age, such as psychological age, sociological age, and biological age. Others are studies such as McGraw's (1940) on toilet training and Gesell and Thompson's (1929) on stair-climbing. (For a summary of these studies, see Munn, 1965, pp. 232–233.) Still others are attempts to accelerate or decelerate the developmental-sequence characteristic of the conservation of substance, weight, and volume by massed acquisition or extinction procedures (for example, Beilin, 1976; Goulet, 1970; Hooper, 1973).

Modification and Optimization of Life-Span Development

A modification and optimization posture (Baltes, 1973) takes one additional step beyond the level of explanation of age functions. It can be written as:

$$\text{Change in } B_A = f(H, E_{pa}, E_{pr}),$$

with "Change in B_A" showing concern for understanding the range of age functions.

The goal of optimization is not only to explain a particular age function via analytic, experimental designs on a short-term basis, as described by Wohlwill (1970a). The added perspective is to modify and optimize individual development in a more robust, long-lasting manner by programmatic individual and ecological intervention. The goal of such modification efforts is a *novel* age function, not merely the explanation of an already existing one.

Life-Span Development and Models of Development

We noted in Chapter Three that there are different models of development (mechanistic, organismic, dialectic, and so on), which are not necessarily true or false but which can serve to some extent as guides for theory construction. Life-span developmental psychology is concerned with finding models that are appropriate for construction of a theory of ontogenetic change over various age ranges.

The question of model appropriateness for distinct periods of the life cycle involves questions of continuity and discontinuity (Huston-Stein & Baltes, 1976; Kagan, 1969). A continuity-oriented approach uses models that have already been developed for distinct periods of the life span and examines whether they work for other periods; for example, Piaget's model has been extended to cover the entire life span (for example, Hooper, Fitzgerald, & Papalia, 1971), social-learning theory to cover adult personality development (Ahammer, 1973), and the operant child-development perspective to cover intelligence in old age (Labouvie-Vief, Hoyer, Baltes, & Baltes, 1974). Perhaps any one of the other models designed for selected domains at selected age spans can be extended to encompass the entire life course.

Another strategy—the discontinuous type—may be to construct or apply qualitatively distinct models to different age spans. White's (1965) two-stage model, with associative responding in the earlier stage and cognitive behavior in the later stage, is one example; another is the suggestion that organismic models are particularly appropriate for child development and gerontological development, and mechanistic models may be better suited for the period of middle life. Reese (1973) has presented a similar discontinuity perspective in arguing that the cognitive-growth model (such as that developed by Piaget) is more useful for childhood memory, and that quantitative, mechanistic models are more appropriate for gerontological memory (although Reese [1976] later suggested that a dialectical model may be appropriate throughout the life span).

Alternatively, it may be necessary to construct an entirely new model for life-span developmental psychology. No one knows what such a new model might look like. Some researchers (Baltes, 1973; Lerner & Ryff, in press; Looft, 1973; Riegel, 1976) have suggested that the models to be developed should either combine or reflect both mechanistic and organismic features. Riegel (1976), for example, has maintained that a dialectic model can resolve not only the numerous problems that arise in mixing models but also the issue of ontogenetic versus historical change.

Life-Span Development and Methodology

In Part I we delineated a series of features that a methodology for life-span developmental research must be sensitive to. In order to familiarize the reader with the argument that a life-span developmental approach has unique methodological requirements, a few additional examples are given here. They will be discussed in greater detail in subsequent chapters.

Time Requirements

To study human individuals across the life span would be an impossible task for any one researcher, just as direct observation of political development in the 20th century in the United States would be impossible for any one historian. Therefore, life-span developmentalists must develop strategies for "compressing" time by using archival data, by engaging in cooperative projects, or by applying special techniques for collecting retrospective and prospective data.

The use of hypnotic age regression (Parrish, Lundy, & Leibowitz, 1968) in the study of illusions is one example; the systematic design of age-simulation studies (Baltes & Goulet, 1971) is another. Retrospective and prospective data are based largely on untested techniques and are therefore fraught with potential errors. Such a criticism, however, does not justify a refusal to search for novel methodology apt to build knowledge about long-term individual change. No methodology is completely isomorphic with the subject matter studied. Giving up an interesting question because no easy or perfect methodology has been found to study it is counterproductive in the long run.

Sample Selection and Maintenance

Another series of methodological issues in life-span developmental psychology is the problem of selecting and maintaining samples. Selecting age ranges and age levels is a complex task that requires careful thought about the behavior class studied, the age/cohort distribution, and the subject variables (education, social class, and so on) that need control or correction.

One of the most critical questions in sample selection and maintenance derives from the fact that the parent population (a specific birth cohort) changes in its composition with age, for example, due to biological mortality. For example, 50-year-olds do not necessarily represent all their peers who were born with them at the same time, since some persons die before the age of 50. Furthermore, 50-year-olds in 1950 may represent a different sample from their birth cohort than 50-year-olds in 1980, because mortality patterns show evolutionary trends (see, for example, Cutler & Harootyan, 1975; Westoff, 1974).

Measurement Equivalence

Finally, a series of questions dealing with the development and application of measurement equivalence (validity, reliability) in differing age/cohort groups is equally important. A number of writers (Baltes & Nesselroade, 1970; Bentler, 1973; Nunnally, 1973; Schaie, 1973) have specified some of the problems involved in establishing equivalence in validity and reliability (see also Chapter Seven).

To illustrate, take the case of an observed age difference between 5- and 15-year-olds in scores on a number test. Is this difference due to a change in the validity of the instrument (number test)? The number test might measure "reasoning" in 5-year-olds and "memory" in 15-year-olds. Or is the difference an ontogenetic change in subjects' behavior repertoire?

Where one locates the source of the change—in the instrument, in the subject, or in an interaction between the two—is an issue that often disturbs researchers and calls for the development of appropriate methodology. Let's illustrate the issue of measurement equivalence by another example. If it is difficult to develop intelligence tests that are race-fair, consider the problem of developing an intelligence test that is age- and cohort-fair when contrasting, in 1976, the performance of a 10-year-old born in 1966 with that of an 80-year-old born in 1896. Similarly, consider the problem of designing an experimental context in which an infant and an adult will attend equally to the test stimulus or target task.

Summary

The tasks of developmental psychology are to describe, explain, and modify (optimize) intraindividual change in behavior and interindividual differences in such change. Change associated with age is "ontogenetic" and change associated with biocultural evolution is "evolutionary," but the two kinds of change are often hard to disentangle because researchers tend to focus on small age spans, restricted biocultural populations, and single—or at best short—periods of evolutionary time. Ontogenetic development can be conceptualized simply as quantitative change in behavior with age, or as qualitative change in behavior structures with age. The first view is that of the stimulus-response behaviorist; the second is that of the structuralist.

Even though most current researchers deal with small age spans, life-span developmental psychology is a growing field and has generated advances in research methodology to deal with problems in describing life-span development. Many of the issues also arise in short-span developmental research.

The description of life-span development, through application of special research methodologies, is only part of life-span developmental psychology, which also attempts to explain the descriptive facts. Although the focus is on change with age, chronological age is considered to be an index variable rather than a causal variable. The causal variables are assumed to be related to heredity, past environment, and present environment; and age itself may be treated as a dependent variable—an effect rather than a cause.

Different models of development imply differences in the nature of change, which is continuous in behavioristic, mechanistic models and is discontinuous in organismic and dialectical models. In life-span psychology, another continuity-discontinuity issue arises: Is the same model useful throughout the life span (continuity), or are different models applicable in different segments of the life span (discontinuity)? Among all the models, a dialectical life-span model may be the most adequate under the discontinuity view.

In addition to the other problems in describing, explaining, and modifying life-span development, three special problems are time requirements, attrition effects, and the equivalence of measures. Thus we see that a life-span approach to the study of development leads to unique requirements in methodology.

Chapter Ten

Targets of Developmental Analysis

In Chapter Nine, developmental psychology was seen as part of a general comparative psychology dealing with the study of behavioral differences and similarities in different subgroups of organisms. Within this general framework of comparative psychology, developmental psychology was viewed as focusing on change and variability in ontogeny (individual development). In terms of statistical concepts, this view led to the conclusion that developmental psychology is concerned with intraindividual change and interindividual differences in change.

In this chapter, two aspects of the change-difference issue will be discussed: (1) the statistical relationship between intraindividual and interindividual variability and (2) the use of additional formal criteria for deciding which behavioral changes are developmental and which are not.

Intraindividual Change versus Interindividual Differences

The relationship between intraindividual change and interindividual differences is not simple, and few attempts have been made to specify its exact nature (see, for example, Baltes & Nesselroade, 1973; Buss, 1974). Figure 10-1 presents two hypothetical examples to familiarize the reader with the notion of intraindividual change and interindividual differences. The examples illustrate quantitative changes and differences in level, on the one hand, and the notions of correlation and stability, on the other. The latter are seen traditionally as being independent of changes and differences in level.

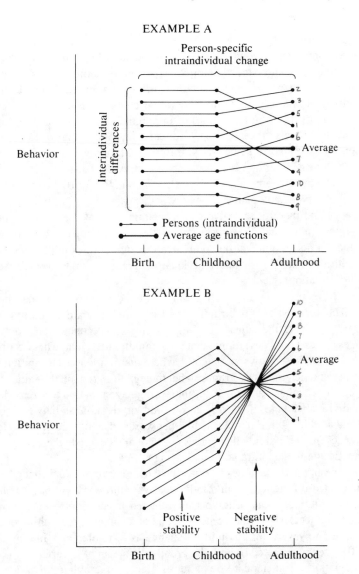

Figure 10-1. Examples of interindividual differences, intraindividual change, interindividual differences in intraindividual change, and positive versus negative stabilities (T techniques).

When plotted on a time continuum, interindividual *differences* refer to differences between individuals in a given behavior at one point in time (for example, at birth). Intraindividual *changes* refer to within-person differences in the same behavior across time. The relationship between intraindividual change and interindividual differences becomes complicated when multiple time points are considered simultaneously.

Typically, interindividual differences at a later time are cumulative results of previous intraindividual changes that differ across individuals. When intraindividual change is plotted across multiple time points for many persons, then, there are interindividual differences in level and form of intraindividual change. First, intraindividual change can occur at different levels. Second, the form (direction) of intraindividual change can differ for different individuals, thus leading to distinct interindividual differences at different time points. In some cases, differing intraindividual change trends can cancel one another out, leading to no interindividual differences.

The two hypothetical examples depicted in Figure 10-1 deal with one behavior observed in the same ten persons at three age levels (birth, childhood, adulthood) and therefore involve change within each of the ten individuals but also interindividual differences among the ten individuals. Note first the difference in developmental outcome, even though both examples started at birth with the same set of interindividual differences (same average, same standard deviation).

In Example A, the outcome in adulthood reflects the same interindividual characteristics as at birth (same average and standard deviation). This outcome may give the superficial impression, if one concentrates only on averages and standard deviations, that no intraindividual change has occurred. That is, Example A shows an outcome where distribution or interindividual-difference characteristics (average, standard deviation) remain the same at the three age levels; therefore, the resulting average age function has zero slope. Intraindividual change, however, does occur for all subjects between childhood and adulthood in Example A. In other words, the absence of age-related differences in interindividual averages does not at all exclude the existence of systematic age-related intraindividual change.

Example B illustrates an outcome where intraindividual change leads to age-related differences in interindividual variability. From birth to childhood, the interindividual difference is reflected in the group average only, since all subjects show the same amount of change. From childhood to adulthood, however, intraindividual change is variable, and interindividual difference is reflected in both the group average and the variability (standard deviation). The standard deviation is greater in adulthood than at birth and in childhood because the amount of change varies among individuals and is greater than the birth and childhood average amounts of interindividual differences.

At this point, two implications need to be emphasized. On the one hand, it should be clear that the term *individual differences* is vague and that it is usually important to specify whether individual differences refer to differences among individuals in level of behavior or to differences among individuals in amount of change. On the other hand, it is important to understand that age differences in interindividual-variability characteristics (average, standard deviation) at two points in time for the same persons must always be, if perfectly measured, a reflection of intraindividual changes between age levels. This statement shows how interindividual differences observed in adulthood can be thought of as the developmental products of distinct intraindividual-change patterns occurring prior to adulthood.

As a matter of fact, if one is willing to assume that there are no interindividual differences at conception (the ideal zero point of development), all interindividual differences observed at a later age under identical measurement conditions must result solely from prior intraindividual change that was different for different persons. In this sense, developmental change is logically and empirically a precursor to a psychology of individual differences; that is, an understanding of how individuals change with age will give one a fairly comprehensive understanding of individual differences. To put it simply, intraindividual change and differential intraindividual change are at the core of interindividual differences.

Covariation and Stability

Figure 10-1 is also useful in presenting the concepts of covariation and stability. Stability is a special case of a set of covariation indexes that can be computed. Stability, in usual statistical analyses, refers not to sameness in *level* of a person but to sameness in *position* of a person relative to other persons. The statistical index is typically a cross-time correlation (comparable to Cattell's S and T techniques; see Chapter Twelve), such as a test-retest correlation.

The birth-to-childhood segments in both Examples A and B in Figure 10-1 reflect perfect between-person stability (the persons maintain their relative positions); Example A exhibits stability with no intraindividual change, whereas Example B exhibits stability with systematic intraindividual change of the same slope for all persons. The childhood-to-adulthood segment in Example A illustrates less than perfect *positive stability* and in Example B illustrates perfect *negative stability*. Negative stability means that persons with high scores on a behavior at one age tend to have relatively lower scores at a later age, and those who score initially low score higher later. Negative stability does occur and runs contrary to classical psychometric guidelines for test construction, where high positive stability is typically a desirable feature. However, the goal of psychometrics is not necessarily identical with that of developmental psychology. Very often, psychometrics focuses on invariance or identity, whereas developmental psychology focuses on change—which can include negative stability.

The relationship between intraindividual change and interindividual differences is further complicated by consideration of the concept of "classes of behavior,'' which as a design parameter permits additional forms of change, difference, and covariation. This concept implies that persons can change not only in one specific behavior, but also from one behavior to another (for example, from anxiety to aggression). This perspective leads to the formulation of multivariate behavior-change concepts, which are discussed in Chapter Eleven.

Intraindividual Change and Development

According to some researchers, not all time-related intraindividual changes are ''developmental'' (see also Chapter Three). These researchers use theory, either explicitly or implicitly, as a basis for defining ''developmental change.''

From the vantage point of world views and developmental-theory construction, a number of criteria have been proposed to distinguish between developmental and nondevelopmental change. Harris (1957), for example, mentioned that among the main features of developmental change is ''movement over time toward complexity of organization, 'hierarchization,' or the comprehension of parts or part-systems into larger units or 'wholes' and an endstate of organization'' (Harris, 1957, p. 3). Similarly, as mentioned in Chapter Nine, Nagel (1957) extracted two essential connotations of development, ''the notion of a system possessing a definite structure . . . and the notion of a sequential set of changes in the system . . .'' (p. 17). In a somewhat different vein, Birren (1959) considered distinguishing between developmental change and aging change, the latter occurring after ''maturity'' and consisting primarily of decline and deterioration.

Wohlwill (1970a, b) has reiterated a fairly restricted view of developmental change that derives largely from Heinz Werner's (1948) position. According to this view, a developmental approach is useful only with behavioral variables that follow an invariant course of development—invariant ''in terms of direction, form, sequence, etc.,'' but invariant only ''over a broad range of particular environmental conditions or circumstances, as well as genetic characteristics'' (Wohlwill, 1970a, p. 52). Wohlwill called variables with such characteristics ''developmental'' variables, and defined ''nondevelopmental'' variables as those that ''show consistent age changes only for individuals subjected to specific experience'' (1970a, p. 52). If the reader recalls the earlier discussion of world views (in Chapter Three), it will be apparent that Wohlwill's proposal is more useful for organicists (developmental change is given) than for mechanists (change is determined by efficient causes), as Overton and Reese (1973) noted. Wohlwill's position also implies that developmental changes are unlikely to be modifiable except perhaps by extreme measures. (But this view can be challenged: see Baer, 1970; Reese, 1976.)

In a similar vein, Fahrenberg (1968) distinguished types of intraindividual variability on the basis of whether the changes are (1) *reversible,* (2) *partially reversible,* or (3) *irreversible.* Examples of reversible intraindividual changes—which can be periodic, quasi-periodic, or aperiodic—are biological rhythms such as diurnal cycles, changes in heart rate, and stress-reaction patterns. Under partially reversible changes, Fahrenberg classified variability associated with specific-learning phenomena and illnesses. Finally, examples of irreversible intraindividual variability are general maturational and aging changes and changes resulting from morphological damage. The category of irreversible change appears closest to Wohlwill's notion of developmental change.

Fiske and Rice (1955) took a different approach. They distinguished three types of variability: In *spontaneous variability,* the change in response is not a function of time-related conditions such as stimulus changes. In *reactive variability,* the response change is determined in part by the individual's reaction to the preceding stimulus or the preceding response (for example, alternation behavior). In *adaptive variability,* the response change is a function of changes in the stimulus or other situational conditions. The distinction among these three types of intraindividual variability is largely based on the notion that response changes are classifiable according to differential antecedents (that is, whether or not response changes are associated with stimulus and situation variations). Apparently, it is *adaptive variability* that in Fiske and Rice's view is at the core of developmental change. In tying their distinction to antecedents, Fiske and Rice implicitly adopted a mechanistic position, unlike the other researchers discussed, whose position is implicitly organismic. (Other mechanistic positions have been summarized by Reese, 1970.)

Such attempts to attach specific theoretical meaning to the concepts of development and aging have never been widely popular, perhaps because they are useful either for organicists but not mechanists or for mechanists but not organicists. However, one should acknowledge that a strong theoretical posture regarding the nature of "true" developmental change has its usefulness when the task of theory-building begins, though within a restricted domain of research questions (see also Baltes & Willis, 1977; Reese & Overton, 1970).

Life-Span Development and Definitions of Change

Even though it is important to be aware of different types of intraindividual variability, there is no clear-cut answer to the question of what kind of intraindividual change should be labeled "developmental."

For descriptive research, the most significant criterion seems to be that the change observed is not random, short term, or momentary. This criterion is also perhaps the most significant for the task of explanation, because change phenomena that are too easily alterable may be largely controlled by concurrent, situational determinants and therefore are of less interest to a process-oriented, historical approach. In this vein, one may decide to adopt the classical view, implying that all changes that are age-related are developmental, whether they are linear or nonlinear, reversible or irreversible. If one adds the notion that <u>age-related phenomena can result from historical-change antecedents</u> (see Chapters Thirteen and Fourteen) <u>as well as from age-related antecedents</u>, this position has additional merit.

There are other reasons for remaining <u>flexible</u> in deciding which changes are properly labeled developmental, especially in a life-span developmental framework (Baltes & Willis, 1977; Huston-Stein & Baltes, 1976). Life-span views need to consider dynamic behavior-environment systems that combine ontogenetic (individual-developmental) and evolutionary (biocultural history-developmental) perspectives. When both ontogeny and evolutionary change are considered, the usefulness of a single world view or model of development for the entire course of life becomes questionable, and the researcher has reason to be flexible rather than rigid in deciding which changes are developmental and which are not.

A researcher should be ready to find any type of intraindividual change when investigating behavioral change through the life span. Whether a developmental approach is useful in explicating the particular change phenomenon observed is perhaps more an issue of the relative empirical power of specific developmental-research paradigms and models when applied to the phenomenon than an issue of the phenomenon itself.

Summary

Intraindividual change in behavior can be described by noting the change in level of performance or by noting the manner of change (for example, the slope of the developmental curve). Interindividual differences may refer to differences in level of performance at one age, or it may refer to differences in the manner of intraindividual change between ages. The first type of interindividual differences, however, must result from the second type if a developmental point is involved, such as conception, at which there are no interindividual differences in behavior. However, even in the absence of an ideal zero point with no interindividual differences, it is still correct to state that any <u>changes in interindividual differences from one time to another must result from differences in intraindividual change between the two points in time.</u>

Positive stability means that individuals maintain their positions relative to one another on a behavioral scale, not necessarily that they maintain their absolute level on the scale. Positive stability can therefore occur even if intraindividual changes are large, but it is not likely to occur if interindividual differences in change are large. Negative stability refers to a reversal in the relative positions of all persons. When this phenomenon occurs, the amounts of intraindividual change are variable and the change is in different directions for different individuals.

Several schemes have been proposed for distinguishing "true" developmental change from other types of change, often limiting the former to change that exhibits an invariant, irreversible sequence. None of the schemes has become widely popular, perhaps because their force and reasonableness depend on the world view or model of development one adopts.

A more neutral view is to include as "developmental" any change that is not random, short term, or momentary, and that is age related. This view (perhaps most prominent among mechanists—see Chapter Three) permits a flexibility not permitted by the other schemes and especially desirable for a life-span developmental approach. Not only are there many gaps in our present knowledge about life-span development, but the empirical evidence for diversity and multidirectionality in adult development and aging seems to require definitional flexibility as well.

Chapter Eleven

Developmental Research Paradigms

One central purpose of this book is to present a persuasive methodological case for a developmental approach to the study of behavior and to recommend a set for "developmental thinking" when formulating hypotheses, designing research, and interpreting outcomes.

Chapter One presented a definition of developmental psychology that includes the notion that developmental researchers search for ways to identify behavioral-change patterns and to explicate them in terms of historical, process-oriented relationships. This chapter further exemplifies the developmental approach by presenting a few prototypical research paradigms (see also Baltes, 1973; Baltes & Willis, 1977) that are considered unique to a developmental view of analytic behavioral research.

Any attempt to derive prototypical paradigms is embedded in some particular world view (Reese & Overton, 1970), as discussed in Chapter Three. However, a presentation of prototypical paradigms, although metatheoretically biased, is useful if it exemplifies and clarifies the framework within which developmental psychologists or human developmentalists operate. For this purpose only, we have selected a mechanistic, behavioristic frame of reference for the following presentation of prototypical developmental research paradigms. The tacit acceptance of such a mechanistic framework is important for the considerations to follow.

The System of Variables and Basic Designs

Within a mechanistic and deterministic metamodel (for example, Kerlinger, 1964; Spence, J. T., 1963), behavior is studied via three systems of variables: *response variables* (R), *organismic variables* (O), and *stimulus variables* (*S*). For the present purpose, response variables refer to classes of behavior in the most general sense; organismic variables involve biological (and not behavioral) attributes of the organism studied; and stimulus variables refer to environmental events. To illustrate once more the significance of one's world view, a strict organicist (for example, Overton, 1973; Riegel, 1976) could argue that such a distinction among three systems of variables is not warranted, because of the organicist postulate that these classes of variables *always* exhibit joint action and interaction and are inseparable.

Within a behavioristic frame of reference, however, the distinction among response, organismic, and stimulus variables is useful. Table 11-1 translates the three-variable system into concrete prototypical research paradigms. The underlying rationale for these paradigms is that a given target behavior is the consequent or dependent variable that needs description and explication through the establishment of predictive relationships to an antecedent variable or antecedent-variable system. Table 11-1 summarizes a variety of prototypical research paradigms on the levels of univariate, multivariate, and developmental (historical) analysis. In each case, the assumption is that changes in the consequent variable relate to, covary with, or are a function of changes in the antecedent variable or antecedent-variable system.

Univariate Paradigms

The initial prototypical paradigms deriving from this three-variable system are the univariate paradigms: $R = f(R)$, $R = f(O)$, and $R = f(S)$.

A concrete example using these three paradigms is the study of anxiety as the consequent behavioral variable (R). Relating anxiety to other behavior categories such as aggression or guilt illustrates the $R = f(R)$ paradigm; the research would lead to a statement such as "the more guilt, the more anxiety." Relating anxiety to organismic, biological variables such as blood pressure or heart rate illustrates the $R = f(O)$ paradigm and leads to a statement such as "the higher the blood pressure (O), the more anxiety (R)." Finally, relating anxiety to an environmental variable such as darkness or isolation illustrates the $R = f(S)$ paradigm and leads to a statement such as "the more darkness (S), the more anxiety (R)."

For any given behavior class, it is probably possible to find illustrations in the psychological literature for each of the three prototypical paradigms.

Concurrent versus Historical Paradigms

It is apparent that the basic paradigms contain a component of change, in that the consequent variable (anxiety, for example) is said to "vary" in conjunction with the antecedent variable. In this context, note that, in true

Table 11-1. Illustration of developmental-research paradigms within a behavioristic framework

Explication	Consequent/Dependent Variable	Process	Antecedent/Independent Variable
	Univariate Paradigms		
A given behavior (R) is related to a single antecedent in form of a response (R), organismic (O), or stimulus (S) variable that is either proximal (concurrent) or distal (historical) to the consequent variable.	R	$= f$	(R)
	R	$= f$	(O)
	R	$= f$	(S)
	*Multivariate Paradigms**		
A set of consequent variables at a given time (t) is related to a set of response, stimulus, and organismic antecedents that are concurrent and/or historical.	$R(1,2\ldots r)T$	$= f$	$(R1,2\ldots r)$ $(O1,2\ldots o)$ $(S1,2\ldots s)$
	Developmental-Multivariate Paradigms		
Time-ordered $(t, t-1,$ and so on) changes in a multitude of variables (age functions) are related to sets of concurrent or historical antecedents via differential (f,g,h) functional parameters.	R	$= f$	(Age)
	Age function	$= f$	(H, E_{pw}, E_{pr})
	$R(1,2\ldots r)T_t - T_{t-t}$	$= f$ g h	$(R,O,S)T_t$ $(R,O,S)T_{t-1}$ $(R,O,S)T_{t-t}$

*The definition of *multivariate* assumes that both antecedents and consequents involve multiple classes of variables. More restrictive definitions have been proposed (for example, Marriott, 1974). Based on Baltes (1973).

experimental designs, between-group (treatment) differences on the dependent variable appear as interindividual differences in the data, but that these differences actually imply intraindividual change. The reader should also recall that—depending on the world view—the nature of this variation in the dependent variable may have to take certain forms in order to be classified as developmental change (see Chapter Ten).

The "covariation" between antecedent and consequent variables can involve small or large segments of the time continuum, depending upon whether the antecedent variable occurred *close* or *distal* in time to the consequent variable. Therefore, Table 11-1 also states that antecedent-consequent relationships can be *concurrent* or *historical*. The distinction between concurrent and historical antecedent-consequent paradigms is an important one, implying, for instance, a time-related continuum of immediate to distal causal or predictive chains. In other words, the task of accounting for changes in a given consequent variable, such as anxiety, can be based on antecedent variables that are concurrent or distal (historical) to the consequent.

Strictly speaking, all causal variables are assumed to occur prior to the event they cause. If an antecedent variable is interpreted as a cause, the distinction between concurrent and historical antecedents is pragmatic—in that the time differential between a consequent and its postulated cause (antecedent) can vary considerably in concrete research examples. Understanding the distinction between concurrent and historical paradigms, however, is crucial, because the usefulness of historical paradigms is at the heart of developmental psychology.

In the case of anxiety, for instance, changes in anxiety would be studied with a historical $R=f(S)$ paradigm if the assertion were that anxiety differences in adult persons (R) relate to the experience of a threatening father (S) in childhood. Many psychoanalytic assertions about adult personality differences are of this type. Another example of the use of historical (distal) paradigms is to relate differences in adult anxiety to hereditary variables, using the historical $R = f(O)$ paradigm, or to relate adult anxiety to dependency in childhood, using the historical $R = f(R)$ paradigm.

Incidentally, the simplest form of a developmental-historical paradigm is the $R = f(R)$ case, with both Rs involving the same behavior class —say, anxiety—but with the Rs being ordered in time. In this instance, the paradigm relates past to present or present to future levels of anxiety, and it reflects simply a time-ordered process of change in a given behavior, such as the description of change in anxiety.

Multivariate Paradigms

Many behaviors are not controlled by a single antecedent variable. Moreover, many "behaviors" are not single behaviors but rather classes of behaviors. Anxiety, for example, is a behavioral class including specific motoric responses, physiological responses, and feelings. Such a perspective leads to the formulation of multivariate-research paradigms. Baltes and Nesselroade (1973) summarized the rationale for multivariate research: "(a) Any dependent variable (or consequent) is potentially a function of multiple determinants; (b) any determinant or antecedent has potentially multiple consequents; and (c) the study of multiple antecedent-consequent relationships provides a useful model for the organization of complex systems" (p. 220).

Table 11-1 illustrates this multivariate expansion of the basic paradigms by showing that a variety of behaviors can be seen as consequent variables ($R1, 2, \ldots r$), and that the empirical inquiry can relate a *class* of consequent variables to a class or *system* of response ($R1, 2, \ldots r$), organismic ($O1, 2, \ldots o$), and stimulus ($S1, 2, \ldots s$) variables. The multivariate expansion shown in Table 11-1 also suggests that the antecedent systems can be concurrent, or historical, or a mixture of both. A historical approach to multivariate paradigms leads to developmental-multivariate paradigms.

Developmental-Multivariate Paradigms

Practically all developmental research is of the *multivariate-historical* kind, at least on a conceptual level (for example, Lerner, 1976).

The focus of developmental research on change suggests the study of multiple levels of a given variable. Furthermore, it was argued earlier that the power or usefulness of a developmental approach increases with the frequency, magnitude, and length of historical, chained relationships with respect to both antecedent and dependent variables. In fact, one could argue that a developmental approach loses most of its appeal if a comprehensive account (description, explanation, modification) of a given behavior could be obtained from a concurrent analysis alone.

With respect to the antecedent component of the analysis, developmentalists often emphasize a multitude of antecedent systems that, through specific forms of behavior-biology-environment interactions, influence the pattern of change in behavior. Patterns and interactions of long-term effects produce the behavior of an individual and interindividual differences at a given point in time (T). The notion that time-related change is the focus of research is expressed in Table 11-1 by giving subscripts to time (T) such as $t, t-1, t-2$, and so forth. The explication of an age function in terms of hereditary (H), past environmental (E_{pa}), and present environmental (E_{pr}) antecedents (see Chapter Nine) is an example of the multivariate-historical approach, since an age function contains multiple levels of at least one variable and there is a multitude of antecedents to consider.

Developmental researchers, particularly those who embrace an organismic world view, often refer to "discontinuous" antecedent-consequent relationships.Therefore, the developmental paradigm shown in Table 11-1 uses not one functional indicator (f) but *multiple functional indicators* (f, g, h). This usage suggests that the form of a given antecedent-consequent relationship can be different at different developmental levels (Baltes & Willis, 1977; Huston-Stein & Baltes, 1976). Although the terms *differential* and *discontinuous* are not precise theoretical concepts, they communicate what is at the heart of many developmental, explanatory analyses: a focus on interactive, nonadditive, nonhomologous antecedent-consequent relationships and structurally different processes.

Examples of Developmental-Multivariate Paradigms

Examples of the use of developmental-multivariate paradigms can be found in a comparison of personality theories. Classic Freudian psychoanalysis, for example, focused predominantly on multivariate, historical $R = f(O)$ relationships (oral, anal, genital), whereas the Adlerian version of psychoanalysis (individual psychology) added multiple historical relationships of the $R = f(S)$ type to the core $R = f(O)$ Freudian framework (see Hall & Lindzey, 1970, for review).

Another example of a multivariate historical analysis of the $R = f(S)$ type is Becker's (1964) attempt to relate child personality structure and differences (R) to multiple dimensions of parental behavior (S) shown both concurrently and at earlier times of parent-child socialization. In the same vein, the Kagan and Moss (1962) monograph on *Birth to Maturity* concentrates on age-related effects of four primary dimensions of maternal behavior (maternal protection, restrictiveness, hostility, and acceleration) on five dimensions of child and adult behavior (passivity-dependency, aggression, achievement, sexuality, and social-interaction anxiety).

Epidemiological theories also offer good examples of developmental-multivariate paradigms. Most disease phenomena—for example, lung cancer and tuberculosis—show persuasive support for multivariate and multiple-causation theories. Lung cancer, for example, does not appear to be a unitary phenomenon or to be tied to a single antecedent; it follows a long-term and variable process of emergence, and it seems related to a variety of antecedents, including inhalation of asbestos and cigarette smoke and experience of stress. Models developed in disciplines other than psychology or medicine also focus on the analysis of multivariate relationships. General systems theory (Bertalanffy, 1968; Sadovsky, 1972; Urban, in press) is one such model that has attracted considerable attention in a variety of disciplines.

Developmental Paradigms and
Prediction/Optimization

The potential strength of historical-developmental research paradigms becomes particularly obvious when long-term prediction and preventive optimization are considered.

Whenever predictive statements extend beyond the immediate situation, it is crucially important to know about the course of probable time-
ordered behavioral chains—whether they are of the *R-R, R-O, R-S,* or multivariate type. As suggested in Chapter Two, knowledge about past, present,
and future conditions is assumed to maximize the success of predictive
statements. Prevention or optimization of development, therefore, is especially dependent on sound knowledge about the course of developmental
change and the key antecedents and processes that mediate development.

Concurrent paradigms can, in principle, maximize development only
at a given point in time and only by means of treatments that are effective here
and now. In contrast, historical-developmental paradigms dealing with prediction and optimization consider (1) the "roots" of a phenomenon, (2) the
context *(R, O, S)* that produced it, (3) the probable future course of development, and (4) the future ecology *(R, O, S)* in which behavioral development
will be embedded.

In this sense, then, developmental prediction and optimization focus
not only on time-related change but also on the multiple person- and
environment-related systems that influence individual development. Attempts
to examine systematic transfer effects (for example, Goulet, 1970), to collect
information about both the individual's behavior and the age-related environment (for example, Bloom, 1964), and to design treatment programs for
children that involve large segments of the family and community contexts (for
example, Danish, in press; Urban, 1975) all recognize that individual development occurs in a time context involving systems of behavioral *(R)*,
biological *(O)*, and environmental *(S)* variables in conjoint relationships.
Whatever kind of theoretical model a given researcher chooses to adopt, it
seems fair to argue that a time-ordered analysis of networks of antecedent
variables will be useful in understanding and controlling behavior. The
specific implementation of historical-developmental paradigms by a given
researcher can take many forms; the methodological focus on time-ordered
analyses, however, is found in all developmental endeavors.

In line with the conclusion that historical research paradigms, often of
the multivariate kind, are at the core of developmental research, the chapters to
follow will present a variety of specific methods all aimed at describing and
explaining behavior change via historical paradigms. The central implication
of these chapters is that, in order for a developmental approach—especially of
the life-span kind—to be empirically powerful, one must have a warehouseful

of methods capable of identifying, representing, and explaining complex long-term historical relationships.

Summary

The developmental view of research calls for unique research designs. The prototypes, or paradigms, of these designs can be classified into three types—univariate, multivariate, and developmental-multivariate—and within-type distinctions can be made on the basis of the nature of the antecedent (independent) variables to which the consequent (dependent) response variables are related.

The antecedent variables are identified as response variables (R), referring to behavior, broadly defined; organismic variables (O), referring to biological attributes of the organism; and stimulus variables (S), referring to environmental events.

The univariate paradigms can be represented as $R = f(R)$, $R = f(S)$, and $R = f(O)$, in which the dependent response variable, R, is related, respectively, to an antecedent response, stimulus, or organismic variable. The antecedent variables may be concurrent or historical with respect to the dependent variable; that is, the antecedents may be proximal or distal. The multivariate paradigms are like the univariate paradigms except that, in the multivariate paradigms, systems of dependent behaviors are related to systems of antecedent response, stimulus, or organismic variables, which again may be concurrent or historical.

The developmental-multivariate paradigms are like the multivariate paradigms but have an explicit historical focus. The task of a developmental analysis is to describe and explain sequential, historical linkages; hence the developmental-multivariate paradigms are often considered to be the most appropriate for a developmental analysis. Furthermore, although the concurrent paradigms can provide information relevant to the alleviation of developmental dysfunctions, the historical paradigms are more useful for prevention and optimization goals.

Chapter Twelve

Time and Change: The Basic Data Matrix

The previous chapters (Ten and Eleven), on the targets of developmental analysis and developmental research paradigms, have shown that any developmental approach (due to its focus on historical paradigms) is intrinsically related to time. Therefore, despite several nebulous issues related to its proper role in scientific explanation, the concept of time commands a great deal of attention in developmental theory and research. Although time is inextricably linked to the concept of development, in itself it cannot explain any aspect of developmental change (see, for example, Baltes & Goulet, 1971; Birren, 1959; Riegel, in press). Time, rather like the theatrical stage upon which the processes of development are played out, provides a necessary base upon which the description, explanation, and modification of development proceed.

In its many operational expressions, such as calendar days or years, chronological age, or pretest-posttest interval, time provides one dimension of a framework within which a series of events can be organized in a meaningful way. The notion of order that it lends—one event preceding the next event, which in turn precedes a third event, and so on—makes time an integral component not only of descriptive developmental research but also of causal demonstration and inference as well. The event-ordering use of time is particularly important in the following sections, which illustrate the nature of various data sets or matrices resulting from translating both concurrent and historical paradigms into concrete empirical observations.

This chapter links Part Two and Part Three. It introduces descriptive developmental designs by outlining a basic data matrix, which results when time is introduced into the study of behavior. This basic data matrix is also the opening stage for assessing intraindividual change and interindividual differences therein. The data matrix is also intended to illustrate the kind of statistical manipulations necessary for representing developmental change.

The Basic Time-Ordered Matrix and Covariation Chart

A general scheme to illustrate several issues pertinent to the collection, analysis, and interpretation of descriptive data via application of concurrent and historical paradigms was developed by Cattell (1946). He presented a three-dimensional "covariation chart" or "basic data relation matrix" to define and illustrate a variety of strategies for organizing observational and data-analysis schemes.

The original figure developed by Cattell was a cube (represented in the upper right portion of Figure 12-1) with one of the three axes representing *persons*, one representing test behaviors, or *variables*, and one representing times or *occasions* of measurement. Any score for a particular person on a single variable, obtained on a specific occasion of measurement, could be located uniquely as a single point within the three-dimensional space.

Represented in Figure 12-1 are three sets of hypothetical data that might have been collected on a sample of persons at three different points in time. Each two-dimensional data set (represented as a matrix or table of numbers) includes a score for each of N persons on each of n variables. If the three matrices in Figure 12-1 were squeezed together along the time line until they touched each other, the resulting figure would be the three-dimensional covariation chart. (Note, however, that hypothetically the covariation chart could include any number of occasions.)

Naturally, many variations of this basic scheme can be imagined, each of which corresponds to a particular problem, research design, and data-collection strategy. For instance, only one variable may be measured on the same N persons at several different points in time—as is done when, say, IQ is measured at different ages. Such a data-collection strategy is symbolized in Figure 12-1 by the data found, for example, in the extreme left-hand column of each of the three matrices. Or only one individual may be measured on several variables at many points in time, as is represented, for example, by the data in the first row of each score matrix. Yet another variation might involve substituting chronological age for time of measurement and measuring three (or more) samples of persons, each representing a different age group, on one or more variables. The number of possible specific data sets that can be identified (and, by implication, the kinds of research problems) within this basic framework is quite large. Not all variations are related to the study of development, however.

The covariation chart was extended by Cattell (1966) to include some

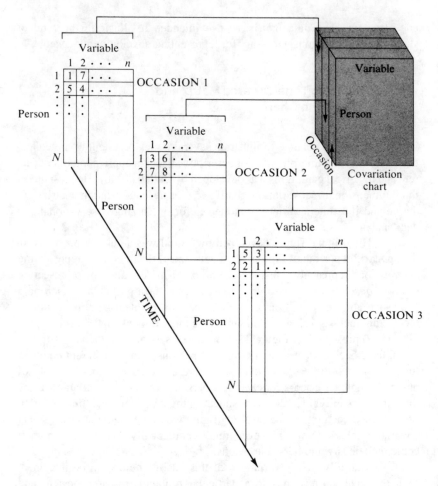

Figure 12-1. Representation of time-ordered data, consisting of scores for N persons on n variables at three times of measurement. This figure also illustrates how the three-dimensional matrix is composed of a series of two-dimensional matrices.

ten dimensions, and Coan (1961, 1966) modified the original covariation chart to give it more developmental pertinence. Coan defined four axes or dimensions: persons, variables representing the persons (attributes, responses, test scores), external stimuli (variables in the environment that influence behavior), and occasions. Within this framework Coan formulated a series of models that provided precise specification of such developmental phenomena as emergence, differentiation, and integration. Nesselroade (1970) also discussed the original three-dimensional covariation chart and multivariate-analysis techniques associated with it, again to emphasize its developmental implications.

The Basic Data Matrix: Questions of Data
Analysis

The basic data matrix contained in Figure 12-1 represents the raw material for statistical analysis and mathematical representation. The nature of data analysis is not only a function of the research question and the research design, but also a function of the nature and level of measurement used. For example, the level of measurement (such as nominal, ordinal, interval, ratio) available for a given behavior is directly related to the kind of statistical inference or mathematical representation that can be made. Thus, questions about the rate of growth—either in one behavior or across many behaviors—or about the origin point of growth can be made only if proper scale characteristics are present (see Chapter Seven and Wohlwill [1973] for more extensive discussion).

In principle, on the assumption that appropriate measurement characteristics are available, statistical or mathematical manipulations of the basic data matrix summarized in Figure 12-1 involve separate and/or joint computation of

> average,
> variability,
> covariation and structural analysis, and
> trend or change analysis.

For each of these, several alternative techniques are available; they are described in most statistics textbooks. Thus, averages and variabilities can be computed for all dimensions in the data matrix: persons, behavioral variables, and occasions. Furthermore, it is possible to represent change across occasions (for either persons or behaviors) by means of mathematical functions.

We have chosen one of the four targets of analysis listed above, covariation, to illustrate how the basic data matrix can be translated into concrete analytic schemes. Some of these analytic schemes are more clearly related to the study of change and development than others.

Correlational Techniques

Cattell's (1946) initial focus was primarily on examining the patterning of relationships among elements representing one dimension of the covariation chart as they varied over either of the two remaining dimensions. Cattell further analyzed these interrelationships to detect basic sources or dimensions of variation among the persons, variables, and occasions. He used the covariation chart to specify, in systematic fashion, six different *correlational techniques* that could be employed by selectively sampling data from the general matrix represented in Figure 12-1. Each of these correlational techniques varies two dimensions of the three-dimensional covariation chart while hold-ing the third dimension constant at one particular level. Although strategies for structural analyses will not be discussed in this book (see, however, Baltes & Nesselroade, 1973; Bentler, 1973), it seems appropriate to point out here that many questions about the pattern or structure of behavioral change can be answered by using multivariate methodology—such as factor analysis—for which covariation information is the starting point.

The six correlational techniques, designated R, Q, P, O, S, and T techniques, are defined in Table 12-1 in relation to the three dimensions of persons, variables, and occasions. It seems fair to conclude that only one of these six techniques (R) is well represented in behavioral research and statis-tics textbooks. As we shall see, however, the R technique is not the technique of greatest interest to developmental researchers.

Table 12-1. Six correlational techniques defined in terms of the three dimensions of Cattell's covariation chart

Correlation Technique	Covariation Focus			Observational Entity		
	Person	Vari-able	Occa-sion	Person	Vari-able	Occa-sion
R		X		X		
Q	X				X	
P		X				X
O			X		X	
S	X					X
T		X		X		

Note: All six techniques involve computing the correlations between pairs of focus dimensions for a sampling of observational entities, with the third dimension fixed at one level. For example, the R technique involves correlating pairs of variables (*Covariation Focus*) over many persons (*Observational Entity*), with *occasion* fixed at one level (each person/behavior combination observed only once).
Based on Cattell (1946).

R and Q techniques. The R and Q techniques both rest upon data representing only a single time sampling of multiple behaviors observed in a sample of persons. As indicated in Table 12-1, the R-technique analysis focuses on the patterns of covariation among different variables (behaviors) as represented in a subset of persons. The Q technique, in contrast, involves the examination of similarities and dissimilarities among persons as reflected by the observed sampling of behaviors.

Several broad implications of these techniques, and a variety of technical issues related to forms of data manipulation, are discussed elsewhere (Cattell, 1946, 1966; Coan, 1966; Nesselroade, 1970). Of special significance here is the fact that even though these two techniques, R analysis especially, are by far the most widely used in behavioral research, they involve only one occasion of measurement and therefore provide for only limited generalizability over time. They are consequently less clearly pertinent to the achievement of developmental research objectives than are any of the remaining techniques, discussed below. Note, for example, that R analysis (because of its restriction to one point in time) does not contain information about intraindividual change.

O and P techniques. As indicated in Table 12-1, the O and P techniques rest upon data sets representing a sampling of behaviors (variables) observed on a number of occasions in only one person. The P technique, which focuses on the patterns of covarying behaviors over time, has been used rather widely to determine patterns of intraindividual change in behavior (Cattell, 1966; Bath, Daly, & Nesselroade, 1976; Luborsky & Mintz, 1972; Mitteness & Nesselroade, 1976). The O technique, in contrast, concentrates on the similarities and dissimilarities of occasions of observation for the person tested as reflected by the particular sampling of behaviors.

S and T techniques. The third pair of analyses defined in Table 12-1, the S and T techniques, are applicable to data matrices representing the observation of a single behavior, but on a sampling of persons at each of a number of occasions. The S technique is used to determine similarities among persons with respect to the particular behavior over the given sampling of occasions of observations. The T technique focuses on the similarities and dissimilarities among occasions of observation of this particular behavior in the sample of persons.

Limitations. The basic data matrix and its associated analytical schemes, such as the various correlational techniques, provide a useful initial framework in which to organize much of the developmental research aimed at description. However, these techniques need to be supplemented by additional research tools. One general but important reason why additional approaches are needed is that each technique focuses on only two of the three dimensions (persons, variables, occasions) and thus, as research designs, all suffer from limited generalizability or external validity.

Implications of the Basic Data Matrix for Developmental Research

On Time and Change

What are the implications of the basic data matrix and its associated analytic schemes for developmental research methodology? First, the study of change requires by definition the inclusion of time as a dimension, either explicitly or implicitly. The time dimension represents a meaningful *ordering of observations*, whereas in most cases the other dimensions (persons, variables) do not. That is, whether Smith or Jones occupies the first row of the data matrix, or whether IQ is the first or last variable entered, is usually of little consequence; but whether a measure of performance on some task requiring manual dexterity is obtained when a person is 2 or 6 years old has significant implications for developmental theory.

The significance of the basic data matrix for a discussion of developmental research design also becomes evident if one considers which data submatrices or statistical schemes are applied in concrete behavioral research. Although specific evaluative information is not available, we believe that most of the current research in the behavioral sciences does not involve the data slices, or subsets, that involve time (occasions) as a dimension. For example, computing R correlations is most likely the standard procedure when the establishment of a covariation is at stake. Yet, for the study of change, S, T, O, and P techniques are conceptually more appealing.

On Measurement of Change

The second salient implication of the covariation chart is that the study of development on the level of both intraindividual change and interindividual differences requires either the assessment of change (for example, is there a difference between two occasions?) or the representation of change (how should we formalize the relationship between occasions?). At present, there are many issues to be resolved in the assessment or representation of change. We can discuss only a few here, but the ones focused on should enable the reader to appreciate the scope of the problem of the measurement of change.

Change as difference. One approach—often used but widely criticized—is to assess change by the difference between the scores on two occasions. This strategy has three major potential deficiencies (see also Chapter Seven). One deals with the required *level of measurement* necessary to interpret differences: what level of measurement (nominal, ordinal, and so on) is required in order to quantify different aspects of change? The second refers to the question of *measurement accuracy* or reliability. When the reliability of observations is low, the reliability of difference scores tends to be even lower. The third potential deficiency involves issues in *measurement equivalence* or measurement validity: how do we know that the difference between scores on two occasions involves change on the same underlying dimension or attribute?

To illustrate these issues, we would like to suggest a few examples from the literature for further reading. Cronbach and Furby (1970), for example, have exhorted psychological researchers to try to structure research questions that are apparently focused on change so that researchers can answer them without having to compute change scores directly. Comparisons between experimental-group and control-group means subsequent to the application of a treatment rather than examination of change scores in an experimental group before and after an intervention is an example of how one might use differences between means as a basis for making inferences about the nature of changes.

Further, Bereiter (1963) discussed several statistical and philosophical points bearing on the interpretability of change measures. For instance, change scores are in many cases considerably less reliable than are their constituent scores. Irregular scale intervals, or other inappropriate aspects of a measurement model at the level of single occasions of measurement, may lead to distortions in the difference scores. Raw difference scores, used to indicate changes, show spurious correlations with the initial and final measures from which they are derived. Ceiling and floor effects, and phenomena such as regression toward the mean, may render the change scores of persons at the extremes of a distribution quite problematic.

To deal with a variety of these issues in the measurement of change, a number of concrete methods have been proposed; but they are rarely accepted by a wide audience. The more recent proposals include the use of *residual scores* (Nunnally, 1967), *base-free change measures* (Tucker, Damarin, & Messick, 1966), *multiple regression* (O'Connor, 1972), and *structural models* to represent causal systems (Bohrnstedt, 1975). Furthermore, with respect to the construction of measurement scales or tests *per se*, Carver (1974) questioned the psychometric approach to measuring change and argued that some tests should have characteristics different from those typically built into a psychometric device. In effect, he suggested that classical test theory be abandoned and new ways of defining concepts like reliability and validity be adopted for judging the accuracy of a measure used to assess changes (see also Nesselroade & Bartsch, 1976, on the "state-trait" distinction).

Toward representation of change. Our view is that many of the issues raised in the literature about the measurement of change (based on the measurement of difference) are legitimate and await better solutions in the future.

However, we believe that focusing on simple difference scores might be, to a large degree, the basis for wide dissatisfaction. Difference scores appear to be tied to a two-occasion situation. At the moment one moves from a two-occasion situation to one involving a large number of occasions (as suggested by the data matrix in Figure 12-1), one can see that the task is less the assessment of a difference than the representation of a multiple-occasion change function.

Representing change functions (for example, by means of trend analysis or mathematical equations; see Wohlwill, 1973), however, does not immediately rely solely on a valid difference between two occasions. Its objective is to use a more comprehensive data base (involving many occasions) in specifying a given change function. We believe that vigorous exploration of such efforts at representation may lead to strategies for the measurement of change that are less susceptible to the criticisms raised against the two-occasion difference score. To illustrate: as one moves to multiple-occasion differences, as in some time-series-analysis models (Glass, Willson, & Gottman, 1972; see also Chapter Eighteen), difference scores can be a powerful way of detecting certain kinds of change functions. Another example is the comparison of multiple-occasion level differences and slope (regression-line) differences (Campbell, 1969).

Therefore, we do not suggest that one should give up efforts to measure change, as implied, for example, in Cronbach and Furby's (1970) conclusions. Many of the measurement issues raised appear to revolve around the use of difference scores in the two-occasion case, which we judge to be a very limited case. What is necessary is the development of new, perhaps elaborate, designs and data-analysis strategies that will assist us in identifying and representing multiple-occasion data in ways that correspond more directly to the study of development. The basic data matrix presented is helpful in pointing out a variety of directions in which such new developments might occur.

Summary

This chapter makes a transition between conceptual arguments and descriptive research designs. It illustrates the role of time-related aspects of behavior. Although time, or age, is not a causal variable, it is an extremely useful index variable—that is, a variable that provides an intuitively clear ordering of events and, therefore, is intrinsic to the study of development.

Time is used in this way in Cattell's classic basic data matrix, or covariation chart. This basic data matrix represents the dimensions of persons, variables (behaviors), and occasions (time) in a three-dimensional matrix. By selecting various combinations from the rows, columns, and slices of this matrix, one can represent most of the descriptive developmental research designs. In addition, the matrix shows how one approaches the computation of various data-analysis tasks involving average, variability, covariation, and change functions or trends.

Examination of the implications of the basic data matrix makes it immediately apparent that some subsets or arrangements of the matrix are more useful for developmental work than others. Those slices or subsets that include time as a dimension of variation are most relevant. However, many of the statistical techniques most frequently used in psychology do not directly focus on time, as we illustrated by contrasting six different correlational techniques (R, Q, O, P, S, T).

An additional implication of the basic data matrix for developmental research is the explicit concern with strategies for the measurement of change. The most obvious measure of change over time—the difference between the scores obtained at two different times—has many technical faults (related to questions of reliability, measurement equivalence, and level of measurement), and psychometric specialists have argued that this measure should not be used. They have suggested several alternative approaches that include statistical manipulation to provide a basis for indirect measurement of changes.

The issues and deficiencies surrounding measurement of change, however, take on a somewhat different perspective as one moves from two-occasion difference scores to scores involving many occasions (time points) as suggested by a developmental approach. The goal becomes one of representing change over time rather than one of assessing a difference between two occasions. Appropriate methodologies for representing change apply such techniques as trend analysis and mathematical functions.

Given the present state of the measurement art and of knowledge about psychological development, there seems to be no universally agreed-upon method or procedure that can be blindly relied upon to make the most sense out of data containing change information. Until better methods are established, the presently available tools—however crude—can be used with liberal amounts of caution. At the same time, the search is on for more effective ways of identifying and describing change.

Part Four

Descriptive Developmental Designs

Descriptive developmental designs are aimed at the identification and representation of intraindividual change and interindividual differences therein. Life-span developmental change can be related to many basic search or organizing variables; one of the primary ones is chronological age. If developmental change is seen within an age-developmental framework, there are two main descriptive designs. The simple cross-sectional method compares different age groups, each observed once at the same point in time. The simple longitudinal method follows one group through several age levels with repeated observations. There is also a simple time-lag design that measures different cohorts, each at the same chronological age.

The major problem with all of these designs is that they lack controls for internal validity. For example, the cross-sectional method confounds age changes with cohort differences, and the simple longitudinal method confounds age changes with such effects as testing and instrumentation.

Many of the deficiencies in simple designs are overcome in complex designs. In order to separate ontogenetic change from biocultural change, sequential strategies have been developed. Cross-sectional sequences consist of a succession of cross-sectional studies. Longitudinal sequences consist of a succession of longitudinal studies. The methods can be combined to yield a design with maximum power.

There are also strategies by which additional issues of design validity can be approached. For example, one problem in descriptive developmental research is that the nature of the population may change with age, yielding positive or negative selection (the survivors will be higher or lower, respectively, in the behavior studied). Needed descriptions of age-related changes in the population are usually unavailable, but subsamples with different survival rates can be compared. Similarly, it is necessary to examine event-specific interindividual differences in change. Terminal change is an accelerated rate of change during the last few years before natural death. Persons who differ in longevity enter the period of terminal change at different ages, but the proportion of dying individuals increases with age, leading to spurious changes in developmental curves constructed from group means.

Other issues especially pronounced in cross-sectional research are related to selection or bias in the samples, disproportionate availability of persons at different age levels, selection of the age levels to be studied, and matching of age groups on demographic variables. Effects of repeated testing have been found to be large in longitudinal research with reactive measures such as intelligence tests, but the methods that permit detecting them also permit computation of corrections to be applied to longitudinal data to remove these effects statistically.

It is fair to conclude that much descriptive developmental work does not focus directly on a representation of change and interindividual differences in change. Therefore, the future will undoubtedly see many new developments in descriptive identification and representation of change.

One such line of march involves the use of mathematical equations and functions. When a developmental theory is available and is precise enough to predict an equation, confirmatory research is used to test whether the equation accurately describes the development processes observed in the data. Otherwise, an exploratory approach is used: that is, the equation is derived directly from the data. The empirically derived equation needs to be confirmed, however, in further research. In both approaches, standard methods of curve fitting or trend analysis can be used.

The use of time series and of Markov models are two other methods that might be appropriate for the descriptive analysis and representation of change phenomena.

Chapter Thirteen

Simple Cross-Sectional and Longitudinal Methods

In the preface to this book, we pointed out that one of the potential deficiencies of this introductory book is its apparent strong concern with age-developmental change rather than with a more balanced treatment of a variety of behavior-change processes. The basic issues are the relationship between theory and methodology, and the world view or theoretical conception of behavioral development a given researcher embraces (see Chapter Three).

Depending upon his or her conceptual preferences, a researcher will select different kinds of behavior changes or behavior-change processes as the focus for developmental investigations (see also Chapter Nine). In our judgment, the different ways of defining developmental change reflect a healthy pluralism in current developmental psychology. Therefore, when presenting developmental research methodology, we need, in principle, to be pluralistic.

In the sections to follow, we have attempted to show that different theoretical orientations require different methodologies. However, since this book does not claim to be comprehensive, many of the concrete examples deal with age-developmental conceptions or derivatives from them. A life-span developmental approach, at this state of its art, is suggestive of such a primary concern with age-developmental conceptions.

We do, however, encourage the reader to generalize from our examples—often involving age—to his or her own theoretical framework. Such other frameworks may include, for instance, specific short-term behavior-change processes (for example, attachment, heart-rate deceleration) or such "age-counterpart" concepts as cohort, stage, developmental progression, or reinforcement history. It is our belief that such generalization is fruitful and stimulating.

The Study of Age Functions

This chapter deals with simple descriptive designs that developmentalists have traditionally used to collect information about individual change. They are simple because their primary paradigm is the translation of time into chronological age, leading to a formulation of the $B = f(A)$ kind. In the use of most of these designs insufficient attention is paid to core design requirements, but their widespread usage suggests that we should give them extensive treatment, if only to demonstrate their inadequacies. The simple $B = f(A)$ paradigm involves comparing different age groups on some measurable behavioral attribute, such as reaction time or span of immediate recall. This paradigm is, in principle, univariate; age is varied as the independent variable and a given behavior attribute is assessed as the dependent variable in the following manner (Baltes, 1968; Kessen, 1960; Schaie, 1965):

$$B = f(A_{1, 2, 3, \ldots, a}).$$

B indicates a given behavior attribute, A denotes chronological age in various levels $(1, 2, 3, \ldots a)$, and f is some kind of functional (covarying) relationship between behavior and age.

The nature of the $B = f(A)$ relationship, which is sometimes also called an age or developmental function (Baltes & Goulet, 1971; Wohlwill, 1970a, b), is the target of empirical inquiry. Note at the outset that such a paradigm is difficult to implement as an *experimental* design, which would require random assignment of subjects to the levels of the independent variable—in this case chronological age.

Chronological age of subjects is an assigned (Kerlinger, 1964), biological variable that cannot be arbitrarily varied and replicated on the level of individual units. You cannot *make* a person be a certain age; you can only wait until he or she attains that age. Accordingly, it is important to realize that $B = f(A)$ designs are usually of the preexperimental type (Campbell & Stanley, 1963; Schaie, 1976). Later it will be shown, however, that simple $B = f(A)$ designs can and practically always should be expanded to include additional treatment parameters and control arrangements, and that chronological age can be conceptualized in ways that allow experimental procedures (see also Chapter Nine).

Cross-Sectional and Longitudinal Methods: A Definition

The two conventional designs used for the examination of an age-functional relationship are generally known as the cross-sectional and longitudinal methods. The *cross-sectional* method compares different age groups

$(A_{1, 2, 3, \ldots a})$ observed (O) at one point in time. The *longitudinal* method follows the same persons through all age levels with repeated observations $(O_{1, 2, 3, \ldots t})$. Baltes (1967a, b, 1968) and Schaie (1965, 1967) have discussed and contrasted these methods in some detail. Figure 13-1 presents examples of the cross-sectional and longitudinal designs. It also illustrates the *time-lag* design, which compares same-age persons from different generations.

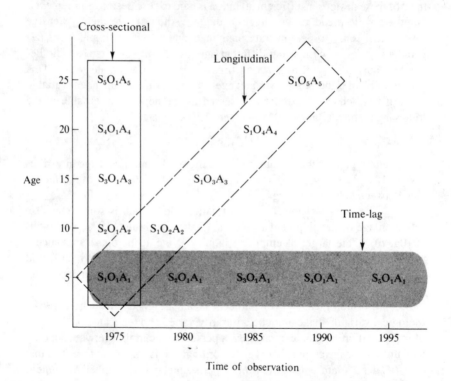

Figure 13-1. A cross-sectional method involves multiple samples (S_1-S_5) of different ages (A_1-A_5) at one point in time, each measured once (O_1). A longitudinal design involves following the same sample (S_1) through all ages (A_1-A_5), using repeated observations (O_1-O_5). The figure also illustrates the time-lag method (Schaie, 1965), which involves contrasting same-age (A_1) but different-cohort samples (S_1-S_5), using one-shot observations (O_1) at different points in time. The time-lag method illustrates the potential significance of historical-evolutionary change in studying development. Based on Baltes (1968) and Schaie (1965).

The example depicted in Figure 13-1 involves the study of 5-, 10-, 15-, 20-, and 25-year-olds. The cross-sectional method, a one-shot comparison of age groups at one point in time, is an *independent-measurement* design;

that is, different persons are observed at different ages. The longitudinal method, extending over a time interval that is identical to the age range studied, follows the principles of a *repeated-measurement* design; that is, the same persons are observed at all age levels.

The Preliminary Evaluation of Simple Designs

Age Differences versus Age Changes

The cross-sectional method does not get at *intra*individual change, and therefore most developmentalists consider this method to yield only approximate conclusions about development. The longitudinal method, on the contrary, yields direct information about intraindividual change and interindividual differences in change.

However, if you can justify making the largely untestable assumption that the different age groups in a cross-sectional study indeed come from the same parent population and differ only in age, then you can interpret cross-sectional age differences as average, intraindividual age changes. That is, cross-sectional *age differences* are equivalent to *age changes* (Schaie, 1967) only if, for example, the 1975 5-year-olds would behave in 1980 (when they are 10) like the 1975 10-year-olds, if in 1985 the 1975 5-year-olds would behave like the 1975 15-year-olds, and so on.

Note, however, that even under the assumption that cross-sectional age differences reflect age changes, inferences from cross-sectional data are limited to *group averages* and do not provide information about intraindividual trends unless a simple, linear, additive, and normative growth model is accepted as a further assumption. The need for the strong assumption of an identical parent population and the lack of information about intraindividual trends are the primary reasons why many design-oriented developmentalists characterize the cross-sectional method as a weak short-cut to the study of change.

Other Sources of Error

When comparing the cross-sectional and longitudinal methods in terms of overall internal and external validity, one must keep in mind that the quality of a design depends on many control factors that go beyond the appropriate variation of the independent variable alone.

Campbell and Stanley (1963), for example, listed eight sources of error limiting the degree of internal validity and four sources restricting the range of external validity (see Chapters Five and Six). A host of potential sources of error affect both the internal and the external validity of simple cross-sectional and longitudinal methods, although not always in the same manner or to the same extent.

In the next section, some key sources of error in descriptive developmental research will be reviewed and then applied to the cross-sectional and longitudinal methods. In general, however, it already seems fair to conclude that both the simple cross-sectional and longitudinal methods show such a lack of necessary control that data collected by application of either of them are for the most part of little validity and little use to the developmental researcher.

The Need for Control and Complex Descriptive Designs

In this section, the case against the use of simple descriptive developmental designs of the cross-sectional or longitudinal type is made on two counts. First, Campbell and Stanley's (1963) list of design errors summarized in Chapters Five and Six is applied to the simple developmental designs. Second, a series of recent studies on cohort effects is cited to illustrate concretely how lack of control in the simple designs influences the interpretation of developmental data. In subsequent sections we will further expand on these issues and propose possible ways of achieving the necessary control.

Sources of Internal and External Invalidity: An Overview

The primary sources of invalidity in Campbell and Stanley's (1963) original list are *history, maturation, testing, instrumentation, regression, selection, mortality,* and various interactions among these factors (see Table 5-1 and related text). In other words, when evaluating whether observed age differences or age changes are indeed internally valid—that is, attributable to age (the independent variable)—the researcher must consider the confounding effects of all the sources of error listed.

For example, a longitudinal age change in intelligence-test performance from age 7 to age 8 might result not from age but from the effect of repeated testing of the subjects, who are required to engage in the same or similar tasks repeatedly; furthermore, the instruments used may have altered their level of calibration. Carefully planned designs are required to control the sources of error or to estimate the magnitude of their effects, and most simple descriptive research has failed in this regard.

Before we examine some concrete examples, let's consider another perspective. Not all sources of error listed by Campbell and Stanley are necessarily true errors. In fact, some (such as history and maturation) probably should be regarded not so much as error variables in developmental research but rather as the defining characteristics of the age variable itself. This observation is not particularly surprising, however, since any of Campbell and Stanley's sources of error can in principle become independent or dependent variables if a researcher is interested in studying them.

For example, a research program on "mortality"—one of the standard error variables—would change the status of mortality from an error variable to an independent or dependent variable. Indeed, the fact that Campbell and Stanley's error variables do operate as antecedents and do produce effects makes them significant in empirical research.

Cohort (History) Effects and Development

Age changes versus age differences versus cohort differences. One design issue that has received much attention in the developmental literature is the effect of biocultural history on observations of individual development (Baltes, 1968; Baltes, Cornelius, & Nesselroade, in press; Buss, 1973; Riley, 1973; Schaie, 1965). This issue, often referred to as the issue of cohort effects, had its origin primarily in the discrepant findings that were obtained with cross-sectional versus longitudinal methodology. In the present context, a cohort is defined as a "generation" of persons born at the same point in time—for instance, in 1900. (See Ryder [1965] and Riley [1976] for good discussions of the cohort concept.)

The classic example is the development of intelligence during adult life. Cross-sectional studies have indicated an early decline beginning around age 30, while longitudinal studies have shown increases or no change in intellectual performance until age 50 or even 60. This finding is sketched in the left part of Figure 13-2.

Figure 13-2 also illustrates how the discrepancy between cross-sectional and longitudinal findings can be accounted for by generation or cohort differences in age-related behavior. The right side of Figure 13-2 shows one possible, simulated outcome pattern. This simulation is based on the assumptions that cohorts differ in the slope of their average age function, and that all cohorts exhibit a linear increase throughout the entire age period studied. A given cross-sectional study involves a given cohort at only one specific age level; for example, in 1960 the 1950 cohort is at age 10, the 1940 cohort is at age 20, the 1930 cohort is at age 30, and so forth. The cross-sectional pattern obtained in 1960 is then an inverted U, similar to the actual data obtained in the cross-sectional research shown in the left part of Figure 13-2.

The important conclusion from this simulation of age-cohort relationships (which is also supported by actual data; see Schaie, 1970) is that cross-sectional age differences potentially represent a confounding between

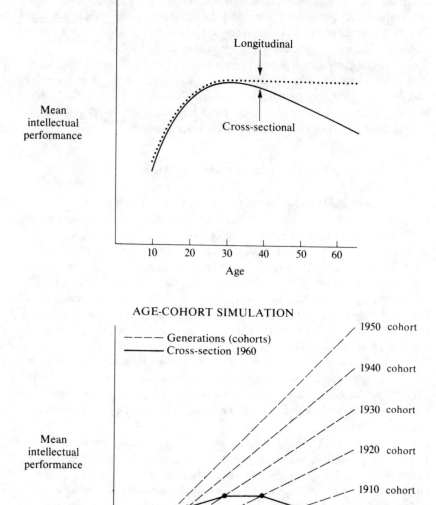

Figure 13-2. Illustration of age-cohort confounds in cross-sectional research and of cohort differences in intellectual functioning. Based on Baltes (1968).

age changes and cohort differences. In this simulation, cross-sectional age differences in 1960 are not an average for all cohorts; neither do they accurately reflect any one of the six cohort-specific age curves, all of which are linearly increasing.

It may be important to emphasize at this point that a very large number of age-cohort simulation solutions could be developed to fit any cross-sectional gradient obtained in empirical research. To make a simulation formally adequate, one need only plot cohort-specific curves that pass through the appropriate age-specific points obtained from the cross-sectional observations for each of the cohorts involved. Nesselroade and Baltes (1974, p. 4) present additional simulation examples.

Empirical illustrations of age versus cohort effects.   Since the bulk of developmental research does not include both cross-sectional and longitudinal studies of a particular topic, the available empirical evidence on the importance of cohort effects is not extensive. The studies to date, however, are overwhelming in their consistency and persuasiveness (Baltes, Cornelius, & Nesselroade, in press).

Wheeler (1942) was one of the first to report systematic cohort and age differences in intelligence. He compared the intellectual performance of Tennessee mountain children (ages 6, 10, and 16) in 1930 and 1940. His two major findings are illustrated in Figure 13-3. First, Wheeler found that children in 1940 scored higher than children who were the same ages in 1930 (time-lag comparison). Second, in both 1930 and 1940, the IQs were progressively lower as age increased from 6 to 16 (cross-sectional comparison); that is, there was an age-related decline in IQ in both 1930 and 1940.

The usual interpretation for the higher performance in 1940 when compared with 1930 is that general improvement in the environment—roads, schools, and so on—produced a cohort change by providing more intellectual stimulation for the children in the later testing. The usual interpretation of the finding of age-related decrease in IQ (both for the 1930 and the 1940 data) is that the relatively isolated and nonstimulating mountain environment produces a cumulative depressing effect on intelligence (as contrasted with the rural and urban samples used to standardize the IQ test), resulting in an age decline in IQ.

To show how complicated it is to interpret data like these, however, consider only the possibility that the brighter teenagers move out of the mountains. Only the less bright 16-year-olds would remain, artificially lowering the intelligence mean for 16-year-olds. Given this possibility, you can see that there is still no good evidence of any age change in this study.

More recently, Schaie, Nesselroade, Baltes, and their colleagues have collected large-scale and better controlled information on the relationship between age-related and cohort-related change in cognitive abilities and per-

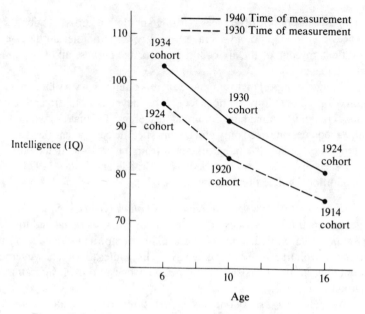

Figure 13-3. Wheeler's data on IQs of mountain children. Beside each data point is the year of birth of the children. Based on Wheeler (1942).

sonality traits during childhood, adolescence, and adulthood. In general, the findings of these studies are extremely consistent and emphasize the strong impact of cohort differences in both intelligence and personality. Figure 13-4 summarizes empirical evidence for two behavior dimensions from this work.

The left-hand panel of Figure 13-4 shows data on crystallized intelligence from a study by Schaie and Strother (1968a, b) as reanalyzed by Nesselroade, Schaie, and Baltes (1972). The between-group results are similar to those of Wheeler's study, in that the time-lag data show that persons tested in 1963 were superior in intelligence to persons who were at the same ages in 1956, and in that the cross-sectional data for both the 1956 testing and the 1963 testing show a decline in performance with increasing age. However, the longitudinal data (points connected by lines) show that the cross-sectional trends are misleading, because every cohort actually increased in intelligence with increasing age.

Results selected from a study by Nesselroade and Baltes (1974) on adolescent personality are presented in the right-hand panel of Figure 13-4. Over the relatively short historical period of only two years (1970-1972), the different cohorts showed different age changes in Achievement, the personality measure selected for our example. Contrast, for instance, the 14-year-olds in 1970, 1971, and 1972. The 14-year-olds in 1970 had one of the highest mean scores of all samples, but their 1972 14-year-old counterparts produced the lowest mean score of all.

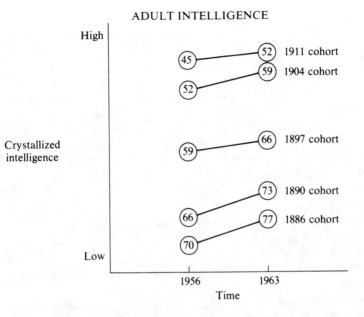

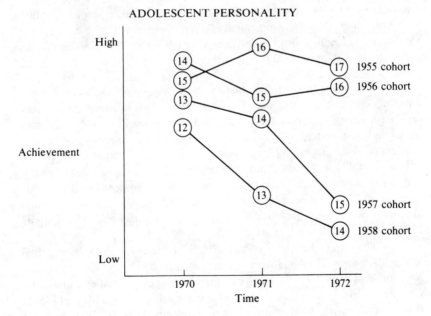

Figure 13-4. Selected results from two studies of adult intelligence (Nesselroade, Schaie, & Baltes, 1972) and adolescent personality (Nesselroade & Baltes, 1974), illustrating separation of age changes from cohort differences. Note the differences between horizontal (longitudinal) and vertical (cross-sectional) comparisons. Ages are given in the circles.

The cross-sectional age comparisons (vertical contrasts) in the right-hand panel are not only inconsistent at different times of measurement but also clearly different from the longitudinal (horizontal) trends and, therefore, misleading about the nature of age change. At the same time, the longitudinal age changes are equally lacking in consistency among cohorts, and they point up the significance of cohort-related interindividual differences.

One can make several theoretical observations regarding the Wheeler, Schaie and Strother, and Nesselroade and Baltes data on age versus cohort effects. At present, however, we are focusing on methodology. It was noted earlier (Chapter Two) that a key requirement for developmental methodology is to identify intraindividual change patterns and not simply interindividual differences. Another key issue raised earlier (Chapter One) is that developmental methodology should be sensitive to the notion that individuals develop in a changing biocultural context. The data presented above relate to both issues.

On the basis of data accumulated so far, it appears reasonable to assume when studying behavioral development that there may be cohort differences, and therefore that cross-sectional age differences represent confounded effects of age and cohort. The issue of cohort differences, however, is also relevant to longitudinal outcomes. Simple longitudinal studies, dealing with only one cohort, are potentially severely restricted in their external validity or generalizability. Age-change curves can differ markedly from cohort to cohort because different cohorts develop in distinct biocultural contexts.

If you are interested in history, you may enjoy knowing that the importance of cohort differences for the interpretation of age functions was discussed (using different terminology) as early as 1741 by a German demographer-minister, J. P. Süssmilch. Süssmilch was interested in various age-related demographic indicators such as marriage, divorce, and prostitution; he found that periods of war and epidemics "interfered" considerably with the establishment of general age norms for the phenomena listed. Accordingly, he argued that it takes "a series of good and average years—if one wants to obtain something reliable on the basis of age comparisons" (Süssmilch, 1741, p. 226; translation by the authors).

The extent to which cohort effects are relevant in developmental research is an empirical question. A recent chapter by Baltes, Cornelius, and Nesselroade (in press) presents an overview. For specific studies and discussions on the topic, the reader is referred to Riegel, Riegel, and Meyer (1967), Baltes and Reinert (1969), Baltes, Baltes, and Reinert (1970), Woodruff and Birren (1972), Schaie (1972), Schaie, Labouvie, and Buech (1973), Goulet, Hay, and Barclay (1974), and Bell and Hertz (1976). There are also reviews, covering data from other research domains, in which cohort effects are interpreted in terms of secular and historical trends (for example, Bakwin,

1964; Meredith, 1963; Tanner, 1962). Novel conceptions of developmental theory are needed, with a joint concern for historical and individual change (see Baltes & Schaie, 1976; Elder, 1975; Huston-Stein & Baltes, 1976; Keniston, 1971; Riegel, 1973a, 1976; Riley, 1976; Riley, Johnson, & Foner, 1972).

Summary

A key descriptive task of developmental psychology is to discover how an individual's behavior changes with age and how individuals differ in their change. If "search" variables other than age (such as stage, progression, critical life events, and so on) are used for the study of developmental change, similar perspectives apply.

The traditional descriptive designs for age-developmental research are the cross-sectional and longitudinal methods, but both methods are flawed. For example, the cross-sectional method compares different age groups, each observed once at the same point in time. Age differences are confounded with cohort (year of birth) effects. Therefore, because intra-individual change is not directly studied but rather is intended to be approximated by age-group differences, it will not even approach accuracy unless cohort effects are negligible. In fact, most of the currently available data in developmental psychology are cross-sectional and hence likely to be afflicted by cohort effects.

The longitudinal method follows one group through several age levels with repeated observations. The major advantage to longitudinal designs is that they give a direct estimate of intraindividual change and interindividual differences. However, since only one cohort is studied, the cohort effect cannot be determined. Therefore, longitudinal studies are restricted in external validity. Moreover, simple longitudinal designs do not control for a variety of sources of error dealing with internal validity, such as repeated testing and instrumentation.

Chapter Fourteen

Sequential Cross-Sectional and Longitudinal Strategies

Chapter Thirteen presented persuasive empirical cases demonstrating the need for complex and well-controlled studies when the goal is to identify intraindividual change. In this chapter we present some design models and control methods that have been proposed to meet this need.

Sequential Strategies

In line with Süssmilch's early contribution, the fields of epidemiology, demography, and sociology have contributed heavily to methodological developments in the area of cohort differences (for example, Bengtson & Cutler, 1976; Riley, 1973, 1976; Ryder, 1965; Whelpton, 1954). Within the behavioral sciences, following up earlier suggestions by researchers such as Bell (1953, 1954) and Kuhlen (1963), it was Schaie (1965) who gave the major impetus to the formulation of designs that would allow for the simultaneous description of age changes and cohort differences.

In 1965, Schaie proposed a "General Developmental Model" based on three components: chronological age, time of measurement, and cohort (year of birth). From this model he derived three strategies of data collection and data analysis, which he labeled the *cross-sequential, cohort-sequential,* and *time-sequential* methods. According to Schaie, successive application of these data-analysis techniques can provide not only descriptive information but also explanations of developmental change. For example, Schaie (1965) argued that it is possible—through various logical and mathematical

using all techniques enables explanation

inferences—to unconfound the multiple effects contained in the sequential data matrices and to identify age effects as being due to maturational processes, time effects as being due to cultural-change phenomena, and cohort effects as being due to genetic determinants.

Researchers agree on the overall significance of Schaie's proposal for the descriptive identification of change, but they disagree on the explanatory usefulness of his model (for example, Baltes, 1967a, b, 1968; Buss, 1973; Labouvie, 1975b; Wohlwill, 1973). One of the present authors (Baltes, 1968) was particularly critical of Schaie's proposals on this point. He argued that the application of Schaie's model is primarily useful for the descriptive identification of change, and that any attempt to interpret the findings of a particular study in terms of specific maturational, environmental, or genetic determinants is highly speculative without additional knowledge or information. In the meantime, Schaie and Baltes (1975) jointly considered this question and concluded that distinguishing between the *descriptive* and *explanatory* functions of Schaie's General Developmental Model has indeed been helpful in clarifying some of the vagueness and answering some of the criticism surrounding the development of sequential strategies.

In any case, there is agreement that Schaie's General Developmental Model is extremely useful for the generation of descriptive data, and it is this focus on *accurate description of change* that is emphasized here. Figure 14-1 presents the type of research strategies necessary to produce a data matrix involving cohort, age, and time of measurement, as suggested by Schaie's General Developmental Model.

The left-hand part of Figure 14-1 shows the three major conventional methods of data collection—cross-sectional, longitudinal, and time-lag—and shows that each of them represents a special case within Schaie's General Developmental Model. This part of Figure 14-1 also illustrates again how a cross-sectional study simultaneously varies age and cohort membership and therefore necessarily confounds age and cohort differences. Apparent, too, are the confounding of age and time-of-measurement effects in longitudinal research, and cohort and time-of-measurement effects in time-lag studies.

The right-hand part of Figure 14-1 represents two ways to collect all the observations necessary to fill the entire matrix defined by an age-cohort-time arrangement. Note first that each column of the matrix represents different birth-cohorts, and therefore that observations within a column must be independent. One person cannot be simultaneously a member of different birth-cohorts. Observations within each row (across ages), however, can be either independent or repeated. That is, as in a classical longitudinal study, one can follow a sample from a given cohort through all age levels, or one can draw multiple independent random samples from a given cohort and observe each of the cohort-specific samples at only one of the age levels. The latter strategy would be equivalent to a "longitudinal study with independent observations,"

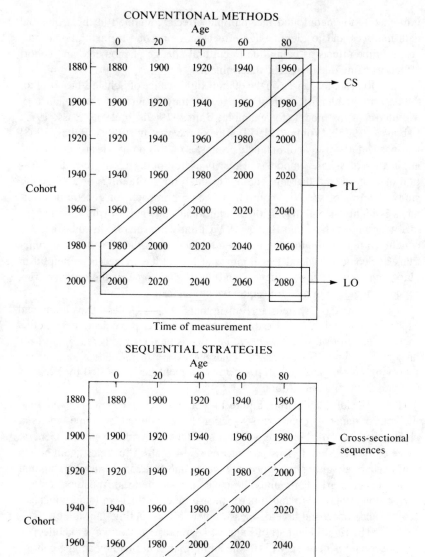

Figure 14-1. Illustration of simple cross-sectional, longitudinal, and time-lag designs (top) and cross-sectional and longitudinal sequences (bottom). Modified from Baltes (1968) and Schaie (1965).

like the comparison between the 1930 and 1940 samples of the 1924 cohort in Wheeler's (1942) study (see Figure 13-3).

Using this distinction between independent and repeated observations, Baltes (1968) has differentiated between two types of data-collection strategies: *cross-sectional sequences* and *longitudinal sequences*. In cross-sectional sequences, independent observations are obtained at all cohort and age levels. For example, in the cross-sectional sequence shown in Figure 14-1, the 1980 and 2000 testings of the 1920 cohort are done with different members of that cohort in order to make these testings independent. In longitudinal sequences, repeated measures are obtained within each cohort. Thus, for example, a sample is selected from the 1980 cohort and the same persons are tested in 1980 and 2000.

The choice of terminology is rather arbitrary, but the conventional terms *cross-sectional* and *longitudinal* may make the designs easier to understand than would the use of Schaie's terminology. Also, Schaie's designs, the "cross-sequential," "cohort-sequential," and "time-sequential" designs, which did not distinguish between the use of independent and repeated observations, are apt to confuse the use of an age-cohort-time matrix as a model for descriptive data collection versus explanatory data interpretation. For the same reason, Schaie and Baltes (1975) agreed that Baltes' terms (cross-sectional and longitudinal sequences) should be used where the task is *description* of change, and Schaie's terms (cross-sequential, cohort-sequential, time-sequential) are preferable if a researcher is interested not only in data-collection strategies but also in the use of Schaie's General Developmental Model for *explanatory* purposes.

In practice, simultaneous application of cross-sectional sequences and longitudinal sequences is always desirable, since they supplement each other by providing for various control arrangements. For example, as will be shown later, data from cross-sectional sequences can be used to estimate the magnitude of retest effects in longitudinal data. Note, however, that cross-sectional sequences alone can lead only to *average* intraindividual change functions. Moreover, cross-sectional sequences require fairly strict assumptions about linearity and additivity if inferences about average change functions are to be useful and valid. Furthermore, unless all the samples for all observations are selected at the beginning of the sequential study, results from cross-sectional sequences cannot be controlled for changes in sample composition, as might have happened in the 1930 and 1940 samples from the 1924 cohort in Wheeler's study.

Data Analysis of Sequential Strategies

The analysis of sequential data can, in principle, make use of a large variety of models (for example, analysis of variance, time-series methodology, correlational techniques, trend analyses) available for matrices involving information about intraindividual change and interindividual differences in change (see Chapters Eight and Twelve). Care should be taken to utilize the repeated-measurement information contained in sequential-longitudinal data in order to chart intraindividual trends, interindividual differences in such trends, and cross-age or cross-time relationships, as evidenced, for example, in stability coefficients. Obviously, if multiple behavioral measures are available, multivariate models for the description and structuring of change can be used (for example, Nesselroade, 1970).

Since sequential longitudinal and cross-sectional data can be arranged in a two-dimensional (or bifactorial) matrix ordered by age and cohort, age and time, or time and cohort, much discussion has arisen as to which of these bifactorial matrices is best suited for developmental analyses and interpretations (Baltes, 1968; Buss, 1973; Labouvie, 1975b; Schaie, 1965, 1970; Wohlwill, 1973). This question bears directly on Schaie's (1965, 1970) initial attempt to develop not only an accurate description of change but also a way to identify the developmental origin (maturational, environmental, genetic) of the observed change.

The selection of any one of these bifactorial matrices establishes constraints on how the effects of the three factors—age, cohort, and time of measurement—can be examined. Specifically, from the standpoint of maximizing the appropriateness of a simple additive-effects model, the two factors of the selected matrix are, by implication, assumed to be important determinants of behavior, and the third factor may be assumed to be unimportant. The reason is that the third factor is confounded with the interaction between the two selected factors; the effect of the third factor is therefore not separately analyzable, but rather constitutes part of the observed effect attributed in the data analysis to the joint effect of the two factors that are analyzed.

Our preference (see also Nesselroade & Baltes, 1974; Schaie & Baltes, 1975) is to treat data from sequential methods descriptively and to settle on one, and only one, of the three possible bifactorial (age-cohort, age-time, time-cohort) data-analysis models for a given data matrix. The selection of a specific bifactorial model is in part a function of parsimony and in part a function of the limits imposed by the available data matrix. Both Baltes (1968) and Schaie (Schaie & Baltes, 1975) now maintain that, for two reasons, the *age-by-cohort arrangement* is typically the most useful for *ontogenetic* research. First, the age-by-cohort arrangement can be used for both independent and repeated observations (relative to age). Second, the age-by-cohort matrix is the only arrangement that is unambiguous with respect to the *direct* description of intraindividual change and interindividual differences therein.

The observed effects in an age-cohort design refer to cohort-specific intraindividual changes and involve the identification of true between-individual differences in intraindividual change (both within and across cohorts). Therefore, of the three bifactorial arrangements, only the age-cohort arrangement provides a *direct* description and assessment of intraindividual change (age changes) and of interindividual differences in intraindividual change (cohort differences). In general, however, as long as only descriptive statements are to be made, the use of any of the three bifactorial arrangements is defensible for purposes of data analysis, depending upon the specific research emphasis.

In our view, the search for the developmental meaning of any observed age, cohort, or time effect is a task that lies outside the proper realm of sequential methodology *per se,* since that realm is primarily descriptive and not explanatory. The pattern of age-, cohort-, and time-related trends can at best suggest hypotheses about the developmental origin of each of these trends. The hypotheses would then need to be tested in further experiments. Similarly, as shown, for example, by Mason and her colleagues (Mason, Mason, Winsborough, & Poole, 1973), if one is willing to assume that any two levels of age, of cohort, or of time of measurement do not differ on the measurement variable, separate estimates of age, cohort, and time effects can be obtained, as initially hoped for by Schaie in his classic 1965 article. Moreover, it is possible to use alternative or supplemental modes of data analysis (such as path analysis; see Chapter Twenty-Four) in order to go beyond the age-cohort-time framework to examine particular causal hypotheses.

From a theory-construction viewpoint, however, it is indeed doubtful whether engaging in complex forms of cross-checking, as proposed by Schaie, is worth the trouble, since it is generally accepted that analysis of variables such as age, cohort, and time *per se* will never result in a meaningful, explanatory interpretation of change. Thus, the general recommendation in analyzing sequential data is to focus on an accurate description of intraindividual changes in various cohorts and to leave explanatory interpretations of the observed changes and interindividual differences in change to subsequent or parallel research and modes of analysis.

Summary

Sequential designs were developed in order to study intraindividual change in a changing world and to separate age changes from cohort effects. Originally, researchers hoped that these designs would be not only descriptive but also explanatory, but it is now generally agreed that their primary usefulness is limited to the descriptive task and that explanation must come through the use of other research designs.

A distinction is made between two types of descriptive sequential strategies: cross-sectional sequences and longitudinal sequences. In the former, independent groups are tested once at all cohort and age levels; in the latter, the selected cohorts are retested at all ages. The advantage of cross-sectional sequences and longitudinal sequences over the simple cross-sectional and longitudinal methods is that they provide a more comprehensive descriptive identification of change phenomena. Specifically, data from sequential strategies permit us to study behavioral development in a changing world and protect us from mistakenly using cross-sectional age differences as the valid targets for subsequent explanatory change analysis.

A greater amount of internal validity is obtained when cross-sectional and longitudinal sequences are used simultaneously in a design. In practice, for the purpose of descriptive analysis, the data obtained from sequential models are organized into a bifactorial matrix—age-cohort, age-time, or time-cohort. For descriptive developmental research, the age-cohort matrix is generally the most straightforward, because it focuses explicitly and directly on the assessment of intraindividual change and interindividual differences both within and across cohorts. The use of Schaie's General Developmental Model for explanatory (rather than descriptive) purposes is judged to have only limited value.

Chapter Fifteen

Developmental Design and Change in Subject Populations with Age

A set of control issues arises in descriptive developmental research because of time-related changes in the parent population under investigation and in the samples drawn from it. In short-term developmental research, sampling issues are obviously less relevant than in long-term developmental research. In long-term development, the nature of a subject population may change. The study of such change is the task of demography.

Changes in Parent Populations and Age Structures

The first step in deciding which sampling technique to use is the accurate definition of the parent population from which to sample. (See Blalock & Blalock, 1968, for review on sampling techniques *per se*.) The task of defining the parent population in developmental psychology is complicated by the fact that the parent population itself (consisting, for example, of all members of a given birth-cohort) is undergoing change as ontogeny and history proceed. On the one hand, the age structure of a given society changes with historical time. On the other hand, as a given birth cohort ages, it is reduced in size by interindividual differences in life span or biological mortality. (See United Nations, 1973, and Westoff, 1974, for comprehensive overviews of population changes.)

The fact of changing age structures is well known to demographers. The issues of biological mortality and changing age structures have been introduced into the developmental literature primarily by gerontologists (for example, Cutler & Harootyan, 1975; Davies, 1954; Riley, Johnson, & Foner,

1972). The concern of gerontologists about changing age structures is easily understood when one recognizes that with advanced age the proportion of adult survivors becomes markedly reduced. Biological mortality, however, is of significance in infant research as well, since during the 1960s approximately 2.5% of all newborns died during their first year in most Western countries (the comparable figure in Africa was about 15%).

Figure 15-1 shows, in abbreviated and simplified form, some data on age structures and mortality probabilities in the United States. The left-hand part of the figure shows (in approximation) the estimated distribution of the population in the United States in 1830, 1870, and 1969, as published by the United States Bureau of Census. It illustrates the changing nature of age structures at different points in historical time, the most recent age structure exhibiting the highest proportion of elderly persons. For example, the left-hand part of Figure 15-1 indicates that, whereas in 1830 about 33% of the living population was 10 years old or younger, in 1969 this age group constituted only 18% of the total population.

In general, the direction of historical change over the last century was toward an older average age and toward more equal frequencies across the age groups. Incidentally, the percentage of persons over 65 is predicted to be about 20% of the population living in the United States by the year 2000. Various publications by the United Nations and by the U.S. Census Bureau (for example, United Nations, 1973; U.S. Bureau of Census, 1974, 1975) contain projections of future population trends (by age, sex, family structure, and so on) for the United States and other countries of the world.

Age structures reflect several kinds of processes or events, such as average life expectancy in a given cohort and birth rate. As estimated by the United Nations, the life expectancy for the living cohorts of the 1970s is approximately 71 years in developed countries, 63 years in Latin America, 57 years in Asia, and only 46 years in Africa. The yearly growth rate (new births minus deaths) also differs markedly among countries. The growth rate in Europe and North America comes close to zero (about ½ of 1%); the growth rate in Asia, Africa, and Latin America is about 2.5%. Age structures also differ for members of different biocultural subgroups within a given country. This factor makes, for instance, the comparison of White and Black adults —within a developmental framework—a difficult task.

The right-hand part of Figure 15-1 shows one variable that influences age structures and changes in these structures. This variable is mortality rate, which varies among different United States samples. Mortality curves indicate the average probability of death at various ages or age ranges. Note in particular that, in contrast to the estimated curve for Ancient Rome, except for an elevation in early infancy due to infant mortality, the mortality curve for 1940 is close to zero for most of childhood, adolescence, and early adulthood. From middle adulthood into old age, the probability of death steadily rises.

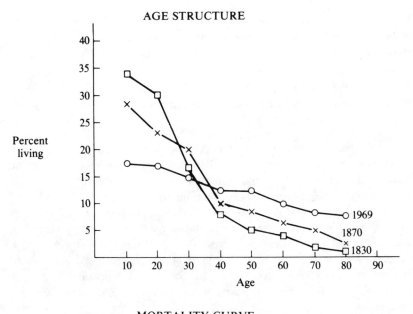

AGE STRUCTURE

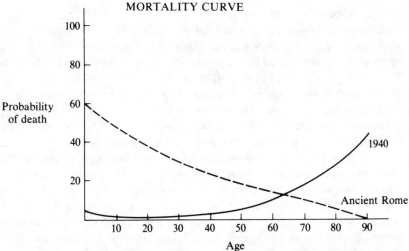

MORTALITY CURVE

Figure 15-1. Examples of data on age structures and mortality. Shown are age structures of the U. S. population at three historical times (1830, 1870, 1969) and estimated mortality curves (probability of death in a given decade) for Ancient Rome and 1940 United States. Based on Davies (1954) and *Current Population Report*, United States Bureau of the Census, Washington, D. C.: U. S. Government Printing Office, 1970.

There are, however, large cultural- and ethnic-group differences not shown in the figure. In 1970, for example, the average life expectancy at birth in the

United States was approximately 73, 70, 67, and 60 years for White females, nonwhite females, White males, and nonwhite males, in that order (Cutler & Harootyan, 1975).

Mortality and Behavior Development

What are some of the implications of demographic changes and age-related changes in the cohort population for developmental research in the behavioral sciences? Aside from requirements for the sampling process itself (dealing with issues of representativeness, and so on), the major issue is that of selective biological and psychological survival. *Selective survival* not only implies that there are distinct subgroups showing different change patterns but also introduces many potential sources of error (Campbell & Stanley, 1963; Schaie, 1976) in developmental research. In principle, age- and cohort-related changes in demography become relevant for the developmental researcher in the behavioral sciences if such changes are correlated with behavior differences.

Sociologists and demographers have spent a considerable amount of time studying the implications population changes have for various aspects of societal functioning. Space does not permit a review here, but interesting summaries are available. For example, following the suggestions of Matilda Riley (Riley, 1976; Riley et al., 1972), Waring (1975) reviewed some of the likely implications of ordered versus disordered "cohort flow" (demographic changes in age structures across cohorts) for life-span sociology. Lacking systematic data, we know very little about historical-evolutionary population changes as they relate to individual development and behavior.

Information about survival and individual development through the life span is beginning to accumulate, however, in the psychological literature. The core argument is that mortality is an independent factor to consider in the interpretation of age differences, whenever life span or length of life is correlated with the target behavior studied. The potential effects of selective survival are illustrated in Figure 15-2. If life span (or survival) correlates negatively with the behavior to be charted developmentally, then with increasing age the effect is to lose subjects who obtain high scores on the behavior. The outcome of such a negative relationship between life span and behavior is *negative selection*; as shown in the right-hand part of Figure 15-2, it leads to a lowering of the average age function. If the relationship is positive, as shown in the left-hand part of the figure, the outcome is *positive selection*, resulting in an increasing average age function.

A complication is that relationships between life expectancy and behavior may not be linear; moreover, relationships may be more or less pronounced for different cohorts and age groups. Consider, for example, the relationship of mortality to intelligence (as discussed, for example, by Baltes,

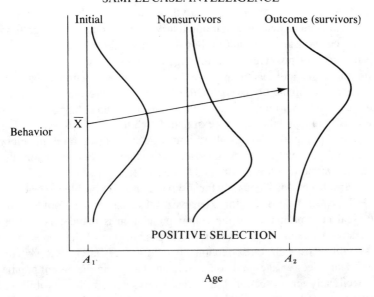

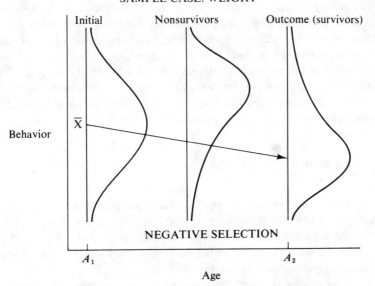

Figure 15-2. Examples of positive and negative selection in developmental research associated with selective survival effects and the mortality curve. From "Adult Development of Intellectual Performance: Description, Explanation, Modification," by P. B. Baltes and G. V. Labouvie. In C. Eisdorfer & M. P. Lawton (Eds.), *The Psychology of Adult Development and Aging.* Copyright 1973 by the American Psychological Association. Reprinted by permission.

Schaie, & Nardi, 1971; Jarvik, 1975; Jarvik & Falek, 1963; Riegel & Riegel, 1972). There is clear evidence that adult survivors are on the average more intelligent than nonsurvivors on a variety of intellectual dimensions. In short, life span correlates positively with intelligence. This positive-selection process produces an age-related increase in simple cross-sectional data and restricts the generalizability of longitudinal findings. Unfortunately, there is little evidence of other relationships between life span and behavior, although one can easily imagine the existence of many such relationships—involving, for example, psychophysiological attributes such as heart rate and blood pressure, and personality dimensions such as achievement orientation, ego strength, aggression, extroversion, and death anxiety.

How to control adequately for survival effects is a problem (see Baltes et al., 1971, and Schaie, 1976, for extensive discussions), but it is obvious that longitudinal information about the cohort population is mandatory. Unless information on relationships between life expectancy and behavior is available from other research, cross-sectional age differences are hopelessly confounded with selective age- and cohort-related changes in the parent population. Specifically, cross-sectional gradients always contain the possibility of a selective survival component that can exaggerate, diminish, or nullify true intraindividual change patterns.

In longitudinal research, whether cohort-specific or cohort-sequential, it is necessary to plot changes separately for the intact sample available at each age and across all ages for the subsample consisting of survivors at the oldest age studied. This technique permits examination of and direct comparisons among subsamples with different lengths of life span. The product can be change patterns for distinct subgroups, or corrections to apply if an estimate of average change functions is desired. (See Baltes et al., 1971, for concrete examples illustrating this procedure.)

Summary

An intrinsic feature of developmental research, especially when large segments of the life span are covered, is that there may be age changes in the nature of the population initially selected for study, and in the composition of the samples drawn from this population. Change may apply to the subject population itself as well as to behavior.

If the change in population structure and composition influences the behavior under investigation, then the direct and indirect effects of age on the behavior are confounded. That is, the direct effect of age on the behavior is confounded with the direct effect of population changes that are age-related. Therefore, the relationship between age-related changes in the population and age-related changes in behavior needs to be assessed.

Little is known about links between demographic changes in population characteristics and behavioral development. However, in age- and cohort-developmental research it is important to recognize that these links may exist. For example, the effect of age-related population changes can be positive selection (survivors exhibit a higher level of the behavior) or negative selection (survivors exhibit a iower level of the behavior). The effect may also, however, be nonlinear, and it may be different for different cohorts and subgroups from a single cohort.

Aside from obtaining relevant information on demography-behavior relationships, which is usually unavailable, two possible solutions appear. First, one can compare at each age level studied the performance of the total sample available at that age level with the performance of the subsample that survived to the oldest age level studied. Second, one can compare subsamples that represent different lengths of life span. The yield could be different developmental trends reported for each subgroup, or the computation of a correction that can be applied to scores to permit estimation of a single developmental trend. Additional issues and strategies for assessment and control dealing with the relationship between demographic changes and behavioral development are discussed in the next chapter.

Chapter Sixteen

Change in Populations and Sampling: Assessment and Control

This chapter expands on issues dealing with age-related changes in parent populations and samples drawn from such changing parent populations, and with the need for control or assessment of these changes in descriptive developmental research. To meet these objectives, we focus on a selected set of concrete research applications.

Mortality and Terminal Change

A first sample case presents a somewhat different perspective on the issue of mortality from that discussed in Chapter Fifteen. In Chapter Fifteen the discussion of relationships between life span and behavior was based on the argument that the effects consist simply of an age-correlated selective dropout of individuals. Such dropouts may produce apparent age changes, resulting from changes in the composition of the parent population and not from changes within individual members of the population. Another perspective on this question is to view death as a significant life event related to major behavioral or developmental change. This perspective sees death as one event in a more general class of "life events" (Dohrenwend & Dohrenwend, 1974; Hultsch & Plemons, in press) related to individual development and biological survival. Other such "life events" might be marriage, divorce, unemployment, and sickness, occurring at different ages in different individuals.

Research on mortality has shown, for example, that not only is there a change in parent populations with age, but there are also changes within individuals related to approaching death. Gerontologists such as Kleemeier, Jarvik, Klaus and Ruth Riegel, Eisdorfer, and others have reported an accelerated rate of change in behavior during the last few years before "natural" death (for example, Jarvik, Blum, & Varma, 1972; Riegel & Riegel, 1972). The phenomenon has been referred to as *terminal drop*. Note, however, that changes occurring just before death can also be increases, such as an increase in death anxiety.

There appears to be a terminal drop in intelligence, which can serve to illustrate general implications of the mortality curve for the description of intraindividual change patterns. The mortality curve indicates an increasing frequency of death as age increases. Thus, an older age sample will contain a higher proportion of persons who are in the process of terminal change. The effect in the group as a whole would be an accelerated rate of change; however, this rate would actually apply only to those in the older sample who are in the process of terminal change related to dying.

Statistically, terminal change is a person-by-age interaction, because different persons die at different ages and, therefore, show the terminal change at different times. The identification of this interaction requires longitudinal observations. Note that, unlike selective mortality, which fallaciously produces change in group data of the cross-sectional type, terminal change involves true intraindividual change, although only for a selected set of persons at any one time. To illustrate the effect of terminal change on the study of age functions, Baltes and Labouvie (1973, p. 174) have presented a chart simulating the cumulative effects of mortality and terminal change. They also discussed why cross-sectional studies cannot identify or disentangle the confounding effects of such critical change events. There are also suggestions in the literature (Baltes, Schaie, & Nardi, 1971) about how crisis-related life events such as death can be taken into account in the planning of sequential research.

Sampling Biases and Sample Maintenance (Experimental Mortality)

In the preceding section we discussed time-related changes in parent populations and the identification of subject-specific rates of accelerated change. This section is focused on techniques and problems in sampling and sample maintenance in developmental research.

Whenever samples are not representative of the parent population, one speaks of *sampling bias* or *sample selection*. Whenever, as in longitudinal research, the initial experimental sample is not fully maintained, one speaks of *experimental mortality* (for example, Campbell & Stanley, 1963). Experimental mortality is selective if it correlates with the independent or dependent variables studied.

We have already shown that time-related changes in the population

different selection for different age groups

structure make it difficult to define appropriate parent populations for long-term developmental research. This problem is further complicated by the differential availability (sample selection) of subjects of different ages. For example, about 95% of children are members of a captive school population, and about 90% of 60-year-olds are community residents. Identifying fairly representative samples and obtaining volunteers seem to be most difficult for research on adults beyond the college years. Thus, much research on *children* comes close to including fairly heterogeneous and at least locally representative samples; but the bulk of research with *young adults* is done with college students, who represent a positive selection from their age cohort, and much research with *older adults* is focused on institutionalized elderly, who generally represent a negative selection of their living age mates. We must draw the general conclusion that the age trend for sample biases (not population changes) in life-span developmental research often goes from representativeness (childhood) through positive selection (early adulthood) to negative selection (old age).

dealing w/ problem

There is little empirical evidence on the effects of sample selection and experimental mortality at different points of the life span. Simple cross-sectional studies cannot deal directly with the issue and are hopelessly confounded. From the few relevant longitudinal studies, the findings are that as the study progresses, the samples become more positively selected on such variables as intelligence, flexibility-rigidity, conformity, and social-class membership (Baltes, 1968; Sontag, 1971). In fact, most longitudinal work deals with highly selected samples, thus markedly reducing external validity. Various ways to deal with incomplete longitudinal data can be found in Anderson and Cohen (1939). A method for dealing with subject maintenance in longitudinal work has been presented by Droege (1971), and various statistical techniques for controlling undesirable age-group differences in sample characteristics are described by Schaie (1959, 1973).

Selecting Age Levels and Range: Statistical versus Theoretical Criteria

One critical sampling issue in developmental research is that of selecting age ranges and age levels for the comparison samples or times of measurement. On the one hand, age ranges and levels can be selected on the basis of previous research and specific theoretical hypotheses about the timing and rate of change (for example, Braun, 1973). On the other hand, if one aims initially for representativeness and predictive validity only, one can consider the form of the age-population distribution and choose between a fixed and a random selection of ages.

Form of Age Distribution and Base Rates

As shown in the earlier discussion of the mortality curve (Chapter Fifteen), the population of a given birth cohort contains fewer persons per age interval as age increases, and cohorts differ in their age structures. There are two methods of dealing with this change. One method is to select sample sizes a priori for different age groups on the basis of the actual frequency in the parent population (for example, choose 100 at age 5, 95 at age 20, 90 at age 40, and so forth, using census data such as those summarized in Figure 15-1). The other method is to correct sample sizes a posteriori, by considering the proportions available in the total age population. The earlier discussion showed that different cohorts exhibit different age structures; hence, whichever method is used, one must know the age structure of the cohorts being studied.

Adjustments for an uneven age distribution and a changing parent population seem especially important in light of base-rate problems (for example, Meehl & Rosen, 1955). Choosing an extreme example, if you compared 100 5-year-olds with 100 80-year-olds, you would be comparing a very small proportion of the total population of 5-year-olds with a large proportion of the population of 80-year-olds. Such a comparison, while descriptively correct for the samples involved, leads to gross misjudgments when the outcome is used for inferential predictive purposes (see Chapter Eight)—as demonstrated persuasively in clinical research on criterion groups involving, for instance, the comparison of normal and schizophrenic subjects (Meehl & Rosen, 1955). Although this issue is important, it has been almost ignored by developmental researchers. Various corrections for base-rate differences in parent populations and noncomparable sample sizes are available (for example, Dawes, 1962) and should be used, especially for cross-sectional research in which sample equivalence was not established prior to the experiment by the use of the age-population distribution.

Longitudinal research is less afflicted by base-rate problems, because, at least with regard to biological mortality, the sample diminishes naturally with time in a way comparable to the change in the parent population. Cross-sectional studies, however, are usually jeopardized in their predictive validity, since the tendency of most researchers is to select age ranges either on a subjective basis (without regard for age distributions) or on the basis of momentary availability, and to select samples equal in size. The last tendency is unfortunately encouraged by various established statistical methods, such as analysis of variance, in which the use of equal sample sizes greatly simplifies the calculations. To get equal sample sizes, researchers often "intuitively" adjust age ranges in the direction of larger intervals with increasing age (that is, 5–10, 10–20, 20–40, and so on). This practice appears to be an uncritical solution to the problem of age-related changes in population distributions.

Fixed versus Random Selection of Age Levels

Another issue in defining age samples is whether to use a random- or a fixed-level approach to the selection of age levels. In practice, most researchers opt for a fixed-level approach, although on statistical grounds a random approach may be more appropriate.

In the random approach, you begin by considering the entire age range to be covered, then decide how many age points you will use to cover the range, and finally select this number of age points at random. Suppose the age range is from 30 to 70, in one-year units, and you want seven age points. The random selection could lead to many outcomes, including the following: 31, 37, 42, 51, 53, 59, 68, or 30, 31, 32, 44, 46, 53, 55. This procedure, *if* sufficient levels are selected to begin with to permit sound generalization, has the desirable feature of allowing the investigator to generalize to the entire age span investigated, because of statistical principles of random sampling. A similar approach would be to select one random sample of persons from the total parent population, and to order the sample subsequently into appropriate age categories.

The fixed-level approach is the one most often used in current developmental research. It consists of defining the age levels and age intervals on an a priori basis, either in a continuous age series (for example, 10–15, 16–20, 21–25) or discontinuous age series (for example, 11–20, 31–40, 51–60). If the latter is chosen, the researcher should be careful not to generalize his or her findings to the entire age range (for example, 10 to 60) but only to the age intervals investigated. A compromise approach, apparently not yet used in psychological research, would be to use an analogue of the stratified representative sampling technique: Select fixed age *intervals* to cover every segment of the age span to be studied, and within each interval select specific age *levels* for inclusion in the study.

Empirical Evidence on Experimental Mortality

Most developmental researchers are not sensitive to the sampling issues discussed so far in this chapter and in Chapter Fifteen. This state of affairs is unfortunate from the standpoint of current research practice, and it raises the possibility that sampling selectivity and experimental mortality substantially affect existing empirical evidence on age differences. Obviously, the problem is greater for cross-sectional than for longitudinal work, since cross-sectional age differences contain such age-related sampling effects for not just one cohort but for multiple cohorts (without the potential for corrective steps). Longitudinal research, if carefully monitored for initial selection and experimental mortality, can at least come up with fairly accurate estimations of the extent of biases involved and, thereby, describe the range of internal and external validity.

For example, in the Baltes-Nesselroade-Schaie sequential-longitudinal studies on adolescent and adult personality (see Chapter Thirteen), an attempt was made to estimate the effects of biological and experimental mortality on the age-change functions obtained for various ability and personality dimensions in adolescence (Labouvie, Bartsch, Nesselroade, & Baltes, 1974) and adulthood (Baltes, Schaie, & Nardi, 1971). In both studies, the basic design involved the comparison of subjects who dropped out (for biological and psychological reasons) with subjects who stayed with the longitudinal study. The comparison was performed on the first occasion of measurement at which all subjects participated (that is, before any subjects dropped out).

As can be seen in the left-hand part of Figure 16-1, persons who continued their participation in Schaie's seven-year longitudinal study showed higher intellectual performance at the initial date of observation than those who dropped out. Statistically, it turned out that this selection occurred in all age-cohort groups. Similarly, in the Nesselroade-Baltes study of adolescents, those who remained in the study represented a positive selection on five of six ability dimensions. Figure 16-1 contains data on two of these five ability dimensions.

Differences between stay-ins and dropouts can be assessed in longitudinal research, yielding specific information about the degree of reduction in external validity of the study. In the case of the Nesselroade-Baltes study (Labouvie, Bartsch, Nesselroade, & Baltes, 1974; Nesselroade & Baltes, 1974) on adolescence, for instance, stay-ins and dropouts differed hardly at all on the personality variables but scored quite differently on the measures of intelligence used.

Other Subject Variables and Age/Cohort Comparisons

There are other subject variables beyond mortality and volunteering that are occasionally considered in the planning of descriptive developmental research, and that turn out to be relevant when change functions are charted. *Sex, social class, race, educational level, occupational level, marital status,* and *health status* are among the most frequently used and evaluated. Occasionally the argument is made that, in order for age comparisons or age functions to be valid, it is necessary to equate—or at least to homogenize—the various age samples for all other subject variables, especially if cross-sectional age groups are involved.

The strategy of homogenizing a sample seems to treat age as a truly

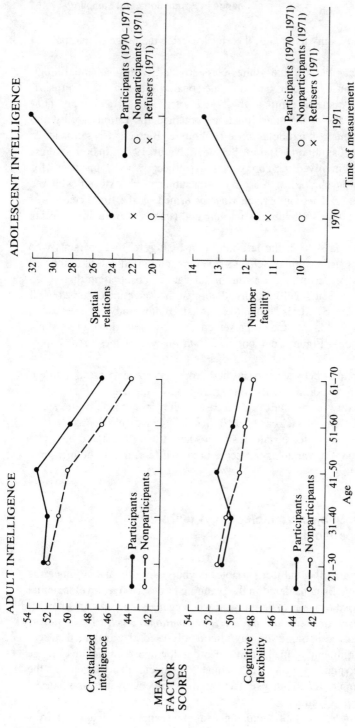

Figure 16-1. Examples of selective survival and experimental-mortality effects in seven-year (1956–1963) longitudinal research on adult intelligence (Baltes, Schaie, & Nardi, 1971) and one-year (1970–1971) longitudinal research on adolescent intelligence (Labouvie, Bartsch, Nesselroade, & Baltes, 1974). Comparisons are based on performance at the time of initial longitudinal observation (either 1956 or 1970). Classification into survivor categories is based on subsequent participation in the longitudinal study. Subjects in the adolescence study ranged in age from 12 to 17. In this study a distinction was also made between unavailable nonparticipants and available but refusing nonparticipants.

independent experimental variable having meaning independent of age-associated processes. Although it is reasonable to argue for a clear definition and analysis of the parent population involved and a precise assessment of interindividual differences in change, it appears doubtful that age homogenization in all subject variables is a defensible strategy except for specific hypothesis-guided research in developmental psychology.

One major reason for this rejection of age homogenization as a generally useful strategy is that aging and interindividual differences in aging are intrinsically linked to many subject variables, such as occupational and educational level. In other words, experiences associated with advancement in educational level, for example, are an intrinsic part of the developmental process. Thus, only in rare circumstances would it be reasonable to study 7- and 10-year-olds who are equated for educational level (see Goulet, 1975, for such an exception). In the same vein, only in rare circumstances would one want to study 45-year-olds and 20-year-olds equated for occupational level or marital status. In fact, one could argue that following age homogenization to its logical extreme would eliminate all differences that result from developmental change. Moreover, age homogenization leads easily to a focus on interindividual differences rather than intraindividual change.

Age or cohort homogenization, then, is sometimes ill-advised and guided by poorly understood principles. The intent in sample homogenization often seems tied less to a theory-based rationale than to the use of simple cross-sectional methodology as a short-cut to the study of change. If the goal of cross-sectional studies is to approximate those conditions that properly identify change, through either sample manipulations or corrections, then the desirable (although indirect and perhaps cumbersome) strategy is a different one.

First, if the goal is to identify interindividual differences in development (change), then the task is to chart the course of development separately for subsamples of the parent population (for example, according to sex or social class). Second, if the goal is to obtain age samples that are equally representative of their own or the same parent population, whether highly selected or representative, the procedure relies on cohort- *and* age-specific adjustments. In cohort-specific longitudinal research, such a goal can be directly accomplished by careful sample description and repeated contrasts of dropouts and longitudinal subjects. In cross-sectional research (if the goal is description of age change), the task is to identify subject variables that may be used to place subjects within the distribution of each of the age cohorts for the purpose of making adjustments if desired. For example, census data may indicate that a mean educational level of 11 years for cohort 1900 at age 70 represents a strong positive bias for that birth cohort, while this mean educational level for cohort 1940 at age 35 is average. Accordingly, it would be desirable to identify comparable cohort-specific levels of education for each of the cross-sectional samples involved.

There is no simple solution to the problem of sample heterogeneity in cross-sectional studies. Selecting subjects for equal standing on subject variables *within* each age-cohort distribution appears the most defensible, although least practiced, strategy. In any case, however, our first general recommendation to the cross-sectional and longitudinal researcher is to collect subject-variable information as carefully as possible and to use it when describing age samples with reference to cohort-specific census-type information. This procedure at least allows the scientific consumer to examine questions of sample bias with reference to both age- and cohort-related issues of internal and external validity.

Our second general recommendation is that statistical control for subject variables in age-comparative research should be used only if the rationale has been made theoretically explicit, and not because it is an established design practice. The established procedure of age homogenization in cross-sectional work of the life-span type often seems ill-advised and poorly justified.

Summary

Especially in long-term developmental research, the population under study may change in ways that are relevant to the behavior studied. In principle, changes in the population with age or time indicate that there are interindividual differences in behavior-change functions. One such change is caused by mortality, which produces age-correlated dropout from the study. Whether age-related changes in the demographic structure and composition of the population result in behavioral effects depends on whether dropout is selective—that is, correlated with behavior.

One example of the likelihood of a demography-behavior correlation is found in the study of adult intelligence, where the phenomenon of terminal drop has been observed. Terminal drop is an accelerated rate of decline in behavior during the last few years before natural death. Thus, because mortality increases as age increases, an older age group will contain more persons in the process of terminal change, reducing the group mean and leading to erroneous conclusions about normal individual development. The drop occurs only in the affected persons (those who are "in the process of dying") and not in their age peers with greater longevity. This situation can be detected statistically in longitudinal research, appearing as a subject-by-age interaction.

In addition to changes in the parent population itself, there are age-related changes in the samples drawn for a given study. An example of sample-specific effects is experimental mortality. Experimental mortality in longitudinal research means that the original sample does not remain intact, not only because of "natural" mortality affecting the sample and the parent population, but also for reasons specific to the experiment or study. Therefore, with time the sample becomes more and more selected or biased and appropriate controls are necessary. The problem of selection changes in parent populations cannot be solved directly in simple cross-sectional research, but it can be dealt with in longitudinal research.

Another question in long-term developmental research (especially if cross-sectional) is whether to have all age-cohort samples equal in size or to have the sample sizes proportionate to the number of persons at each age in the population. In addition, the researcher must decide whether to use randomly selected age levels for study, or to select the age levels systematically. Finally, researchers must decide what to do about sex, social class, race, marital status, and so on, when defining their samples. It is sometimes argued that the age samples should be equated or homogenized on variables such as these in order to yield valid age comparisons, especially in cross-sectional studies. However, the strategy of homogenizing the samples also redefines the population to which generalizations can be made, and the redefined population is often so restricted or restructured in composition that the generalizations and inferences drawn are uninteresting or misleading.

Chapter Seventeen

Selected Issues in Developmental Assessment

The frame of reference developed by Campbell and Stanley (1963) for the evaluation of internal validity contains three sources of error that are particularly relevant to descriptive developmental research and need additional emphasis: *testing, instrumentation,* and *statistical regression* (see also Chapter Five). These sources of error affect the internal validity of designs and, in interaction with age or cohort, external validity as well. Basic to these effects is the general issue of establishing measurement equivalence across occasions and persons (see also Chapters Seven and Twelve).

Comparisons and Measurement Equivalence

Conducting an experiment implies making at least one comparison (Campbell & Stanley, 1963; Eckensberger, 1973). In the study of intraindividual change, the immediate comparison is between or among observations made at more than one point in time. As emphasized elsewhere in this book (Chapters Five, Six, and Seven), careful attention should be applied to research design to ensure that the comparisons made are meaningful and give unambiguous answers to questions related, for example, to the identification of change or the effectiveness of treatments.

One must recognize and appreciate the importance of the role played by measurement variables, both in comparisons and in the empirical process in general. Measurement variables often provide the only precise and communicable definition one has of a construct, and they bear the burden of registering empirical evidence for the identification of change, whether ''due'' to time or to planned treatments occurring in time. In Chapter Seven issues related to measurement were discussed at some length, and we pointed out that measurement involves the meaningful assignment of numbers to objects to represent amounts of attributes. Meeting such fundamental objectives is crucial in any quantitative comparison.

The extent to which we rely on measures to develop an interpretation of empirical phenomena should underscore heavily the necessity that measures be valid for the various uses to which they are put. Assessing changes—or differences that are interpreted as implying changes, as is frequently done in studying developmental phenomena—usually requires that one proceed as though what is being measured is conceptually the same or equivalent each time, or in each group, in order for comparisons to be meaningful. Or, just as the layman admonishes that one should not add oranges and bananas, neither should one subtract one from the other in computing changes or differences.

Examples of Measurement-Equivalence Issues

The general concept of measurement equivalence has been focused on extensively and defined in elegantly precise terms (Eckensberger, 1973), but the basic notion may be formulated in a number of contexts. For example, if the average score of a group of persons on a particular test changes as they grow from 10 to 15 years of age, is it the persons themselves or what the test is measuring that has changed? Or is it some of both? Or suppose we give a test of achievement orientation to a group of males and a group of females and observe a ten-point difference in the average score when the two sexes are compared. Does this difference mean that one sex has more achievement orientation than the other, or that the accuracy of the measure is different for the two sexes, or that the test measures somewhat different attributes in the two sexes?

Finally, suppose that the achievement-orientation test is given to a sample of Chinese and a sample of American Indians. Would a difference in average scores indicate a difference in the achievement orientation of members of these two cultures, or would the observed difference simply indicate that the scores are not directly comparable between the two cultures? (For examples of the question of measurement equivalence in learning research, see Chapter Twenty-Two.)

Our intention here has been only to highlight the problem of equivalence of measurement and related issues and to call attention to how they have plagued researchers in a number of areas, including the study of developmental changes. Moreover, even though strategies for dealing with measurement-equivalence problems have been advanced by researchers, no universally satisfactory criteria for how measurement-equivalence problems should be resolved have yet been found.

Questions of Strategy
of how to make measures equivalent

A distinction has been made in the literature between *identity* of measures and the weaker concept of *equivalence* of measures (see Eckensberger, 1973, for review). In two different contexts, for instance, a given instrument may indeed be measuring the same attribute. In two other distinct situations, a given instrument may measure the same attribute, but it may need to be calibrated differently. In still other cases, two different measures, one for each context, may be needed to measure the same psychological construct. In the latter case, note that the "same" construct must be defined independently of the measurement devices. It seems clear that, before quantitative statements about developmental change (such as age comparisons) can be justifiably made, these measurement issues must be faced and resolved by one means or another.

One way to establish measurement equivalence is simply to define the test scores as representing the same thing from one case to another. Using that approach, a score on a ten-item test composed of items requiring spatial transformations is considered neither more nor less than a score on a set of ten items requiring spatial transformations. This is a short-sighted remedy, however, because, as soon as one attempts to incorporate empirical evidence thus derived into a useful theoretical scheme, generalizations to more abstract concepts must be made, and it then becomes risky to talk about the more theoretical notion of spatial-transformation ability. Such a blunt approach is simply not satisfactory to many developmentalists because they desire, from a theoretical perspective, to formulate relationships in terms of more abstract properties, such as general spatial-transformation ability. One may ask, then, whether it is possible to produce evidence that justifies treating the scores of different individuals or groups of individuals as reflecting the same basic dimension so that the differences in the scores may be interpreted as quantitative difference.

Other writers have stressed the creation of rather sophisticated analytical and statistical procedures to strengthen the interpretation of measurement equivalence for a particular measure or set of measures. Cattell (1970), for example, proposed a technique for establishing the nature of a basic unit for a given measuring device, which then might be used to recalibrate the scores of different individuals or different groups of individuals so that meaningful comparisons could be made on their scores. Baltes and Nesselroade (1970; see also Corballis & Traub, 1970) discussed strategies by which measurement equivalence is established (rather than assessed) by means of factor-analytic rotation. Another generally useful strategy is the formulation of an external "invariant" and known measurement space within which the study-specific "new" measures are evaluated. This procedure—as demonstrated by Labouvie and her colleagues (Labouvie, Frohring, Baltes, & Goulet, 1973) for short-term learning research—appears to have major potential if a set of well-established criterion-referenced tests is available. Conceptually, this strategy is comparable to the use of a *tertium comparationis* (two things are compared to each other by comparing each to a third known attribute or phenomenon). Eckensberger (1973) discussed various other statistical approaches aimed at a solution of the measurement-equivalence problem. Such procedures always rest on a number of assumptions that other researchers may or may not be willing to accept.

We do not propose a single, universal solution to the measurement-equivalence problem here. The reader should simply grasp the nature and extent of the problem and, until it is more convincingly resolved, realize that the validity of data-based interpretations depends on measurement-equivalence issues and that one should, therefore, qualify conclusions accordingly. Caution is desirable in most cases anyway. Such profoundly engrossing and even embarrassing issues may be with us for a long time to come, but their existence must not be allowed to stifle attempts to proceed with the establishment of a useful body of knowledge concerning developmental phenomena. Openness in this regard enables others to form independent evaluations of outcomes and fosters the development of alternative courses, some of which may be more scientifically useful than the initial one.

be cautious on age, sex, cultural leaps

In the following sections, selected aspects of measurement equivalence are discussed in more detail. This approach emphasizes a broad conception of measurement equivalence as it pertains to developmental research. Additional concrete research examples dealing with development-related differences in the validity of measurement in the context of learning research are presented in Chapter Twenty-Two.

Definitions of Testing and Instrumentation Effects

Testing and instrumentation effects refer to changes in the dependent variable. The changes are called *testing effects* when they are attributable to changes in the subjects as a result of repeated testing; they are called *instrumentation effects* when they result from changes in the testing context, the tester, or the validity or reliability of the test.

In the preceding section we noted that both the validity and the reliability of measurement instruments can change with development, although the instruments may continue to exhibit surface equivalence (equivalent face validity). In this section, we emphasize not such developmental changes in test characteristics but testing-instrumentation effects that result primarily from repeated observation *per se* and not from development.

The confounding effects of testing and instrumentation in repeated-measurement designs are well known in the behavioral sciences. Many of the instruments used involve reactive and obtrusive measures (Webb, Campbell, Schwartz, & Sechrest, 1966). Therefore, measurement is often not independent of the process of observation, and the thing observed may be changed by the process of observation in complex ways—a phenomenon somewhat analogous to the Heisenberg principle of indeterminacy in the physical sciences (Labouvie, 1975a). Thus, presenting the same assessment situation repeatedly to the same person can be an experience that alters the observer, the observation medium, and the person observed. The exact magnitude of testing and instrumentation effects is largely unknown for most psychological instruments, especially because the magnitude, form, and duration of such effects may vary across developmental levels.

Intraindividual Change and Testing-Instrumentation Effects

The issue of testing and instrumentation effects as sources of error in developmental research becomes conspicuous as soon as one accepts that the meaning of development is intraindividual change, an assessment of which requires at least two time-ordered observations. The importance of these sources of error lies in evidence from learning research that repeated presentation of the same stimulus material leads to performance changes, which are regulated by a variety of learning parameters. Thus, the later measurements, necessary for the assessment of intraindividual change, may reflect not only an individual's status on the same attribute as was measured initially, but also learning effects irrelevant to that particular change-assessment objective.

Similarly, on the level of psychometric-test construction, there is evidence that short-term repeated presentation of personality tests (Windle, 1954) and ability or achievement tests (Vernon, 1954) results in distinct effects. In personality tests, for instance, one general effect is toward "better" adjustment profiles as familiarity with the test increases, and in intellectual tests the trend is usually toward higher performance, at least during initial phases of the retest situation. These trends, however, are differentially strong for different behavior dimensions and for different age/cohort groups.

With respect to long-term developmental research, it is often argued that testing and instrumentation effects occur primarily in the team of researchers (who often change with time), the testing context, and the data interpretation, rather than in the subjects themselves. Such optimism, however, is not supported by recent evidence gathered in carefully controlled long-term longitudinal research, even with trait-oriented psychometric instruments constructed to exhibit stability rather than change. This evidence is summarized in the next section.

Assessment and Control of Testing Effects in Longitudinal Research

Testing effects are generally accepted as an important source of error in short-term longitudinal research, but not in long-term developmental research. Therefore, the evidence presented here to illustrate these effects is taken from long-term longitudinal data involving a retest interval of at least one year. In both Schaie's (1970, 1973) studies on adult intelligence and Nesselroade and Baltes' (1974) study on adolescent intelligence and personality (see also Chapter Thirteen and Figure 16-1), control groups for testing effects were incorporated. The overall outcomes clearly supported the need for adequate control groups even in long-term longitudinal studies.

In principle, the design for control of testing effects requires that random samples from a parent sample be randomly assigned to levels of testing frequency that they will have experienced at a given age, as shown in Table 17-1. Table 17-1 presents a simple design that includes four samples, each given its first test at a different level among four age levels. One of these samples $(C_1 S_1)$ is also the target longitudinal sample.

Table 17-1.   Simple design for control of testing effects in longitudinal research with one cohort

	Age/Observation			
Random Sample	*5*	*10*	*15*	*20*
$C_1 S_1$	O_1	O_2	O_3	O_4
$C_1 S_2$		O_1	(O_2)	(O_3)
$C_1 S_3$			O_1	(O_2)
$C_1 S_4$				O_1

Note: This is only one possible design. If other error sources or nonlinear testing effects need attention, more complex designs are necessary (C = Cohort, S = Sample, O = Observation). The observations in parentheses may be omitted. See Campbell and Stanley (1963) for alternative arrangements.

Nesselroade and Baltes (1974) used this kind of design in their study of ability and personality development in adolescents. In general, testing effects were significant and strong for all ability measures, but they were negligible for all but one of the ten personality dimensions assessed. Figure 17-1 represents the magnitude and direction of the testing effects by the length and direction of arrows, separately for each of four cohorts (ages 12–13–14, 13–14–15, 14–15–16, and 15–16–17). The testing effects were assessed by comparing the third testing of the longitudinal samples with the performance of samples from the same cohorts tested only on the third occasion.

The left-hand part of Figure 17-1 shows a testing effect on number series, amounting overall to about 50% of the age variance obtained in the core

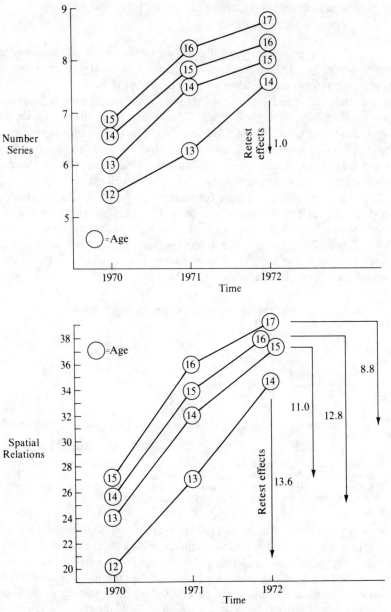

Figure 17-1.   Empirical examples of the effects of repeated testing on longitudinal assessment of ability in adolescence (selected from Nesselroade & Baltes, 1974). Magnitude and direction of testing effects are indicated by the length and direction of arrows. Each retest comparison is based on contrasting the longitudinal sample (three testings) with a control group tested for the first time in 1972.

longitudinal sample. The right-hand part of the figure, dealing with spatial relations, summarizes a more complicated case, since the statistical analysis showed that testing interacted with age/cohort. By and large, the older the subjects, the less strong was the retest effect. The retest effect on spatial relations amounted to about 95% of the longitudinal age difference for the 12–13–14 cohort, 85% for the 13–14–15 and 14–15–16 cohorts, and 70% for the 15–16–17 cohort.

The magnitudes of the testing effects on ability measures in the Nesselroade-Baltes study are indeed astonishing, as they account in all cases for at least 40% of the longitudinal age variance. We mentioned before that the bulk of past longitudinal work has not included appropriate testing controls or corrections. The possible testing effects in all those studies—some of which had as many as 40 testing occasions—are a source of concern when the measurement instruments used were reactive and obtrusive. The same is obviously true for experimental learning and memory research, in which long-term longitudinal data are beginning to appear in the literature (for example, Arenberg, 1974).

One way to correct for significant testing effects is to *adjust the core longitudinal data appropriately*. This adjustment process (see Labouvie, Bartsch, Nesselroade, & Baltes, 1974, for detailed description) may also need to take into account joint effects of testing and selective dropout or experimental mortality, if the latter turn out to be significant in a given study. The reason for this added complication is that dropout effects may be larger in the core longitudinal study (because of its multiple-observation feature) than in the retest control group, which is observed only once. In principle, extended controls or corrections are always necessary if testing interacts with other sources of error, or if the trend of the testing effects is nonlinear or multidirectional. In sequential research, the simultaneous application of longitudinal and cross-sectional sequences permits an initial control for testing effects.

Incidentally, a comparison of testing effects in simple longitudinal and simple cross-sectional studies might initially lead one to extol the virtues of the cross-sectional method, since cross-sectional subjects are observed only once. This conclusion, however, is not completely justified if we recognize that the different independent age/cohorts in cross-sectional studies may have experienced different amounts of preexperimental test exposure. For example, in comparing present-day 80-year-olds with 20-year-olds on an intelligence test, how often have both age groups participated in similar settings before? In this case, the major grace of the simple cross-sectional method is that the investigator is unaware of the groups' *pre*experimental testing history.

Another strategy for control of testing and instrumentation effects is taken from verbal learning research (Goulet, 1973). The strategy is to engage all subjects in sufficient *preexperimental warm-up* to reach peak performance before the key observations begin. It appears, however, that this technique needs careful examination, since it has been shown not only that different age/cohort groups exhibit different average instrumentation effects, but also that these effects show complex interactions (see also Chapter Twenty-Two). In a study by Furry and Baltes (1973), for example, extended work on ability tests aided adolescents but hindered old persons.

Regression toward the Mean and Developmental Assessment

Statistical regression toward the mean (see Chapter Five for definition) is another type of error related to measurement equivalence that needs attention when developmental change is charted. The effect of statistical regression toward the mean is particularly important when change data are charted across two occasions. If the task of identifying change extends beyond two occasions (Baltes & Nesselroade, 1976), the issue of statistical regression toward the mean loses much of its significance.

Regression toward the mean is important when the task is to describe interindividual differences in intraindividual change (Baltes & Nesselroade, 1976; Baltes, Nesselroade, Schaie, & Labouvie, 1972; Campbell & Stanley, 1963; Furby, 1973; Lord, 1963). Because of measurement error, subjects who are located toward the extremes of a score distribution at one occasion of measurement tend to converge toward the overall mean at another occasion of measurement. According to the conventional interpretation of reliability, this statistical effect is stronger the lower the reliability of the measurement instrument.

In principle, error of measurement operates in the following manner on change scores from one occasion to another (Furby, 1973; Lord, 1963). The underlying conception is that measurement error is uncorrelated across occasions; that is, at each occasion a random process operates that superimposes positive, negative, or zero error on the individuals' true scores. The high and low extremes of the distribution, therefore, at a given occasion contain a larger proportion of persons with large positive (high scorers) and large negative (low scorers) error components. Accordingly, members of extreme-scoring groups on one occasion will tend, on the average, not to receive the large positive and negative error components on another occasion. The result is that the mean score of an extreme scoring group on one occasion will tend to be less extreme when it is computed for another occasion of measurement. The outcome is called regression toward the mean: the mean of high scorers has a tendency to decrease (reflecting their loss of positive error), and vice versa for the low scorers.

Statistical regression toward the mean, then, becomes relevant if one divides a sample into subsamples on a measurement continuum (for example, high, medium, low) and examines intraindividual change separately for each of the subsamples on the same measurement variable. Developmental researchers need to distinguish, therefore, between "true" error-free interindividual differences in intraindividual change and "fallible" ones due to statistical regression toward the mean. Two concrete examples from the developmental literature are the intellectual development of gifted, normal, and retarded subjects, and the development of anxiety in persons initially high versus persons initially low in anxiety. Regression toward the mean can also have a substantive source as well as a statistical source. For example, the sources of change may become more homogeneous with increasing age of the subjects, thus reducing the range of developmental variability (see Baltes & Nesselroade, 1976, for discussion).

In principle, there are *several strategies for control* of regression toward the mean. One strategy is to use highly reliable measures for classifying subjects; another is to increase the number of times of observation (for example, Baltes & Nesselroade, 1976; Campbell, 1969), thus producing a baseline pattern of change trends to permit the separation of reliable from fallible change sequences; still another is the application of time-reversal designs (for example, Baltes et al., 1972). Each of these strategies has its own merits, depending upon the specific case and the investigators' intentions (see Baltes & Nesselroade, 1976, for further discussion).

A further note of caution is needed on the relevance of statistical regression toward the mean. Statistical regression toward the mean is clearly relevant in the *two-occasion case* when instruments with low reliability are used and samples are divided on the basis of pretest scores. However, in the case of *multiple-occasion data*, it may be equally important to focus on the description of change in terms of raw data rather than within a framework imposed by a given analysis technique, such as the least-squares-estimation framework of linear regression. Furthermore, as argued by Baltes and Nesselroade (1976), multiple-occasion data (in analogy to the baseline component in a single-subject design; see Chapter Twenty-Three) provide a direct assessment of the magnitude of regression toward the mean that is not possible in the two-occasion case.

In some cases, the application of a statistical-regression-based model can *impose* regression effects that are a function more of the model used and the two-occasion situation than of the measurement instrument (for example, Baltes & Nesselroade, 1976). This possibility reminds us that, in the search for intraindividual change, it is important to understand not just some but all of the effects of manipulations of the data before doing them and to move beyond a two-occasion situation whenever possible.

Summary

The use of observations from multiple occasions for inferences about change requires assumptions or information about measurement equivalence. Unless we can assume or demonstrate that differences in observations are not confounded with development-irrelevant sources, we are not justified in using multiple-occasion data as direct indicators of change.

Strategies for the establishment of measurement equivalence are not yet well formulated. Aside from the general issues involved—which are often metatheoretical—there are a few specific problems that must be dealt with before differences between multiple-occasion observations can be used as indicators of change.

One known source of error is testing effects. Testing effects are changes in the subjects as a result of repeated testing. A second source of potential error refers to instrumentation. Instrumentation effects are changes in the testing context, the tester, or the validity or reliability of the test. The magnitude of these effects is largely unknown and is believed to vary across developmental levels. Some relevant research that has been published has shown that testing and instrumentation effects may account for 40% or more of the differences between ages in a longitudinal study. Thus, when these effects are taken out of developmental curves, the true intraindividual changes (independent of the effects of repeated testing) are found to be considerably reduced. The solution to this latter problem is methodological: include a longitudinal sample tested repeatedly, and include independent samples tested only once each, a different sample for each testing occasion. The latter samples serve as controls for the effects of repeated testing, and their data can be used to adjust the longitudinal data appropriately.

Another major concern in the descriptive study of change deals with regression toward the mean. This issue is particularly relevant if the objective is to study interindividual differences in change. Statistical regression is a tendency for persons who initially obtain extreme scores on a test to converge (at the second occasion) toward the mean when given the same test again. The tendency results from error of measurement assumed to be uncorrelated across occasions. The effect is especially pronounced when the test is low in reliability.

As one moves from a two-occasion situation to observations on multiple occasions, statistical regression becomes less important. In any case, however, regression toward the mean illustrates how important it is to separate the effects of imprecise measurement from "true" change or "true" interindividual differences in change. Fortunately, several strategies are available for control of statistical regression, particularly if the task of description extends beyond the two-occasion case.

Chapter Eighteen

Modeling Change over Time: From Description to Explanation

Developmentalists have begun to recognize the advantages offered by valid mathematical and statistical representations of relevant phenomena. The gains in economy and precision of description, and in predictive and inferential power, given by accurate mathematical expressions are necessary if significant advances in empirical approaches to the study of development are to be realized.

Although developmentalists typically have not been in the forefront of innovation in measurement and statistical methodology, a variety of tools showing some promise for the task of studying systematic changes over the life span are available from other disciplines. This chapter will provide a cursory examination of selected procedures sometimes used to provide a rigorous, quantitative representation of sequences of observations of the same experimental units. The strategies highlighted are especially appropriate for structuring observations related to time or dependent upon one another through time. As we will see, two of them especially focus directly on the nature of the temporal dependency of the observations.

Data and Mathematical Representations

Given observations on two or more variables at one, two, or more occasions, one may proceed to examine the data in a variety of ways for evidence of relationships among the variables (see also Chapters Eight and Twelve). Standard statistical tests for detecting differences among group means, techniques of multiple and partial correlation, and other well-known coefficients and devices may be used to provide answers to questions of magnitude of effect, strength of relationship, proportion of variation accounted for, and so on.

In some circumstances, and developmental research is a good example, an investigator desires not merely to establish that a relationship exists between two or more variables, but also to specify or determine the actual form of that relationship. There is an obvious difference, for example, between the assertion that 19-year-olds are taller than 13-year-olds and the assertion that the relationship between height and age is a negatively accelerated function during the teens. An even more precise statement, which specifies an actual formula relating height to age, might be constructed for a given data set.

The necessity for mathematical and statistical tools by which to structure temporal relationships is widely acknowledged, and one may, in accord with the distinction made earlier between confirmatory and exploratory analyses (Chapter Eight), approach the business of determining the functional (mathematical) nature of a relationship in quite different ways. If the relationship is sufficiently dependent upon a theory that the form can be specified before the data are seen, one can determine statistically whether or not the function specified does indeed fit the data satisfactorily. Performing a test of goodness of fit between observed data and a hypothesized curve or function also provides a test of the credibility of the theory. Or one might consider alternative functions—say, two provided by competing theories—and test to see which provides the better fit to observed data. Both of the examples above are instances of confirmatory research.

An exploratory approach might involve, for example, initially determining what function or curve best describes a given set of data by developing a formula directly out of the data themselves. Subsequently, a series of tests might be performed to see if the relationship developed from one set of data on an exploratory basis can be confirmed in another set of data, drawn independently of the first set.

Procedures for fitting different mathematical functions to data in a systematic manner are discussed in various statistical texts, often under the general title of *curve fitting*. The term *trend analysis* is sometimes used in this very general sense, although in other instances it is reserved for the fitting of polynomial relationships in data representing repeated measurements of the same experimental units. Developmentalists often discuss related procedures in terms of fitting *growth curves* (Tanner, 1962; Wohlwill, 1970b; 1973). Naturally, more refined and powerful analyses place greater requirements on the quality of the measurement and data-gathering procedures (such as scale level and reliability) employed in an investigation.

In recent years social and behavioral scientists have turned in many directions to seek useful ways to describe and structure interesting change processes. Interest has grown dramatically, for example, in the application of mathematical models that enable one to study the interrelationships among

observations over time (for example, Kowalski & Guire, 1974). Such efforts
are particularly important if one assigns major theoretical weight to the nature
of developmental functions (for example, Wohlwill, 1970a, b; 1973). Also of
potentially great value at the present stage of developmental theory-building
are models that lead to predictions about future events in terms of probabilities
rather than absolute certainties.

Markov Processes

The term *Markov process* designates a particular structure or set of
characteristics that may be exhibited by a variable observed in an organism or
system over time. Brand (1966), for example, defined a Markov chain to
include both a set of states in which a process can be found and a set of
conditional probabilities specifying the likelihood that the system goes from
state i at time t to state j at time $t + 1$. Like any mathematical model, the
Markov process is an idealization, but to the extent that a Markov model
adequately fits a set of real-life observations, it may be used to predict from the
present condition or state to some future state of the organism or system being
observed. If, for example, the process being modeled will eventually stabilize,
the model may be used to determine what proportion of the time the system
will be in a given state.

Essentially, if one "taps" into some ongoing process by means of
repeated observation of a set of outcomes, and if the probability of occurrence
of each outcome in the set of outcomes is conditional (depends) only upon the
immediately prior outcome, the series of outcomes may be called a Markov
chain. Lohnes (1965) pointed out that models like the Markov chain, which
rely on the *dynamics* of a model itself for prediction, are quite different from,
for instance, trait-oriented approaches, which base the prediction of one
variable on the values of others correlated with but distinct from it. Of course,
some amount of stochastic indeterminacy, or random error, may prevent the
Markov model from fitting the data exactly, but the degree of fit may still be
good enough to warrant representing a given set of observations as a Markov
chain.

Markov models have been applied to data from various areas of the
social and behavioral sciences (Spilerman, 1975), and a few attempts to fit
Markov chains to developmental change processes can be found (Gribbons,
Halperin, & Lohnes, 1966). Below, a somewhat contrived example will
illustrate features of the Markov model and how it might be used to represent
developmentally interesting behavior.

The formation of friendship pairs and other dyadic relationships
occurs across the life span. How well might aspects of pair bonding be
characterized by a simple Markov model? Let's consider a very concrete

instance. Suppose we focus on a child named Billy and observe him during nursery school play period each day. Suppose further, for purposes of illustration, that Billy plays either with Johnny or with Mary in any particular play period. Given a set of observations on Billy's playmates we might produce the data in Table 18-1, indicating the probability (transitional probability) of each of two present events—(1) play with Johnny or (2) play with Mary—depending upon whether Johnny or Mary was played with in the preceding period. Such a table of transitional probabilities is called a *transition matrix*.

Table 18-1.   Illustration of simple Markov transition matrix: Probabilities of Billy's play partner sequences across adjacent time periods

Play Partner in Period t	Play Partner in Period t + 1	
	Mary	Johnny
Mary	.40	.60
Johnny	.30	.70

The hypothetical transition matrix in Table 18-1 indicates that if Billy plays with Mary in one period, the probability that he will play with Mary in the next period is .40. The probability that Billy will play with Johnny, given that he played with Mary in the preceding period, is .60. The two probabilities sum to 1.00, signifying that playing with either Mary or Johnny exhausts the possible events. The numbers in the second row of the transition matrix indicate that if Billy plays with Johnny in one period, the probability of playing with Mary in the following period is .30, and the probability of playing with Johnny two periods in a row is .70.

If the elements in the transition matrix apply to every pair of adjacent occasions in which Billy, Mary, and Johnny interact, and if the interaction process has only a one-step memory (probabilities of present outcomes depend only on the immediately preceding occasion), we may use the power of the Markov model to make various predictions about the interaction process being studied. For example, it can be shown that the probability that Billy plays with Mary on Friday, given that he played with her on Monday, is 1/3. Alternatively, the probability that Billy plays with Johnny on Friday, given that he played with Johnny on Monday, is 2/3. Actually, the process converges—in the sense that, regardless of whom Billy played with on a given day, after a few sessions the probability that he will play with Mary stabilizes at 1/3. Such disparate relative frequencies of interaction often seem to be the most useful definitions of such abstractions as "friendships."

Wide applicability of Markov models for representing developmental processes remains to be demonstrated. Spilerman (1975) pointed out that, although there is some overlap between the objectives of merely predicting the occurrence of some phenomenon and being able to explain it, the two are not the same. Markov processes emphasize the former aim—prediction. However, the introduction of independent variables into Markov chains, as proposed by Spilerman (1972), may turn out to provide a powerful tool for developmentalists interested in explaining change processes. Markov chains' primary usefulness will probably be for studying phenomena that involve relatively short portions of the life span, due to the apparent complexity and number of influences and determinants of behavior.

Time-Series Analysis

Another interesting and, to developmentalists, potentially useful class of procedures for analyzing observations reflecting certain kinds of temporal processes is a family of techniques and models called time-series analysis (Box & Jenkins, 1970; Campbell, 1969; Glass, Willson, & Gottman, 1972; Porges, in press).

A time series involves successive observations of one or more variables. A time series obtained on a given experimental unit (or group of units) represents observations that are potentially dependent upon each other due to some underlying process or processes. Inferences about the nature of such processes are desired, but the lack of independence among observations violates the assumptions underlying many of the conventional statistical techniques that would otherwise be used to evaluate the data. Methods for analyzing a time series are, for that reason, somewhat specialized. Time-series analyses remain descriptive if they aim simply at examining whether ordering observations with respect to time itself provides a useful data representation. They become explanatory if, in addition, assessments of the effects on the series of interpolated treatments or interventions are conducted.

In developing a case for the usefulness of time-series designs in developmental psychology, Porges (in press), for example, suggested that the designs commonly used in psychology are inappropriate for analyzing development because they are based on a notion of static data points rather than a notion of continuous data. If development is continuous, Porges argued, then the static-point approach is faulty, and techniques such as time series need to be exploited more fully.

A time-series analysis, then, may be employed simply to determine whether or not something more systematic than random events is represented in a string of successive naturalistic observations; or it may be used to ascertain whether or not an intervention has produced an effect in the measurement variables of interest. Discussing the application of time-series models, Glass and his colleagues (1972), for instance, distinguished between the use of time-series analysis to develop mathematical expressions describing components of an observed data set and the use of time-series analysis to evaluate the results of treatments, either naturally occurring or experimentally applied.

Highly sophisticated procedures may be applied to give mathematical and statistical expression to a series of observations extending over time. Glass and his colleagues pointed out, however, that these techniques are probably reasonable only if the data represent continuous or nearly continuous observations numbering in the hundreds—data such as EEG records, for instance. Except when studying processes indexed by, say, physiological variables, developmentalists typically do not produce data records extensive enough to be appropriately analyzed by these extremely powerful methods (Porges, in press). However, statisticians currently are working on time-series-estimation procedures that will permit inferences from less extensive data bases.

In addition to application in developmental psychophysiology, other applications of certain time-series models may prove helpful to developmentalists, both for descriptive purposes and for tactical experimentation on change processes. For example, identifiable interventions that fall within a string of repeated observations, and that may be expected to affect either the level or direction of the values in a series of observations, may be examined by the procedures discussed by Glass and his colleagues (1972), Gottman, McFall, and Barnett (1969), and others. Time-series analysis has been used to assess the effects of events such as the enactment of laws or highly publicized interventions such as safety campaigns (Campbell, 1969).

The developmentalist might employ time-series methods to assess the effects on individuals of critical incidents occurring at essentially predictable points in the life span (for example, first grade, marriage, retirement). Time series could also be used to evaluate the effects of treatments designed to explain developmental change via simulation studies (see Chapter Nineteen). Again, such an approach marks the transition from a descriptive to an explanatory posture.

In Figure 18-1 a fictitious example is presented to illustrate the application of time-series logic. Represented are extensive observations of anxiety and depression levels surrounding the death of a spouse. Let's consider only anxiety for a moment; the data suggest that the rapid increase in level of anxiety might well be attributed to that event. Appropriate analysis procedures would show that anxiety increases significantly following the death of the spouse. Reaching valid conclusions about changes in level of score is a legitimate objective of time-series analysis. Now consider the depression variable. Depression level changes in essentially the same form as anxiety level during the short time period immediately surrounding the critical event. Given the more extensive information available about the nature of the depression curve, however, and the proper time-series analysis, one would not conclude that the increased depression is due to the death of the spouse, even though it coincides with that event. Depression level is under the control of some more regular phenomenon, such as monthly money supply, for example.

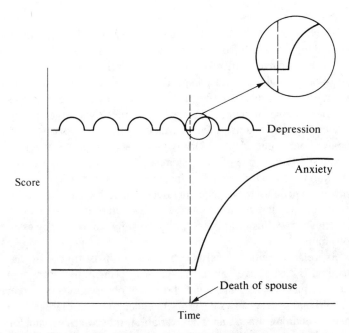

Figure 18-1. Hypothetical scores on dimensions of anxiety and depression over a time interval that includes a critical event.

Thus, time-series procedures offer a more objective way of ascertaining (with some level of confidence) whether or not a given intervention (death of spouse) may be responsible for a change in some measurement variable (anxiety or depression). In Chapter Twenty-Three, the use of the rationale of time-series analysis will be further illustrated, in the context of single-subject designs.

Summary

The study of behavioral change can be approached by means of mathematical representations. In fact, the most economical and direct way to represent a phenomenon is to represent it mathematically—that is, to represent relationships among the relevant variables by means of an equation. Such an equation specifies a function, in the mathematical sense, and hence is said to represent the functional relationship among the relevant variables.

Moving from exploratory description to theoretical prediction and explanation, one can distinguish between two strategies. In the exploratory approach, data are collected and an equation is derived to fit the data. The empirically determined functional relationship should be tested in further, confirmatory research. A second approach to determine the functional relationship among variables is to use another kind of confirmatory approach: a theory about behavioral change is used to predict the functional relationship, then research is conducted to test the agreement between the predicted relationship and the relationship observed in the data. If the agreement is close, the research is said to have confirmed the theoretical relationship.

When a mathematical perspective is applied to the study of change over time, various kinds of curve-fitting procedures can be used to specify relationships among variables. Processes studied over time may be represented by special models, such as Markov chains, involving probability statements about events. If the Markov model is appropriate, precise predictions about the future state of the system can be made. A major drawback is that the simple Markov model is inappropriate for many developmental phenomena, especially those occurring over long age spans, because preceding events often interact in complex ways to determine future events (see Chapter Eleven for illustration), violating the simple dependency assumed in Markov chains.

A related method consists of various forms of time-series analysis. This method is descriptive only in its simplest form. In that form, it may be used to determine whether an extended series of observations is systematic or random. When the time-series design is intended to incorporate time-specific treatments (retaining time as an index variable), it becomes explanatory. It is then possible to discern whether a treatment introduced into the series has an effect on the dependent variable. In many ways, the logic, design, and use of time-series analysis are consonant with the basic objective of developmental research. However, its full-blown form has not yet been applied and tested. The exception is the use of single-subject designs to be presented in Chapter Twenty-Three.

Part Five

Explanatory-Analytic
Developmental Research

The designs presented in Part Five are aimed at explaining developmental change in terms of time-related antecedents and mechanisms. In a strict sense, it is impossible to distinguish between descriptive and explanatory designs. Description and explanation always go hand in hand, and the distinction is one of degree.

All of the explanatory-analytic designs presented involve "simulation," some more explicitly than others. Whenever researchers cannot intervene directly in the normal course of development—and they usually cannot—they must study artificial situations designed to represent the real situation. The artificial situation serves as a model, or simulation, of the real situation, and the external validity of the simulation depends on its isomorphy and homology to reality. Examples of simulation research will be described in Part Five to demonstrate the utility of the simulation strategy for the explication of developmental processes.

Cross-cultural research is part of comparative developmental psychology, which also includes cross-species, cross-generation, and other criteria-group contrasts. When used in explanatory developmental research, the comparative approach involves the simulation strategy in that the existing cultures, species, generations, and so on are construed to simulate life histories of individuals. The methods are useful in spite of not being experimental-manipulative, and in spite of internal and external validity problems.

Another nonexperimental approach, used in heredity-environment research, is to compare groups differing in genetic similarity, such as identical versus fraternal twins, and differing in environmental similarity, such as reared together versus reared apart. The correlations within pairs can be compared across groups, and can be used to derive the heritability coefficient. The heritability coefficient is an estimate of the relative contributions of heredity and environment—that is, *how much* each of these variables contributes to variability in a behavioral phenomenon. The approach is potentially useful for explanatory developmental research, but so far it has seldom included the critical developmental variable, an index of time.

Experimental-manipulative methods are also used in developmental-learning research, which can be descriptive or explanatory in intent. The developmental study of learning is important because, for many psychologists, learning is the process of development. In short-term group designs on learning, longitudinal methods are often inappropriate because subjects "learn how to learn" when they are repeatedly given the same task, even with different materials each time. Therefore, combinations of longitudinal and cross-sectional arrangements are desirable.

Single-subject designs are also used in developmental-learning research; they are especially useful for the functional analysis of development. The functional analysis of development is a three-step program: (1) simulate development in the laboratory, showing that it is controlled by contingent stimuli; (2) determine whether contingent stimuli occur in the natural environment (a check on external validity); and (3) intervene by manipulating the natural contingencies in the natural environment (a further check on external validity and initiation of the optimization goal).

When experimental-manipulative designs cannot be used, it is sometimes possible to use the methods of path analysis and structural models, which unlike other nonexperimental methods can yield causal statements. However, in order to use such methods it is necessary to state the theory tested in precise form, such as in a mathematical equation, a condition seldom met in developmental psychology. Nevertheless, it is exactly this lack of theoretical explicitness that explanation-oriented research and theory in developmental psychology needs to overcome.

Chapter Nineteen

Toward Explanation: The Simulation of Developmental Processes

Overview

Part Four, on descriptive designs, addressed methods of properly identifying developmental change. Occasionally, it became evident that complex descriptive designs (especially if enriched by control groups) may also provide explanatory information. As we stated before, the distinction between descriptive and explanatory research is less logical than didactic and heuristic.

In Part Five, we present a series of designs aimed at "explaining" developmental change in terms of time-correlated antecedents and mechanisms. The ideal of explanatory-analytic research is to demonstrate causes of development or, at least, to approximate direct demonstrations by inferences about causes. In explanatory research, age-change functions or alternative developmental phenomena typically are seen as part of the dependent variable (Baer, 1970; Baltes & Goulet, 1971; McCandless & Spiker, 1956; Wohlwill, 1970a, b), and researchers' efforts are aimed at finding the controlling variables and processes.

At this point, it may be important to convey the bias of the authors as to the nature of the "philosophical model of causation." In our view, the search for causation is an important goal of any empirical science. What needs to be recognized is that there is no single, "true" principle of causation for any given phenomenon, but rather that a search for multiple and diverse forms of causation should be encouraged. The question of what is *the* proximal cause (see Chapter Four) for a given event is a good case in point.

It is important that explanatory attempts begin by focusing on the proper kind of change phenomenon. For example, the reader should now appreciate that simple cross-sectional and longitudinal age differences are not necessarily equivalent to age changes but may contain many sources of error. As a consequence, much explanatory developmental research—which is based on age differences—may be plagued by the fact that researchers look for age-associated antecedents even though a search for cohort-related antecedents may be more appropriate or, at least, should be considered with equal intensity. Similar conclusions may be derived from the impact that retesting effects seem to have on longitudinal change data.

Therefore, before embarking on explanatory-analytic research on age changes, the researcher should reflect carefully about the realm of internal and external validity characterizing the target change phenomenon. The extent of concern with the initial validity of change data also differs, of course, among researchers; and, again, their conception of what constitutes developmental change is a major factor.

The coverage of explanatory-analytic developmental designs in this part of the book is not intended to be complete. The selection of methods and designs was based on whether they appear to have general value for most areas of developmental research. Therefore, many worthwhile explanatory strategies (for example, verbal-learning paradigms: see Goulet, 1968, 1973; Kausler, 1970) are not given extensive treatment because their primary usefulness is limited—to the memory area, for example. In addition, in agreement with a life-span developmental view, the methods selected for detailed examination are ones involving an explicit effort to explain long-term intraindividual change patterns.

Part Five of this book attends to issues concerning both rationale and method in the use of experimental and nonexperimental research design. Topics focused on include comparative developmental psychology, ecological methodology, designs for heredity-environment research, group designs on learning, single-subject designs, path analysis, and other structural models. These presentations are preceded by an examination of simulation strategies.

The simulation of developmental process is the initial focus of discussion for two reasons. First, the term *simulation* calls attention directly to the issue of reality correspondence in empirical research, a particularly troublesome problem in research on "assigned" (Kerlinger, 1964) subject variables such as age and sex. Second, full recognition of simulation as an orientation to research design helps to clarify the strategy involved in formulating and testing hypotheses about any cause of development. Simulation is useful as an aid to teaching, thinking, and conceptualizing.

Rationale and Definition of Simulation

Whenever researchers cannot experiment *in vivo* with their subject matter, they design artificial situations that represent the real target phenomenon as closely as possible. This strategy of simulating reality is used in practically all empirical sciences. The experimental laboratory, as a place for the isolation of and controlled study of variables, is the classic paradigm for simulation. More specific examples from other sciences are the construction of moon-like geographies to aid engineers in the building of moon vehicles, or of air tunnels to assist engineers in the design of automobiles or aircraft with optimal resistance characteristics.

In all these cases of simulation, the simulation situation presents an operating model. It is assumed that the model is relatively isomorphic and homologous to reality. As Raser (1969, p. 9) stated it: "Change over time in a model corresponds to changes over time in the system being modeled . . . . The functional relationships among components being modeled are isomorphic with that being represented."

Simulation strategies, then, are not unique in empirical inquiry. They only make very explicit, from a somewhat different perspective, what our earlier discussion (Chapter Three) on the relationships among theories, models, and data has already elaborated. The scientific view of reality is not identical with reality; a scientist building knowledge transacts with reality, or even constructs reality—if one is willing to follow the philosophical assertions of many researchers of the "constructivist" orientation.

In developmental research, the simulation strategy is perhaps more conspicuous than in other areas of psychology (for example, Baer, 1970, 1973; Baltes & Goulet, 1971; Kuhn, 1974), because the developmental study of behavior is defined as dealing with complex and long-term phenomena. In addition, the target phenomenon (developmental change) involves, at least at the outset, person- and time-related variables (such as age) that cannot be manipulated arbitrarily. Thus, it seems fair to conclude that all developmental research has strong simulation properties, and that the generation of developmental knowledge will benefit if developmentalists face up to this aspect of their work.

The Strategy of Age Simulation

A Hypothetical Example

Baltes and Goulet (1971) demonstrated how simulation could be used for the explanatory study of age changes. In doing so, they paid tribute to Heinz Werner's (1957; Hooper, 1973) concept of "microgenetic" techniques for analysis of developmental processes with adult subjects.

Within the framework of studying age-related change, Baltes and Goulet viewed age simulation as the *time-compressed (short-term) modification of age functions* by application of behavioral, stimulus, and biological variables or processes that are assumed to be age associated. Age was regarded as part of the dependent variable, as in Wohlwill's (1970a,b) suggestion to define developmental functions as the dependent variable.

Specifically, an age-simulation study contains at least the following steps:

1. Define the age function (or the key developmental process) to serve as criterion;
2. Develop at least one hypothesis about which key age or development-associated variable or process could be involved in the "production" of the criterion age function (or criterion process);
3. Design a study with which to test the stated developmental hypothesis by finding conditions (experimental or quasi-experimental) that vary or by manipulating the key developmental variable in desired directions and under controlled circumstances;
4. Assess the accuracy (statistical probability) of the stated hypothesis; and
5. Examine and/or discuss the external validity (isomorphy, homology) of the simulation study.

The steps listed are summarized in Figure 19-1, which is based upon a simple hypothetical example of age simulation. The example chosen is non-controversial in that it is unrelated to an existing theory or body of data. In our example, the researcher is interested in age changes in dart-throwing accuracy and finds in the literature that someone has studied this phenomenon carefully and obtained the age-change function designated in Figure 19-1 as the criterion age function. This criterion age function shows 20-year-old adults highest in accuracy, with 50-year-olds and 10-year-olds following in that order.

Reflection about the causes for this observed age change in dart-throwing accuracy could produce a long list of possible hypotheses. When formulating such a list, a developmentalist will tend to focus on historical paradigms (see Chapters One and Eleven)—that is, variables and processes that accumulate in their form or effect over the life history prior to the age level under consideration—rather than focusing on situational determinants *per se*. In the case of dart-throwing accuracy, for instance, one could hypothesize that two treatment variables are significant: *practice level* and *anxiety level*, both of which are usually related to psychomotor performance.

Specifically, according to the hypothesis that practice is the explan-atory variable, the assertion would be that 20-year-olds are more accurate because they have experienced the most preexperimental practice in dart throwing; and 50-year-olds and 10-year-olds have less preexperimental prac-tice, in that order. Accordingly, one would hypothesize that short-term treat-ments involving practice in dart throwing (say, five times a week for 15 minutes each day) would lead to a significant performance increment in children and older adults. Young adults, on the contrary, would benefit comparatively little from this experience, since their preexperimental life history contained a level of practice in dart throwing that brought them close to

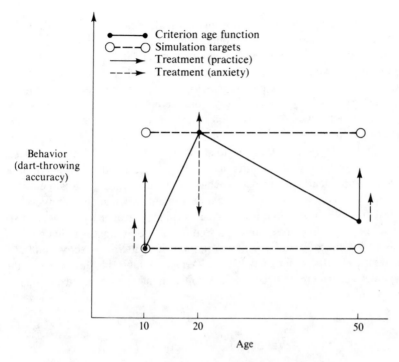

Legend:
- ●——● Criterion age function
- ○– – –○ Simulation targets
- ——→ Treatment (practice)
- – – –→ Treatment (anxiety)

Behavior (dart-throwing accuracy)

Age
10   20   50

Figure 19-1. Design of age-simulation research. An observed criterion age function is explained by variation of treatments hypothesized to be age-associated. Length of arrows indicates magnitude of treatment effects. Based on Baltes and Goulet (1971).

their asymptotic level of performance in that behavior. From a statistical viewpoint, this hypothesis involves an age-by-treatment interaction (see Baltes & Goulet, 1971, for further discussion), since the assertion is that—due to life-history differences—different age groups respond *differentially* to the same treatment.

In the case of anxiety level, the hypothesis would be oriented toward increasing the performance in the two extreme age groups and decreasing it in the group of young adults. The line of reasoning could be as follows. Level of anxiety relates to performance in an inverted U-shaped function, as suggested occasionally for arousal-behavior relationships. Too much and too little anxiety produce the lowest levels of performance.

In competitive situations, young children and older adults have anxiety levels that are too high for optimal performance (see Eisdorfer, Nowlin, & Wilkie, 1970, for a similar argument in the aging literature; Reese & Lipsitt, 1970, for similar arguments on age-related performance-set differences in the child literature); but young adults have an anxiety level close to the optimal level, according to this hypothesis. The application of a treatment such as preexperimental-relaxation therapy, which is designed to reduce anxiety in competitive situations, should produce effects in children and older adults opposite of those it produces in young adults. In this case of an age-by-treatment interaction, young children and older adults would increase in performance (since they would come closer to the optimal level of anxiety), whereas young adults (moving away from the optimal level toward less than optimal anxiety) would be expected to exhibit a decrease in dart-throwing accuracy.

Figure 19-1 is designed to show the hypothesized treatment-effect patterns. For the "practice" treatment, the youngest and oldest age groups increase most markedly in performance. For the "anxiety" treatment, the sample of young adults shows a clear decrement, whereas the youngest and oldest groups exhibit minor improvements. In statistical analyses by analysis of variance, the outcome would be a significant age-by-treatment interaction. It is important to recognize, however, that the pattern of incremental and decremental effects obtained in the interaction must be the same as the hypothesized pattern. Otherwise, the significant interaction would not support the hypothesis.

The External Validity of Simulation

Although issues of external validity should be given serious consideration by the investigator at all phases of a simulation study, upon completion of the project additional discussion and evaluation of the external validity (see Chapter Six) of the obtained simulated change is needed, assuming that there is no reason for concern about aspects of internal validity in the design. Perhaps the most persuasive on this point was Werner (1937; see also Baltes & Goulet, 1971; Baer, 1973; Hooper, 1973; Sutton-Smith, 1970; Wohlwill, 1973). Contrasting developmental processes with induced changes in performance, Werner stated:

> A fundamental issue is involved. Does the genesis of "learning," "abstraction," "reasoning," or whatever term one chooses to use, mean the development of a unitary function? Or does it mean the history of an accomplishment achieved by process-patterns which were quite different at different age levels [Werner, 1937, p. 353]?

The general question is whether it is possible to produce behavioral changes in a short period of time that are indicative of and isomorphic with long-term ontogenetic changes as they occur in nature. Werner's concern with age-invariance of processes is one part of external validity and the isomorphy-homology issue. His question is whether performance differences can be used to infer underlying processes.

There are at least two aspects of the homology inference that affect simulation experiments. On the one hand is the ubiquitous question of whether the treatment conditions manipulated actually do mirror real life-history differences. Only systematic naturalistic observations can provide us with the necessary evidence. On the other hand is Werner's concern for homology in processes (see also Baltes & Goulet, 1971; Hultsch & Hickey, 1976). How many different treatments or treatment combinations (for example, variations in instructional sets, illumination of the dart-throwing target area, changes in dart board size, and so on) would produce outcomes that are similar to the initial simulation study? We owe a nice example of the homology question to Nancy Denney (personal communication, July 1975). Aspirin is often used for the treatment of headaches. It is often effective, but no one would argue that a deficit of aspirin is the "cause" of headaches.

How can a researcher differentiate between simulation outcomes that, even though they "hit," are of low external validity, and those that indeed represent valid key developmental factors? There is no easy answer to this quest for homology, which, as we stated earlier, applies in principle to any type of experimentation. The most widely accepted general strategy is to design programmatic research involving a concerted effort at theory construction with a view to both internal and external validity (see also Chapters Five and Six). In this sense, the issue of the external validity of simulation, or any other kind of explanatory research, will never be completely resolved. It is under continuous test as the refinement of theories about development proceeds and the knowledge generated is put to application.

In behavioral research on development, there is also disagreement about the significance of the homology question. On the one hand, organicists (Hooper, 1973; Sutton-Smith, 1970; Wohlwill, 1970a, b) usually see it as crucially important. On the other hand, mechanists, especially of the operant kind (for example, Baer, 1970, 1973), tend to be less concerned with the question of whether performance changes are indeed developmental.

The Simulation of Development: Research Examples

In principle, all developmental research that is aimed at the analysis of causes of age changes or ontogenetic processes includes, at least implicitly, simulation perspectives. One can argue that any well-designed developmental research with a focus on historical paradigms should be easily translatable into the steps of a simulation. In this section, we present several examples to illustrate this argument.

The Simulation of Sensory Age Changes

Sjostrom and Pollack (1971) have provided a particularly persuasive example of simulation research. They were interested in two kinds of visual illusions: one kind increasing in magnitude through the life span, the other decreasing. According to Piagetian theory, the illusions that increase with age are influenced by cognitive processes that increase with age, whereas the illusions that decrease with age are controlled by perceptual processes (acuity, and so forth) that show decrements in old age. This theoretical formulation, covering longitudinal change from childhood to old age, is what Sjostrom and Pollack (1971) attempted to simulate, testing college students.

One group of college students was equipped with yellow lenses that reduced their visual input to about the level of elderly persons. The prediction was that college students, thus receiving simulated aging changes in sensory input, would behave like elderly persons. Since the simulation was designed to affect perceptual and not cognitive processes, a further prediction was that the simulation would affect the two kinds of illusions differently. Only the kind of illusions that, according to the theory, are controlled by perceptual processes were expected to show decrements in the college students.

The outcome of this simulation of sensory aging changes was generally positive. The kind of visual illusions believed to be controlled by perceptual processes was affected in the expected direction by the simulation treatment; the putative "cognitive" visual illusion was not. Thus, Sjostrom and Pollack were able to produce change within one age group (college students) that looked like ontogenetic change. Furthermore, they produced no change in the case where, according to the theory, no age-simulation effect should have been obtained—an added nicety in any simulation experiment.

An experiment by Parrish, Lundy, and Leibowitz (1968) provides another example of a sensory-perceptual simulation. They used the strategy of hypnotic age regression and, like Sjostrom and Pollack (1971), selected two visual illusions that, on the basis of cross-sectional data, either increase in magnitude from childhood to adulthood (the Ponzo illusion) or decrease during the same age period (the Poggendorff illusion). In line with these differential age trends, the researchers expected that hypnotic age regression would lead to differential outcomes; that is, when their performance under hypnosis was compared with their typical performance, hypnotically age-regressed college students should exhibit a weaker Ponzo illusion and a stronger Poggendorff illusion.

As shown in Figure 19-2, the findings supported this expectation. This outcome is remarkable because it can be assumed that the subjects did not

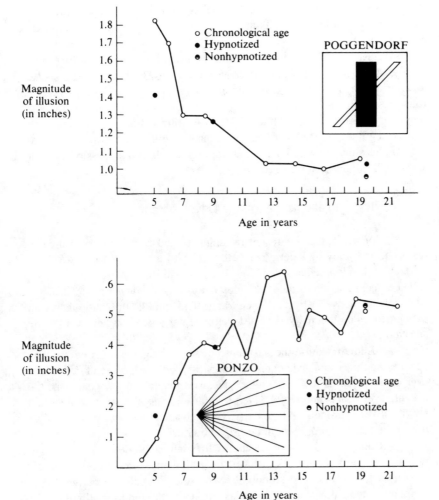

Figure 19-2. Bottom: The equally long vertical lines in the Ponzo illusion (inset) appear unequal in length. The graph describes the magnitude of this illusion as a function of chronological age (open circles); superimposed are the data obtained under hypnosis (solid circles). *Top:* The diagonal line in the Poggendorff illusion (inset) is continuous but appears discontinuous. The graph describes the magnitude of the illusion as a function of chronological age (open circles); superimposed are data obtained under hypnosis. From "Hypnotic Age-Regression and Magnitudes of the Ponzo and Poggendorff Illusions," by M. Parrish, R. M. Lundy, and H. W. Leibowitz, *Science,* 1968, *159,* 1375-1376. Copyright 1968 by the American Association for the Advancement of Science. Reprinted by permission.

have prior knowledge about the differential age functions for the two illusions (see, however, Barber, 1962, for an early critical review of studies of hypnotic age regression).

Pastalan (1971) has also simulated sensory losses in old age by testing college students (see also Lawton & Nahemow, 1973). In Pastalan's study, architecture students wore diffusing lenses, ear plugs, and film over the fingertips to simulate the average impairment of vision, hearing, and tactile sensitivity in 80-year-olds. Although Pastalan utilized this massive simulation treatment primarily for educational rather than scientific purposes, it is illustrative of the simulation rationale and appears to offer rich possibilities for analytic developmental research.

The Simulation of Language Development

For the reader interested in language and cognition as an area of research, one study by Palermo and Howe (1970) may serve to illustrate the strategy of developmental simulation. Palermo and Howe designed what they called an "experimental analogy" study to examine the developmental acquisition of past-tense inflection in children. This simulation study shows an explicit focus on the analysis of a developmental process rather than simple age change.

Children acquire the past tense of some irregular verbs before they acquire the three regular phonetic endings for "ed": /t/, /d/, and /id/. However, upon acquisition of the regular rules, overgeneralization occurs, and the irregular verbs are incorrectly given regular endings even though they had previously been pronounced correctly. Palermo and Howe wanted to simulate this developmental progression, described by Ervin (1964).

College students were taught different single-letter responses to two-digit auditory stimuli. As with verb inflection, there were three "regular" responses to the auditory stimuli, each of these regular responses being contingent upon the nature of the last digit of the auditory stimulus (for example, F was correct for auditory stimuli ending with 7; G was correct for auditory stimuli ending with 1; and C was correct for auditory stimuli ending with 2). In addition, however, Palermo and Howe included a condition that simulated irregular-verb tenses. In this case, attention to both digits of the auditory stimuli was required, and different single letters were designated to be correct (for example, 26–I, 42–A).

The results of this study simulated the developmental trend nicely. The college students (like children) learned first the irregular pairs (analogous to irregular past tenses), using predominantly rote learning. The pairs simulating regular past-tense forms, and requiring rule-governed learning rather than rote learning, were acquired second. Furthermore, once the rule-governed strategy was learned by the college students, they overgeneralized to the pairs involving irregular forms and therefore produced errors similar to the ones exhibited by young children.

In addition to simulating a process (such as rule-learning) that could underlie language development in children, Palermo and Howe identified another aspect of their data that further explains the process of past-tense acquisition in children. They found that the probability of an overgeneralization error (from a regular to an irregular verb) is a function of the frequency of the irregular pair or word in language usage. Such an additional finding, suggestive of further research on the acquisition process in children, is a desired by-product of any simulation study.

The Simulation of Multivariate Change Phenomena

For a final illustration of the simulation rationale, two examples from the literature on personality and ability development are presented. Both examples involve the production of multivariate change patterns via application of multivariate environmental, time-correlated treatments.

Denenberg and his colleagues (for example, Denenberg, Karas, Rosenberg, & Schell, 1968; Whimbey & Denenberg, 1967) set out to investigate the development of interindividual differences in rats on 49 behaviors, including emotionality, open-field behavior, response to novel stimuli, avoidance learning, activity indicators, and other behaviors. They created different life histories by applying 16 different combinations of environmental treatments to random samples from a homogeneous group of young rats. Because the rats were assigned to the treatment conditions at random, genetic effects were ruled out.

The investigators found that the 16 different programs of life history produced different age functions for most of the dependent variables, thus creating interindividual differences shown to be systematically related to life histories. The investigators were also able to show (through comparative factor analysis) that the behavior structure of the individual differences in the adult rats was remarkably similar to behavior structures observed in untreated adult rats. In this simulation experiment, then, the artificial creation of different life histories in rats produced interindividual differences in age functions and in adult behavior structures that appeared highly similar to the interindividual differences observed in more natural situations. This simulation study therefore helped identify sets of environmental influences as possible key developmental factors.

A multivariate simulation experiment by Baltes and Nesselroade (1973; see also Baltes, Nesselroade, & Cornelius, in press) was also addressed to the question of how age-related environmental inputs can produce age changes in the structure of behavior. Baltes and his colleagues did not apply treatments to real persons but, rather, generated sets of hypothetical data using explicit rules to manipulate numbers to correspond to the effects of different treatments. The target developmental change to be simulated was the sequence from structural integration to differentiation to trait/state differentiation, a sequence observed in the development of intelligence (Horn, 1970; Reinert, 1970). The application of three environmental treatments (general environmental differences, behavior-specific environmental differences, environmental stability versus variability) to six measures of cognitive ability was simulated. The three environmental treatments were applied successively (representing a simple cumulative learning model) in order to simulate an age-related process of environmental input.

The outcome of the Baltes-Nesselroade simulation was as persuasive as the studies by Denenberg and his co-workers with respect to demonstrating the susceptibility of behavior patterns to the influence of deliberately planned treatments. The simple model of cumulative environmental input "led" to systematic multivariate changes of the integration-differentiation type. For example, general environmental differences produced "integration" of intelligence-factor structures, and behavior-specific environmental differences resulted in subsequent "differentiation" of the intelligence structure.

The remarkable feature of these multivariate simulation studies is that the development of rather complex intraindividual change patterns and constructs such as "multivariate factors" was brought under experimental control, both in the rat and in the computer laboratory. Obviously, all the issues mentioned earlier relative to isomorphy and homology apply here and should be considered. The search for explanation of age changes, however, is advanced by such studies even if they provide only highly artificial evidence on what the process of development may look like. Explaining development requires the successive refinement of the key variables involved. It is a continuous process of approximation and of testing networks of antecedent-consequent relationships.

Summary

When a researcher is interested in a phenomenon that cannot be studied experimentally in nature, he or she may be able to study an analogue of the phenomenon in a simulation experiment. For example, experimental manipulation of some normal life experiences would be unethical, but it may be possible to simulate the manipulation experimentally and thereby to test a hypothesis about the effects of the life experience.

The steps in the simulation are (1) define the developmental phenomenon that is to be simulated; (2) formulate hypotheses about the age-related variables that might produce the developmental phenomenon;

(3) design a study to test the hypotheses by simulating age changes in the hypothesized explanatory variables; (4) test the hypotheses against the data obtained; and (5) try to determine the external validity of the simulation.

The external validity of a simulation is the extent to which the simulated changes are isomorphic and homologous to the real changes. Do the treatment conditions actually mirror real life-history differences? Would other treatments produce similar outcomes? In short, do the treatments indeed represent valid key developmental factors? At best, the initial answers will be tentative, and they may change as knowledge accumulates and theories are refined.

Examples of simulation research demonstrate the utility of the simulation strategy for the explanation of developmental processes. For instance, age changes in sensory and perceptual processes have been simulated in college students. In one study, yellow lenses were used to simulate the yellowing pigmentation of the eyes with increasing age, and the treatment was shown to reduce the magnitude of a type of illusion that theoretically is related to perceptual processes while having no effect on a type of illusion theoretically related to cognitive processes. In another study, hypnotic age regression was found to simulate increasing and decreasing developmental trends for two types of illusion.

Another example of developmental simulation involved an aspect of language development in children. Generalization of regular past-tense endings to irregular verbs has been simulated in college students, by teaching them an artificial "language" with regular and irregular "endings." An additional finding was that the probability of the generalization error was related to the frequency of usage of the irregular word, suggesting a potentially important refinement in the developmental hypothesis. Finally, multivariate changes have been simulated in rats and in the computer, using simulated conditions of life histories and environmental-influence patterns as antecedents.

In simulation experiments like the research examples presented, the primary objective is to design artificial situations that will, we hope, aid our understanding of the development process through successive approximation.

Chapter Twenty

Cross-Cultural and Comparative Developmental Psychology

Rationale

The simulation strategy discussed in Chapter Nineteen is also part of the strategy for analytic-explanatory research used in comparative developmental psychology. Comparative developmental psychology involves the systematic and theory-guided analysis of developmental change in behavior as seen in various subpopulations of living organisms (Eckensberger, 1973; LeVine, 1970). Baltes and Goulet (1970), for example, distinguished among comparative-species, comparative-culture, and comparative-generation developmental psychology, a list that could be easily expanded.

In the context of this chapter, our intent is not to show how comparative research leads to an independent body of developmental knowledge for each of the subpopulations involved (such as a particular African tribe or a particular species), but to show how a comparative developmental approach is used to explain developmental change. It is important to recognize that what is at stake here is not the value of research with distinct classes of organisms themselves, but the use of comparative-research evidence for the explanation of individual development within a particular target culture or nation, such as the United States. This strategy of deducing knowledge about general development from comparative analysis had been suggested by Baldwin (1906) and Wundt (1911), and was later most compellingly demonstrated by Heinz Werner (1926, 1948).

In principle, a comparative developmental approach involves the use of a quasi-experimental design, mostly in the form of a criterion-group contrast. Naturally existing behavior variations in different species, cultures, or generations are utilized to examine assertions about causes of individual development. In cross-cultural developmental psychology, which will serve as our example, this orientation has been succinctly stated by researchers such as Eckensberger (1973; see also Boesch & Eckensberger, 1969), Child (1968), Furby (1971), Frijda and Jahoda (1966), and LeVine (1970).

In the search for explanation, cross-cultural developmental psychology ranges from the mere establishment of norms of variation in behavior development, or cultural differences, to the theory and hypothesis-guided testing of specific assertions about developmental principles. In a sense, then, naturalistic variation in behavior and in genetic-environmental conditions is used to simulate developmental arrangements that could be created within one culture only with great difficulty or not at all. Following Campbell's (1969) general proposal, the cross-cultural researcher seeks situations in which "Mother Nature" has arranged conditions that turn out to approximate the researcher's own intentions as closely as possible.

Examples

In Campbell and Stanley's (1963) terminology, most simple cross-cultural developmental designs are of the type shown in Table 20-1. These designs involve one-shot (O_1) cross-sectional age (A) samples (S) within each of the cultures (C) and, of course, typically no random assignment to cultures or ages. The fact that no random assignment to cultures has been used is indicated by the dotted line separating the comparison samples. This simple design contains two putative treatments (culture, age) and can be expanded in various ways—for example, by inclusion of various treatment and control groups within each culture or by extending the design longitudinally and/or cohort-sequentially (see Chapter Fourteen; also Eckensberger, 1973).

Table 20-1. The basic design of simple cross-cultural developmental research

Sample	Culture	Age	Observation
S_1	C_1	A_1	O_1
S_2	C_1	A_2	O_1
S_3	C_2	A_1	O_1
S_4	C_2	A_2	O_1

Note: Various controls are necessary to examine aspects of internal and external validity (S = Sample; C = Culture; A = Age; O = Observation).

Historically, the preponderant aim of cross-cultural developmental psychology has been to demonstrate the impact of environmental variation on the form of behavioral development. In this sense, it was assumed that cultural variation in behavior results in large part from environmental antecedents and not from genetic antecedents. Accordingly, although mostly with some rec-ognition of genetic or interactive effects, the finding of large differences in behavior development was overwhelmingly accepted as strong evidence for the importance of environmental factors, especially in the heredity-environment debate of the 1930s but also in that of the 1970s. Contributions by anthropologists such as Mead (1928, 1930) and Benedict (1938), focusing on large cultural variation in personality characteristics (for example, sex-role development), also follow this line of thought. The assumption that cultural differences are predominantly environmental is not consistently accepted. However, in the present context, this issue is secondary to the task of describ-ing the methodology of cross-cultural developmental work.

Cross-cultural studies by Mead, Dennis, Ainsworth, and many others (see LeVine, 1970, for review) on infant motor development represent another set of examples of the traditional rationale of cross-cultural developmental psychology. One of the primary hypotheses in these studies on the rate and sequentiality of motor development was that the socialization environment for motor behavior differs markedly in different cultures. For example, some cultures, such as that of Ganda, emphasize early motor behavior, whereas others, such as that of the Navajo Indians, provide a rearing context that is often rather constraining. Accordingly, the traditional hypothesis was that comparison of cultural settings, either rich or poor in motor stimulation, would provide a naturalistic variation of the "maturation plus learning" type. In the case of infant motor development, the cultural comparisons were interpreted by and large as supporting the conclusion that maturation and stimulation (but not response-learning) processes are the primary contributing factors, as long as a generally supportive nutritional and health context is provided.

Another example of cross-cultural developmental analysis that the reader may want to consult is the comparative analysis of auditory acuity in older African Mabaan and American persons (see Chapter Two). The studies by Rosen and his colleagues (Rosen, Bergman, Plester, El-Mofty, & Satti, 1962; Rosen, Plester, El-Mofty, & Rosen, 1964) strongly supported the contention that adult decrements in auditory acuity are produced largely by a life history of high noise exposure. More recently, Kagan and Klein (1973) have presented a series of cross-cultural developmental comparisons of be-havior development in American children and Guatemalan Indian children. The Kagan-Klein study contains some interesting examples of the use of language-free or putatively culture-fair tests (measures of attention, memory, and perception), intracultural control groups, and theory-guided approaches.

Methodological Perspectives

Cross-cultural comparisons, despite their intriguing rationale, are surrounded by methodological pitfalls that make their usefulness for explana-tory analysis often questionable. (See LeVine, 1970, for a lengthy discussion.)

Because a cross-cultural contrast by necessity involves groups that are not randomly assigned to "natural variation" conditions, it is difficult to rule out the entire gamut of error factors (history, selection, instrumentation, and so forth) described by Campbell and Stanley (1963) and discussed in Chapter Five. Furthermore, it is often difficult to ascertain whether the intended cross-cultural treatment difference (for example, much leg-muscle activity versus none) did indeed exist, since the treatments are typically not produced by the experimenter but are only assumed to operate. Similarly, as mentioned above, it is difficult to tease out genetic differences between subpopulations living in different cultural surroundings.

This large number of uncontrolled error sources has resulted in a rather cautious use of cross-cultural developmental evidence for tests involving precision of a theory (rather than scope and deployability). Murphy and Murphy (1970) and Eckensberger (1973) recommended this cautious position and, for the most part, maintained that systematic intracultural comparative research usually provides a sounder basis for pinpointing causes of developmental differences than does cross-cultural work. The implied message of such cautionary statements is that, with increased cultural variation, internal validity usually decreases. Therefore, the frequent finding of huge cultural differences in behavior development also means that there is a huge number of possible environmental, genetic, or error sources whose effects are difficult to isolate and to disentangle.

In spite of this cautionary stance, and the frequent emphasis placed on conducting hypothesis-guided and controlled quasi-experimentation, cross-cultural developmental research will continue to have its admirers. Once sufficient attention is paid to constructing equivalent measurement instruments (Eckensberger, 1973), to selecting comparative groups carefully on the basis of other putative homologies (for example, in some cases it may be more appropriate to contrast different generations rather than cultures), to the use of extended time series in addition to one-shot arrangements (Campbell, 1969), and to the systematic comparison of both inter- and intracultural subgroups for control purposes (for example, Baltes, Eyferth, & Schaie, 1969), cross-cultural developmental research may become more valuable in explaining ontogenetic and biocultural change components than it is today.

We believe that the current value of cross-cultural developmental research *vis-à-vis* the building of explanatory knowledge lies predominantly in hypothesis generation and pilot testing associated with the task of mapping the *scope* of developmental phenomena. As the *precision* of a theory increases, the general usefulness of comparative developmental work probably decreases. Therefore, whenever a hypothesis or the beginning of a theory about a particular key developmental influence begins to emerge, it is reasonable to engage in comparative developmental work in order to examine initial face validity and the range of the target phenomenon. This strategy was used in early developmental research on heredity-environment questions, and it is seen in the use of Piaget's tasks in cross-cultural research to demonstrate general invariance of cognitive stages under various environmental conditions. Similarly, there is a current need for comparative work on the effects of nutritional factors on intellectual development in children and on the range of social and cognitive behavior in the aged.

In a way, cross-cultural developmental psychology—as a vehicle for explanatory research—is like the opera as described in Mozart's *The Impresario*: "Opera occasionally loses skirmishes, but it invariably wins the battle for survival." Indeed, although full of potential methodological headaches, cross-cultural research is rewarding and fun for many researchers because of its many accidental excitements and benefits.

Intracultural Criterion-Group Comparison

The rationale of a comparative developmental approach also applies to intracultural comparisons of behavioral development in subgroups, which is perhaps the most frequently used way of studying human development from a sociological perspective. Subgroups can be formed on the basis of person variables such as sex, race, cultural membership, or cohort membership, or on the basis of more specific life-history variables such as education or language. Often multiple memberships or contrasts result—for instance, from geographic-location or migration patterns (for example, bilingualism, immigrant status, first versus second generation, Northern versus Southern Black, urban versus rural residence)—and these contrasts can also be used in explanatory research.

It is not necessary to describe the methodology of such intracultural designs in great detail, since the objectives and problems parallel those summarized in the foregoing section on cross-cultural developmental psychology. The prime rationale here is not to use these designs for the study of variation in behavior development *per se*, but to exploit such variation for quasi-experimental hypothesis-testing in the explanatory search for developmental antecedents and principles. The potential weakness of such intracultural criterion-group comparisons lies in a potential lack of theory-guided strategies and the dilemma associated with the high probability of many rival interpretations (error sources) for the obtained group differences.

The greatest strength of intracultural comparisons rests, again, on developing a proper perspective for the range of variability in development and its fertility for hypothesis generation in the beginning steps of theory construction. Consideration of adequate control groups, the use of strategies for establishing measurement equivalence, and the use of extended time series is apt to increase their power. In this context, it probably pays to accept the contention of Murphy and Murphy (1970) and Eckensberger (1973) that intracultural comparisons typically provide sounder inferences about causal relationships than intercultural contrasts. Aside from the fact that intracultural theories are usually more advanced and precise than those achieved on an intercultural level, this argument rests on the assumption that homology, and therefore simulation validity, is probably on the average greater intraculturally than interculturally or interphyletically (see also Lockard, 1971).

Perhaps the best known examples of intracultural, comparative developmental studies attempt to explicate age changes in intelligence by contrasting environmentally enriched children with environmentally deprived children at various ages. This research often follows the design outlined in Table 20-2. In this paradigm, E represents an environment, which is varied on two levels (for example, enriched versus deprived). Following the convention used earlier, the two rows are separated by dashed lines to indicate that the two groups are not based on random assignment of subjects.

Table 20-2.   Illustration of an intracultural criterion-group design for the explanatory study of development using cross-sectional age contrasts

	Sample	Condition	Age
	S_1	E^+	A_1
	S_2	E^+	A_2
	S_3	E^-	A_1
	S_4	E^-	A_2

Note: Various controls are necessary to maximize internal and external validity (S = Sample; E^+ = Rich environment; E^- = Deprived environment; A = Age).

The core design of such intracultural criterion-group comparison is, of course, affected by multiple sources of error and needs expansion in various directions. Suggestions for improving research on comparative developmental questions can be found in the preceding section and the earlier sections on cross-sectional and longitudinal studies (Chapters Thirteen and Fourteen). In any case, from a methodological perspective a highly cautious approach seems appropriate when interpreting intracultural criterion-group comparisons with a view toward explanation rather than description.

Summary

Comparative developmental psychology involves systematic and theory-guided analyses of development in subpopulations. Comparative developmental psychology focuses on interindividual differences in change and the use of differential change (in subpopulations) for explanatory analysis of key developmental processes. The subpopulations used may be different species, different cultures, different generations, or different social-class and ethnic memberships, among others.

In this book, comparative developmental research is not discussed in its function of accumulating knowledge about subpopulations. The focus here is on the use of a simulation rationale to interpret comparative developmental trends. That is, the naturally occurring differences among species, cultures, generations, and so on are assumed to simulate life-history conditions that vary between individuals. For example, much of the cross-cultural research on development was intended to demonstrate the importance of environmental variations in determining behavioral development, on the assumption that genetic differences between cultures are minimal. There is considerable debate about the validity of this assumption.

A major problem in cross-cultural research is to determine the internal validity of the "treatments"—that is, of the assumed cultural differences believed to cause the observed behavioral differences. In addition to the assumed differences—which may or may not actually operate—there are a host of other possible environmental, genetic, and error differences that could be causal. The problem arises because in the real world persons are not assigned randomly to the "treatment" groups; rather, the researcher finds them already assigned to their cultural groups. Therefore, cross-cultural comparisons seem to be most useful for preliminary work, for the generation of hypotheses, and for tests of the range of the developmental phenomenon of interest. Its usefulness in advanced theory-testing is likely to be limited.

In comparative research within a single culture, the subgroups compared may differ in sex, social class, race, cohort, education, and so on. The objectives, methods, and pitfalls are the same as in cross-cultural research, and the greatest usefulness of the method for explanatory purposes is, like that of cross-cultural methods, in the preliminary stages of theory construction. However, for reasons of greater homology, intracultural comparative work may often be more fruitful than intercultural research.

Chapter Twenty-One

Heredity-Environment Research and Development

Although in 1958 Anastasi had already called for a major overhaul of explanatory research on the relationship between hereditary and environmental contributions to development, this area of research is still alive and is even showing a recently accelerating pace of significance and interest.

Anastasi's (1958) suggestion was to study the "how" rather than the "how much"—that is, how heredity and environment contribute to development, not how much each contributes. The two questions may imply different conceptions of development, different world views (see Chapter Three). The search for the "how"—the processes and mechanisms involved in development—is the type of quest that pleases an interactionist of the organismic kind. The inquiry into "how much" is of more significance to those who view development from the perspective of additive, mechanistic models. This relationship between metamodels and the nature of heredity-environment conceptions has been discussed in great detail in the literature (Furth, 1973; Overton, 1973; Riegel, 1973b).

This chapter focuses on quantitative heredity-environment designs in developmental research—that is, designs aimed at "how much." This emphasis is not comprehensive; neither is it necessarily the most important. However, the recent surge of the so-called Jensen controversy suggests that it is important to attend to the methodology of this research and to show why the existing heredity-environment research often falls short of being "developmental."

Quantitative Heredity-Environment Designs

For the quantitatively and psychometrically oriented behavioral scientist, it is tempting to separate the totality of influences on development into two classes, hereditary and environmental, according to a $B = f(H, E)$

paradigm. The problem, however, begins with the fact that the definition, taxonomy, and measurement of both concepts—heredity and environment—are traditionally not the province of the psychologist (see also Schaie, Anderson, McClearn, & Money, 1975).

Heredity has been primarily the domain of the biologist; the environment has been studied in a host of disciplines (geography, sociology, and so on). The consequence of this multidisciplinary situation is that, in focusing on heredity and environment, developmental psychologists for the most part select for explanatory research a set of independent variables or antecedents that they do not understand well. In addition, even for the biologist, geographer, sociologist, or social psychologist, the concepts of heredity and environment lack empirically precise definitions. The area of developmental genetics, therefore, is often clouded with misunderstandings and confused arguments, which, however, should not discourage further research.

Quantitative heredity-environment designs are generally aimed at the "how much" issue. The relative contributions of heredity and environment to the determination of behavior was discussed long ago by Darwin. Jensen's (1969) treatment of the hereditary components of intellectual development and racial differences therein is perhaps the best known recent expression of the "how much" position. Some general methodological issues and concepts in quantitative heredity-environment research are discussed in this chapter (for further elaborations, see Cattell, 1973; Jensen, 1969; McClearn, 1970; Schaie et al., 1975).

Rationale of Quantitative Heredity-Environment Research

The core rationale of traditional heredity-environment research is either to find or to produce variability in hereditary (genetic) and/or environmental similarity and to examine correlated differences in behavior and behavioral development.

Ideally, perfect identity in genetic make-up would be obtained in litter-mates after continuous inbreeding over many generations, or in such identical offspring as identical twins. Perfect environmental identity would be achieved by exposing different organisms to completely controlled and matched environments. If genetically identical organisms were exposed to different environments, the effect of environmental variation on behavior could be assessed. Similarly, if identical environments could be created for genetically distinct organisms, the effect of hereditary components could be quantified.

Unfortunately, especially in the field of human development, perfect identity of heredity and environment is strictly impossible. Conditions, whether found or created, can only approximate ideal design arrangements. For example, due to age-related mutational processes, even identical twins cannot be assumed to possess identical gene structures throughout their life spans.

A Heredity-Environment Similarity Matrix

The traditional rationale for most designs used to obtain quantitative information on the "how much" of hereditary and environmental contributions to human development can be described by constructing a matrix involving dimensions of *environmental similarity* and of *hereditary similarity,* as shown in Figure 21-1. It will be demonstrated later that the classical twin-control method and the conventional method of computing heritability coefficients are special cases using this general heredity-environment similarity matrix.

Figure 21-1 orders hereditary and environmental influences along dimensions of similarity. This ordering is accomplished by comparing the magnitude of similarity for members of pairs who are classified into different cells of the heredity-environment similarity matrix. This procedure leads to both within-pair differences and between-pair differences on a given behavior. The magnitude of these differences then can be compared for different levels of hereditary and environmental similarity and expressed, for example, in correlation coefficients.

Hereditary similarity is described in Figure 21-1 in four levels: (1) identical twins, (2) fraternal twins and siblings, (3) half-siblings (one parent in common), and (4) unrelated children. Researchers traditionally describe environmental similarity in two levels: (1) individuals reared together, and (2) individuals reared apart. In this case, the assumption is that persons reared in the same environmental context (such as in the same family) experience a more similar environment than members of a pair reared in different environments (such as in two families). The definition of similarity among levels of heredity and environment is not free of controversy.

Rationale and Strategy for Heredity-Environment Quantification

The heredity-environment similarity matrix can be used to compute quantitative indices. The logic for most indices is contained in Figure 21-1 and is described below.

If *hereditary differences* were the sole determinants of behavior differences (in Figure 21-1 described as "heredity determinant"), the expectation would be that whether pairs were raised together or apart (the variation in

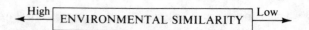

Developmental condition	Pairs reared together		Pairs reared apart	
Hypothesis →	Determinant		Determinant	
	Environment	Heredity	Environment	Heredity
Identical twins	1.00	*1.00*	.00	*1.00*
Fraternal twins and siblings	1.00	*.50*	.00	*.50*
Half-siblings	1.00	*.25*	.00	*.25*
Unrelated	1.00	*.00*	.00	*.00*

Figure 21-1.   Matrix illustrating variation of members of natural and artificial pairs of persons along a continuum of hereditary and environmental similarity. Expected hypothetical effects on within-pair correlations are indicated in nonitalic numbers (environment is sole determinant) or in italic numbers (heredity is sole determinant). The correlations would be computed between members of a pair across a sample of pairs for a given behavior. The higher the correlation, the greater is the within-pair similarity when contrasted with between-pair differences. The numerical outcomes represent limiting values (1.00, .00) or estimated values (.50, .25).

environmental similarity) would make no difference; that is, differences between and within pairs would be entirely attributable to genetic differences. The extent of similarity within a pair as expressed in correlation coefficients would simply follow the magnitude of hereditary similarity. Accordingly, in Figure 21-1 the correlational values entered for corresponding rows are identical under the label "heredity determinant"; that is, pairs of identical twins would be equal and highly similar to each other whether raised together or apart. The magnitude of the decline in behavior similarity from high (identical twins) to low (unrelated children) hereditary similarity would be only a function of the magnitude of the differences in hereditary similarity.

    If *environmental differences* were the sole determinants of behavior differences ("environment determinant"), the expectation would be that the magnitude of correlational similarity would be ordered by columns rather than rows. If members of pairs were reared together (high environmental similarity), then the expectation would be high behavior similarity within pairs, independent of the amount of hereditary similarity.

Quantifying Indexes

The procedures used for quantifying the magnitude of hereditary versus environmental influences are based on core formulas involving the variance (V) of an observed behavior, or "phenotype":

$$V_P = V_H + V_E \,,$$

where V_P = observed *phenotypic* variance (differences) in a population, V_H = hereditary, or *genotypic*, variance, and V_E = *environmental* variance.

The arrangement described in Figure 21-1 would provide estimates for these kinds of variance; V_P would represent the total behavior differences observed in all individuals, V_H would be estimated by within-pair differences between levels of hereditary similarity, and V_E would be estimated by within-pair differences between the two levels of environmental similarity. There are several computational strategies—not presented here—for estimating these variances (see, for example, Cattell, 1973; Jensen, 1969; Vandenberg, 1966).

One index that has attracted considerable attention is the *heritability coefficient* (h^2). The heritability coefficient is typically based on a comparison of identical and fraternal twins only. It was originally proposed by Newman, Freeman, and Holzinger (1937) as a measure of the "relative effects of nature-nurture factors upon the differences found between members of twin pairs reared within a family" (quoted in Vandenberg, 1966, p. 333). The heritability coefficient can take many forms, but psychologists typically define it in its simple form as:

$$h^2 = \frac{V_H}{V_P} \,.$$

Holzinger's restricted version of the heritability coefficient (h^2) was:

$$h^2 = \frac{\text{correlation}_{IT} - \text{correlation}_{FT}}{1 - \text{correlation}_{FT}} \,,$$

where *IT* refers to identical twins and *FT* to fraternal twins. This formulation can be used to illustrate the computation of heritability coefficients using Figure 21-1.

In Figure 21-1, for example, Holzinger's h^2 for the "environment determinant" case (see the first two entries in the first column) would be:

$$h^2 = \frac{1.00 - 1.00}{1 - 1.00} = \frac{0}{0} \,,$$

suggesting that heritability is 0 for the case of sole environmental determinacy. (We recognize, of course, that this outcome is mathematically indeterminate, because division by zero is not defined. Less extreme configurations would not lead to an indeterminate solution.)

For the "heredity determinant" case in Figure 21-1 (first two entries in the second column), the solution is:

$$h^2 = \frac{1.00 - .50}{1 - .50} = \frac{.50}{.50} = 1.00,$$

suggesting that heritability is *1.00* for the case of sole hereditary determinacy. Between these two extreme values, the traditional heritability coefficient is intended to describe the proportion of behavior variance that can be attributed to genotypic variation, or heredity. Typically, heritability values are somewhere between .00 and 1.00, indicating that the outcome is rarely "all or none" (Jensen, 1969, p. 42).

Examples

The area of intellectual development as assessed by psychometric tests offers many examples of explanatory research on the heredity-environment issue and the use of within-pair correlations and heritability coefficients.

Figure 21-2 summarizes a large number of studies on hereditary and environmental determinants of general intellectual performance. In line with the rationale presented above, these data represent correlations between pair-members across a sample of pairs for a given subset, such as identical twins reared together.

Note that the decline in behavior similarity shown in Figure 21-2 is rather dramatic as one moves down the hereditary-similarity continuum from identical twins (.85, .73) to unrelated children (.23, .00). The difference between the two levels of environmental similarity (reared apart versus reared together) is equally consistent although less pronounced.

The Evaluation of Heredity-Environment Designs

A host of design issues should be considered when the researcher evaluates the usefulness of heredity-environment designs for explanatory research in developmental psychology.

The Concurrent versus the Developmental View

The focus in this book has been on developmental research, defined as research aimed at the examination of time-ordered processes. It is clear that the basic heredity-environment paradigms do not explicitly vary time indi-

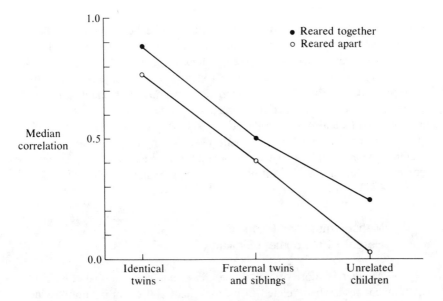

Figure 21-2. Median values of correlations between pair members from a large number of studies on intellectual performance. Note that differences between levels of hereditary similarity are greater than between levels of environmental similarity. Based on data from Erlenmeyer-Kimling and Jarvik (1963).

cators such as chronological age. The basic designs, in principle, examine heredity-environment effects at a given point in time. What appears mandatory in future research is to emphasize age or other indices of developmental processes as parameters. For example, to what degree do the proportions of variance associated with hereditary and environmental variation change with the age of subjects? This question is important but remains largely uninvestigated. As McClearn (1970, p. 61) put it, in the context of developmental genetics: "Developmental processes are subject to continuing genetic influence and different genes are effective at different times." The same generalization holds for age-related effects of the environment.

From the developmental viewpoint, it is immediately obvious that heredity-environment effects are time-specific, that levels of hereditary and environmental similarity may change with time, and therefore that a given heritability coefficient is only one of many selected from a developmental spectrum. For example, to what degree do identical twins remain fully identical as they grow older (consider mutations), and to what degree is the level of environmental similarity for "raised together" similar at different stages of development and for different lengths of life histories? That genetic control extends over the total life span has been shown by Jarvik and her colleagues (for example, Jarvik, Blum, & Varma, 1972), who have examined intellectual performance in aged identical and fraternal twins. The patterning and sequence of developmental functions in quantitative heredity-environment work will need to be a major area of inquiry in future explanatory research.

A similar view was expressed by Jensen (1969, p. 43) when he said "heritability . . . is not a constant." It is a statistic whose value is affected by the genetic and environmental characteristics of a population and its ecology. Heritability estimates are specific to the population sampled and the point in time sampled (see also Scarr-Salapatek, 1971). Similarly, in 1933 Hogben had already argued that "no statement about a genetic difference has any scientific meaning unless it includes or implies a specification of the environment in which it manifests itself in a particular manner" (cited by Jones, 1954, p. 632).

Measurement and Range of Heredity-Environment Similarity

Another major design issue plaguing conventional heredity-environment research is related to measurement and quantification. Aside from the question of the dimensionality of the environment (for example, Frederiksen, 1972), there is the significant question of the level of scaling (for example, ratio versus interval versus rank-order). It was stated earlier that hereditary and environmental variation are not measured directly and are not directly manipulated in traditional designs. In fact, we do not even know the range of genetic and environmental similarity. The variation of hereditary and environmental similarity, as we know it, is on a rank-order scale; we do not know its limits, its zero point, or the magnitude of the difference between the levels of similarity.

Accordingly, it is important to recognize that the available heredity-environment research is tremendously restricted in scope (not necessarily in precision). Quantified results are of the *fixed-level* type and restricted to a highly specific comparison case; the results are indicative of what *is* in a highly specific case and clearly not of what *could be* (see also Hebb, 1970, 1971). Consider, for example, the fact that the variation on the continuum of environmental similarity (raised together versus raised apart) is probably rather small. How big is the environmental difference (when compared with extreme environmental enrichment versus deprivation) between persons who are raised together and apart in the United States? In contrast, it seems fair to conclude that the variation in hereditary similarity (identical twins versus unrelated children) is disproportionately larger, since it covers most of the spectrum available for generational transmission.

In all fairness, therefore, one must raise the question of whether the dimension of environmental similarity is adequately varied in the type of design described above. Consequently, it is important to repeat what Jensen (1969, p. 43) made so clear in his theoretical (although not necessarily in his empirical) presentations: "What the heritability might be under any environmental conditions" is not represented by values of h^2 reported in the literature. It seems worthwhile to add that the environmental variation considered in traditional designs is probably minute, especially if life-span developmental changes and cross-cultural differences in environmental contexts are considered.

Another kind of measurement issue is related to the choice of an instrument to measure intelligence. In most of the research on hereditary and environmental influences on intelligence, the instrument selected yields a single index or measure of global intelligence. However, most researchers who study intellectual *development* abandoned the concept of global intelligence long ago in favor of a concept of intelligence consisting of several relatively independent abilities. In fact, the developmental research shows that many of these separate abilities exhibit different patterns of growth and decline (for example, Baltes & Labouvie, 1973; Horn, 1970).

Thus, from the point of view of most developmental researchers, the behavioral geneticists have been studying the hereditary and environmental influences on a variable (global intelligence) that is at best a poor reflection of actual intelligence and that is at worst fictitious. This criticism is especially pertinent because heredity-environment research involving specific abilities indeed suggests that they have different heritabilities (for example, Vandenberg, 1966).

Models of Heredity-Environment Linkage

Thus far, the rationale presented has assumed that hereditary and environmental influences act independently. Most researchers accept the view that in real life there is an interaction between these sets of influences. The nature of the interaction between hereditary and environmental influences needs to be defined, however, and its definition will reflect the metamodel of development and behavioral genetics a given researcher uses in conducting research and constructing theory.

For example, some investigators (for example, Jensen, 1969) focus on a statistical model of interaction (in the analysis-of-variance and -covariance sense). Others, such as those who adopt the dialectic metamodel (for example, Overton, 1973), argue that the statistical version of interaction is a "weak" model of interaction. They contend that it is necessary to formulate a strategy in which the relationship between hereditary and environmental influences is such that their interaction is nonadditive; they also explicitly postulate mutual influences on hereditary and environmental antecedents themselves.

Anastasi's (1958) paper on the "how" of heredity-environment research reflects such a posture, as does a recent issue of the journal *Human*

Development, edited by Riegel (1973b). For example, a "strong" view of heredity-environment interactions may postulate that the environment can alter the nature of genetic systems (such as through mutation), that organisms with different genetic endowments may "actively" seek different kinds of environments, and so on.

A Concluding Perspective on Heredity-Environment Designs

We stated at the beginning of this chapter that there are different methods of conducting explanatory developmental research of the heredity-environment type. The reader is again referred to publications by McClearn (1970), Riegel (1973b), and Schaie, Anderson, McClearn, and Money (1975) for more detailed expositions of the various lines of approach. Traditional quantitative heredity-environment genetics was selected as a sample case.

In our view, the paradigms of quantitative heredity-environment research represent powerful avenues toward explanation. The many methodological difficulties in developing a taxonomy, and in developing adequate measures of genetic and environmental influences and their interaction, should not be taken as insurmountable obstacles. Developmental psychologists have developed postures and theories that include both environmental and biological antecedents and interactive processes as legitimate sources of influence on behavioral development; therefore, the formulation of corresponding research designs is desirable.

The current status of quantitative heredity-environment research in developmental psychology, although in a pioneering stage and often clouded by philosophical and political arguments, has clearly demonstrated the potential usefulness of both the "how much" and the "how" questions. The future, we hope, will see a further clarification of the relationship between metamodels of development and the research paradigms employed, as well as a concerted effort to introduce a developmental, time-related view into the design of heredity-environment research, whatever its specific form.

Summary

Much heredity-environment research has been performed to determine *how much* heredity and environment contribute to a phenomenon, rather than *how* these variables contribute. The research designs have therefore usually been quantitative (aimed at determining the hereditary and environmental proportions of variation in the phenomenon) rather than qualitative (aimed at determining the mechanisms that underlie the hereditary and environmental contributions). Only the quantitative designs are considered in this chapter.

Hereditary similarity is usually varied by comparing identical twins (the most similar genetically), fraternal twins and nontwin siblings, half-siblings, and unrelated children (the least similar genetically). Environmental similarity is usually varied by comparing individuals reared together and individuals reared apart. These two dimensions of similarity form a "similarity matrix." By comparing correlations between pair-members in different cells of the matrix, one can estimate the relative contributions of heredity and environment to the behavior being studied. The estimate is based on the assumption that phenotypic variance (variation in the observed behavior) is the sum of genotypic variance (variation in hereditary similarity) and environmental variance (variation in environmental similarity). A widely used estimate is the heritability coefficient, intended to reflect the proportion of phenotypic variance attributed to genotypic variance.

From a developmental viewpoint, traditional heredity-environment research is flawed. Time indicators such as chronological age are rarely varied; but because different genes are effective at different times, and the effective environment changes with age, heritability estimates should also vary with age. Another problem is that the measures of hereditary and environmental similarity are psychometrically gross; similarity is measured on a rank-order scale with unknown limits, unknown zero point, and unknown magnitudes of difference between levels of similarity. Furthermore, in most heredity-environment research on intelligence the index used has been global intelligence, even though intelligence is now generally thought to consist of separate abilities, which have been shown to have different heritabilities.

Still another problem is that the rationale of the heritability coefficient requires the assumption that hereditary and environmental influences are additive and do not interact except in the statistical, quantitative sense. Yet many researchers believe that genetic and environmental systems interact qualitatively; environmental variables can produce genetic mutations and can influence the way genes function, and individuals with different genetic endowments may seek different kinds of environments.

Nevertheless, the paradigms of quantitative heredity-environment research are potentially useful for explanatory developmental research when age-related parameters are added to the similarity matrix and the limitations of the underlying paradigms are clearly understood.

Chapter Twenty-Two

Developmental Research on Learning: Group Designs

General Considerations

Learning theory has an intrinsic focus on behavior change, and consequently provides at the outset the most powerful psychological concepts aimed at studying a process of development. The central question for our purposes (for example, Baer, 1970, 1973; Lerner, 1976; Sutton-Smith, 1970) is whether learning is identical to development or, at least, whether development can be conceptualized as consisting of some kind of accumulation of units of learning. In many ways this question, again, reflects metatheoretical differences and touches on questions of homology (see Chapter Nineteen on simulation).

For example, organicists would argue that learning is not a comprehensive representation of development. Simple learning paradigms typically involve manipulation of environmental conditions only, thereby minimizing the import of biological-maturational influences. Organicists argue that developmental processes *always* reflect interactive systems. In practice, nevertheless, learning researchers have often investigated behavior-change processes that are specific to maturational contexts—for example, in learning research on critical periods (for example, Hess & Petrovich, 1973).

From the viewpoint of developmental psychology, we need to distinguish between two major emphases on learning. One emphasis is simply on the study of learning in different age groups, without a major concern for the use of developmental paradigms or an explanation of a development process. Another emphasis deals with a systematic analysis of the conditions and processes characterizing development as a system of behavior change related to learning. In this latter emphasis, the focus is on intraindividual change as a learning process and on the type of interindividual differences in learning histories that produce different developmental outcomes.

In the final analysis, the usefulness of learning research for the explanation of long-term development will be assessed against its success in dealing with the relationship between development and learning histories rather than with short-term learning processes. Short-term learning, by definition, is often of trivial significance to many developmentalists. In this chapter and in Chapter Twenty-Three, however, we recognize the fact that, for many psychologists, learning is *the* developmental process. To study developmental changes in learning is, therefore, to study psychological development. The research should, of course, be aimed not only at description of developmental changes in learning but also at explanation of these changes and at the optimization of learning processes.

Learning and Development

Learning theory has been a major emphasis in American psychology and has strongly influenced developmental psychology. This influence appears in developmental theories of intelligence (for example, Ferguson, 1954, 1956; Staats, 1971; see also Rohwer, Ammon, & Cramer, 1974), problem solving or learning (for example, Goulet, 1973; Kendler & Kendler, 1962), personality (for example, Staats, 1971), education (for example, Gagné, 1974), and other fields.

As might be expected, there has been a tremendous amount of developmental learning research. The majority of this research, however, deals with the study of learning *per se* in different age groups and less with the use of learning for the explanation of development. In addition, the bulk of this research deals with learning in childhood, the period to which most of the theories are addressed. Nevertheless, the kinds of research problems encountered in developmental research on child learning are also encountered in developmental research on learning in other age ranges, including the life-span range. These problems are discussed in this chapter.

A Sample Task: Memory Span

To illustrate the methodological problems in developmental learning research, we will generally refer to the memory-span task as our example. It may therefore be helpful to describe this task in detail. First, however, we should explain that, although "learning" and "memory" refer to different processes, everything we say in this chapter about "learning" also applies to "memory," and vice versa.

In a memory-span task, the experimenter selects a set of items that are not obviously related to one another and arranges them in an arbitrary sequence. Suppose that the items are pictures of everyday objects. The pictures are presented to the subject one at a time, and each picture is exposed for a predetermined amount of time. After the items have been exposed and removed, the subject is asked to recall them in the same sequence as they were presented.

The recall test can be given immediately after presenting the last item in the sequence, or it can be delayed for some predetermined amount of time. The recall can be verbal—requiring the subject to name the objects pictured—or it can be nonverbal. An example of requiring nonverbal recall would be to show the pictures in various sequences during the test, and then to ask the subject which sequence is the same as the one shown originally. Suppose for our sample task that verbal recall is required. Sometimes when we refer to this sample task we will introduce procedural variations, but the basic task will remain the same.

Methodological Issues

The methodological issues that arise in developmental learning research are most easily understood if the background of the research is understood. Therefore, we shall outline the methodological issues at the end of this section, after first discussing their sources—the definition of learning and the theoretical interpretations following from this definition—all viewed from the perspective of the life-span approach.

Learning Performance and Learning Process

Learning is usually defined as a process underlying performance. Research on learning is complicated because the learning process cannot be observed directly; only the performance is observable, and it must serve as the basis for inferring the nature of the underlying learning process. The distinction between learning *performance* and learning *process* has not always been clear enough in developmental research.

For example, early in this century researchers were interested in finding out whether young infants are capable of learning in the classical-conditioning task—that is, whether the classical-conditioning process occurs in young infants. Their research revealed that little if any conditioning occurred before the age of 3 months, and they concluded that the young infant is immature with respect to the capacity to be classically conditioned. That is, they concluded that the conditioning *process* is deficient in the young infant. However, modern research has shown that even newborn infants can be classically conditioned (for example, Fitzgerald & Brackbill, 1976).

One possible interpretation of this discrepancy in results is that there has been a cohort change in conditionability, but the most widely accepted interpretation is that the early research was methodologically inadequate. The experimental conditions used in the early research are now known to have been much less than optimal, and therefore it is now concluded that the young infant is conditionable but will not exhibit this process when inadequate methods are used. The point is that the subject's *performance*—failure to emit conditioned responses in this example—may not accurately reflect his capacity with respect to the learning *process*.

At this point we should clarify our usage of *ability, capacity*, and *process*. To be brief, we use them interchangeably. Thus, learning *ability* and learning *capacity* refer to the use of a particular learning *process*.

Developmental Learning Theories

It is possible to distinguish two kinds of developmental theories derived from the learning-theory tradition. In principle, the two kinds of theories lead to the same research problems, but as we shall see later there are some differences in the points at which the research problems arise.

One kind of developmental learning theory assumes that there are several kinds of learning processes, ordered in complexity. The acquisition of each more complex one is assumed to depend on the prior acquisition of the simpler ones, which transfer to the new learning situation and facilitate the acquisition of the new process. This *multiprocess* theory has generated research on the transfer of various kinds of processes, and on the sequence of acquiring more and more complex kinds of processes.

For example, researchers have found that young children—toddlers—do not do well on the memory-span task, even with a short series of items. Apparently, part of their problem is that they do not name the items and therefore cannot recall the names in the recall test. Toddlers also have another problem in that they have not yet acquired one of the learning processes that enhances memory span—rehearsal. Rehearsal is a more complex process than naming, but it cannot be acquired without the prior learning of the naming process, and it cannot function unless this prior process transfers to the memory-span task. Even nursery-school children are often deficient in rehearsal and do not perform well on memory-span tasks. They name the items but do not rehearse them sequentially. Older children, in contrast, not only name the items but rehearse them in sequence spontaneously and efficiently (see Brown, 1975; Hagen, Jongeward, & Kail, 1975).

The other kind of developmental learning theory, *uniprocess* theory, assumes that there is only one kind of learning process (or only one important kind). However, this theory also assumes that the way the process affects performance depends on systems that are not themselves identified as learning processes but that support the learning process (see also the distinction be-tween ability-intrinsic and ability-extraneous performance variables; Furry & Baltes, 1973). These support systems include organismic attributes such as attentiveness, motivation, and response capabilities, and environmental or task characteristics such as the nature of the material to be learned, the manner of presenting the material, and the amount of study permitted. Another relevant variable is the effectiveness of the rewards, or "reinforcers," used.

Extensive research has been done on the ways these and other vari-ables influence the learning process. For example, it has been found that memory span for long lists of items declines in old age. The decline has been attributed not to a decline in memory *capacity* but rather to a decline in attentiveness to the material (Horn, 1976). That is, old people are as capable of learning the sequence of items as younger people, but they do not learn it as well because they pay less attention to the items as they are presented. The decline, in other words, is in *performance*, and it results from decline in a system (attentiveness) that is not itself a learning process but that supports learning. If the material is not attended to, it is not registered and cannot be learned. An implication is that if the old person is somehow induced to pay attention to the task he or she can learn the material as well as a younger person.

Validity Problems

According to multiprocess theories, different learning processes should be aroused by the same task at different age or developmental levels. In addition, the theories lead to expectations about which specific processes should be aroused at the different levels. Thus, although it is expected that the meaning or validity of a task will change with age, the meaning or validity expected at each age level is specified. A problem is to determine whether the task has the specified validity at each age level (see also Chapter Seven).

According to uniprocess theories, there is only one learning process, and it should be aroused by a learning task at all age levels. The research task is to determine whether the efficiency of the learning process changes with age, or to determine how support systems interact with the learning process at different ages. The problem is to ensure that the task does in fact arouse the learning process at all age levels, and to ensure that the support systems are comparable. That is, the problem is to determine at each age level whether the task is a valid indicator of learning, and whether the experimental manipula-tions validly reflect the status of the support systems.

Unfortunately, few researchers with either theoretical orientation have been concerned with the validity of learning tasks. We shall see, how-ever, that the majority have probably been careless or negligent in overlooking the importance of validity.

Unexpected Age Changes in Validity

The validity of a task may change in unexpected ways. For example, Levinson and Reese (1967) studied "learning to learn," a type of transfer discussed later in this chapter, and used a cross-sectional design covering the range from nursery-school age to old age. They obtained marked age differences in performance, particularly by separating old groups from younger groups.

For the old persons in one group, buttons were used as tokens to indicate correct responses, and it was noted that some of the old persons responded to the task as a guessing game, "Button, Button, Who's Got the Button?" There was no indication that the younger groups responded to the task as anything other than a learning task. Therefore, part of the age difference observed may have resulted from the changed meaning or validity of the task; the old persons did not learn efficiently, but they did not think they were being given a learning task (see also Hultsch, 1974).

The reliability of performance can also be affected by age changes in the validity of a task. For example, the performance of persons who respond to a learning task as a guessing game may be higher than for persons who respond to it as a learning task. Guessing is likely to result in stable performance at the chance level, but individual differences in the use of learning processes could reduce the stability of performance. A point worth noting is that researchers have tended to be as little concerned with the reliability of learning tasks as with their validity.

Within-Task Changes in Validity

The validity problem is further complicated by evidence that the processes underlying performance can change *within* a task. For example, in a study with college students (Labouvie, Frohring, Baltes, & Goulet, 1973), memory-span performance on early trials was found to be more strongly related to memory ability than to intelligence; but on later trials these relationships reversed, and performance was more strongly related to intelligence than to memory ability. The task apparently changed in meaning over trials. At first it seems to have been responded to as a rote-memory task, and later to have been responded to as a problem-solving task requiring active processing of the material. Thus, in order to use performance as an index of learning processes, the researcher may need to take into account the amount of practice subjects are having with the materials currently being presented. (See also the discussion on learning to learn presented later in this chapter.)

From the point of view of multiprocess theories, it is likely that the change in validity within a task will not be the same at different age levels, further complicating the problem of age changes in validity. For example,

Hultsch, Nesselroade, and Plemons (1976) compared the relationship between a free-recall task and various memory tests (abilities) in five adult age groups, using Tucker's (1966) procedure for developing generalized learning functions. These investigators found that the relationship between learning and ability indeed varied with age and stage of learning. For younger adults, memory abilities were highly predictive of free-recall performance at early stages of learning, but not at later stages. In contrast, for older adults memory abilities predicted free-recall performance equally well at all stages of learning. Much more of this kind of multivariate research on the changing validity of learning and memory tasks is needed.

Changes in Support Systems

In order to make valid inferences about age changes in a learning process, the researcher needs to control possible age changes in the systems that support the learning process. For example, research has shown that conditioning is more easily demonstrated in older infants than in younger ones. A possible inference is that conditionability (the learning *process*) is better developed in the older infants. However, the validity of this inference is questionable because the age difference in performance could reflect differences in support systems (for example, Lipsitt, 1970).

For example, it has been found that conditioned head-turning, where head-turning is defined as a rotation of at least 30 degrees, requires considerably more training for newborn infants than for 3- and 5-month-old infants. The conclusion that there is a developmental increase in conditionability could be unwarranted, however, because of an age difference in the ability to make the criterion response.

Spontaneous head-turns as great as 30 degrees occur relatively often in older infants, but they rarely occur in newborn infants (Siqueland, 1970, p. 109). In addition, neural mechanisms operate more slowly in newborn infants than in older infants (Hirschman & Katkin, 1974); the younger infant sleeps more than the older infant, hence may be in a different state during the conditioning task (see Hutt, Lenard, & Prechtl, 1969); and there may be age differences in the sensitivity of the sensory receptors to the stimuli presented (for example, Brackbill & Fitzgerald, 1969; Fitzgerald & Brackbill, 1976). There may also be other age differences in the systems that support learning. All of these points call into question the validity of the inference that the age difference in conditioning performance reflects an age difference in the conditioning process itself.

Floor and Ceiling Effects

Another kind of validity problem arises when floor or ceiling effects are present. A floor effect means that the task is so difficult that essentially all subjects in a group fail to learn; a ceiling effect means that the task is so easy that essentially all subjects in a group learn very rapidly.

Consider the hypothetical data in Figure 22-1. The figure shows no difference between experimental and control conditions in younger subjects, and a large difference in older subjects. Do the data mean that the younger subjects lack the ability to benefit from the experimental treatment? In order to answer this question, you would need to know what the "floor" is on the task. Suppose that the hypothetical data in Figure 22-1 are from a task in which subjects must choose between two objects, one of which is correct and the other incorrect. By chance, or pure guessing, a subject would be correct on half of the trials; hence, the floor is at the chance level, or 50% correct. In Figure 22-1, the younger group is clearly at the chance level. The performance of the younger group therefore demonstrates that the task is too difficult for them, not necessarily that they are incapable of benefiting from the experimental treatment.

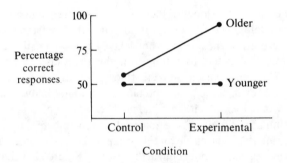

Figure 22-1.   Hypothetical data for younger and older subjects in control and experimental conditions in a learning task. If the chance level of performance is at 50% correct responses, the curve for the younger group reflects a floor effect.

Figure 22-2 shows hypothetical data indicating a ceiling effect. Here, the younger group exhibits an effect of the experimental treatment, but the older group does not. However, the failure of the treatment to benefit the older subjects obviously results from the fact that there is no room for performance to improve. Performance is already so efficient in the older control group that it is impossible for the older experimental group to do better.

The existence of floor or ceiling effects can completely defeat the experimenter's purposes. For example, if a short memory-span list is presented and memory is tested immediately, the number of items correctly recalled can be interpreted to reflect the acquisition process; that is, it reflects the amount of material taken in or registered. When the recall test is delayed for longer and longer times, the number of items correctly recalled will usually decline, and the slope of the curve relating correct recall to amount of delay can reflect the rate of forgetting.

Considerable research has been aimed at determining whether age and intelligence influence the rate of forgetting. The evidence looked for is a

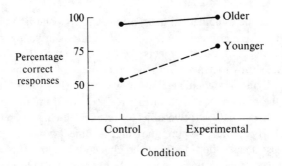

Figure 22-2.   Hypothetical data for younger and older subjects in control and experimental conditions in a learning task. The curve for the older group reflects a ceiling effect.

difference between the slopes of the curves for different age groups or groups of different intelligence. However, if no material is registered—reflected by no correct responses when recall is not delayed at all—then the response curve does not reflect the rate of forgetting. If nothing was taken in, nothing can be forgotten. Thus, the existence of this floor effect in any group would make group differences in slope uninterpretable. We do not know what the forgetting curve would look like if there had not been a floor effect.

Similarly, if all of the material is remembered by one group at short-delay intervals, the curve for this group will not be so steep in slope as the curves for groups that do not begin at this ceiling. Figure 22-3 shows hypothetical data illustrating this kind of ceiling effect. The group differences in slope are uninterpretable because we do not know what the slope in the older group would have been if there had not been a ceiling effect. For further discussion of these points, see Belmont and Butterfield (1969).

In order to avoid floor and ceiling effects, some investigators have used longer lists, or more complex items, for older groups than for younger ones (for example, Milgram, 1967). In general, however, the intent of such a manipulation is not only to avoid floor and ceiling effects but also to equate task difficulty across the groups studied. The problems with this approach are discussed in the next section.

Control by Equation and by Systematic Variation

Control by Equation

In attempting to equalize task difficulty across groups in order to make performance levels exactly comparable, researchers sometimes change the material presented. For example, pictures might be used with younger

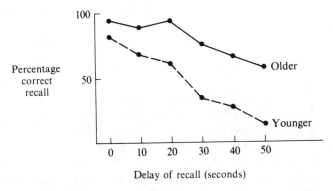

Figure 22-3. Hypothetical data for younger and older subjects in a memory-span task with varying delay of the recall test. Although the curve seems to be steeper for the younger group, the ceiling effect in the older group at the shorter delays makes the apparent difference in slope uninterpretable.

subjects and printed words with older subjects; or concrete words might be used with younger subjects and abstract words with older subjects. Most often, however, researchers have attempted to equate the tasks by varying the *amount* of material to be learned. A problem is that the change in the amount of material may change the meaning or validity of the task. (The same problem arises when the nature of the material is varied.)

For example, when memory for a short list of items is tested with no delay, no special mental activity is required for good performance. People automatically remember short lists, like the seven digits in a telephone number, when the retention interval is extremely short. However, longer lists are not remembered well unless an appropriate mental activity is used. One such activity is rehearsal, which would be required when the telephone number to be remembered includes the three-digit area code. Thus, the younger groups may be given a list that requires no special mental activity, whereas the older groups are given a list that does require some special mental activity. If so, the groups are not being given tasks with comparable meaning, and performance by the different groups cannot be interpreted unambiguously.

Suppose the groups perform relatively poorly. For the younger subjects, this result would indicate a deficiency in the registration of the material or in the capacity to store it in memory. For the older subjects, the result would indicate a deficiency in the use of the required mental activity. Even though the performance levels are the same, then, the groups would not be equivalent in the processes underlying their performance. It is a well-established principle that same performance does not necessarily mean same cause; groups may have the same behavior for different reasons. In the case just described, the problem of interpretation would also exist if the older group performed better than the younger group, because the good performance of the older group would not necessarily reflect better utilization of processes that are deficient in the younger group.

Control by Systematic Variation

The attempt to equate tasks so that they are equally difficult for all age groups may be futile, because changing the details of the task may change its validity. There are also other reasons to believe that "the prospects for control by equation are slim indeed" (Bitterman, 1960, p. 707).

Because of these problems, Bitterman suggested the method of control by systematic variation as an alternative. Using this method, the researcher studying memory span, for example, would not attempt to equate task difficulty across the age groups but, rather, would systematically vary task difficulty. Lists varying in length would be selected, and all lists would be given to every age group. Curves relating performance to list length would be drawn for each group. If the curves had the same shape at all ages, then it would be reasonable to infer that the learning processes were the same. If, however, the curves differed, then it could be concluded that the processes differed, and the nature of the differences among the curves might suggest *how* the processes differed.

Similarly, rather than trying to equate age groups in attentiveness, the researcher would try to vary attentiveness systematically at each age level, and would relate performance to the varying levels of attentiveness. Again, similarity of performance curves would imply similarity of the learning processes, with the effect of attentiveness taken out by being varied systematically.

Cross-Sectional versus Longitudinal Methods in Learning Research

The discussion up to this point in this chapter has referred to research designs in which groups of different ages are compared. It should be noted that the age groups can be either cross-sectional or longitudinal, without changing any of the points raised about validity and reliability. (See Chapters Thirteen and Fourteen for a general discussion of cross-sectional and longitudinal methodology.) There is, however, a problem with the use of simple longitudinal designs in developmental research on learning. The problem is the occurrence of "learning to learn." (See also the discussion of testing and instrumentation effects in Chapter Seventeen.) This problem is particularly acute if the research on developmental learning is the kind that focuses on the study of learning *per se*. The problem is potentially so severe that it is doubtful that simple longitudinal designs can ever be used successfully to study short-range age effects on learning.

Learning to Learn

If a memory-span task is given repeatedly with short intervals between the repetitions and with the same items in the same sequence each time, performance will improve because of learning. Even if the task is repeated with different items each time, however, performance improves. The latter phenomenon—improvement over a series of tasks of the same kind, all with different specific materials—is referred to as learning to learn. There is evidence that, when any kind of learning task is given repeatedly with different materials each time, performance on new problems gets better and better. Thus, subjects can "learn to learn" any kind of task. In fact, this learning-to-learn effect has been assumed to play a powerful role in all kinds of development involving learning (for example, Goulet, 1970, 1973; Hultsch, 1974; Staats, 1971).

Learning to learn seems to result from the acquisition of more effective or more efficient learning processes. Thus, performance on the first task in the learning-to-learn series does not have the same meaning, or validity, as performance on tasks late in the series. The first task reflects relatively inefficient learning processes; the later tasks reflect efficient learning processes. It is therefore impossible to interpret performance on a task unless the learning history of the individual subject is known. Is this the first time he or she has encountered this kind of task, or has the subject already had so much experience with tasks of this kind that he or she has "learned how to learn" them?

Goulet (1973) has described several research designs that could be used to describe the acquisition of learning-to-learn skills. For example, the researcher could (1) compare age groups on the initial problem in the training series to get an estimate of the processes at the beginning of training; (2) assess the performance level after a specified amount of training to get an estimate of the speed of progress; (3) determine the amount of training required to attain a specified performance level as a further estimate of the speed of progress; (4) compare the groups at their maximum level of performance to get an estimate of the extent to which the groups are capable of benefiting from the training; or (5) combine any of the foregoing to answer more complex questions.

An example is a study by Levinson and Reese (1967), already mentioned earlier. They compared nursery-schoolers, fifth-graders, college students, and several groups of elderly persons in a learning-to-learn task. The researchers were primarily interested in the two types of comparisons listed as (3) and (4) above, and they examined not only performance as indexed by the number of correct responses but also performance as indexed by consistent patterns of responses. The results showed that, although all age groups were capable of attaining the same maximum performance level, indexed either way, they required different amounts of training to attain that level. Furthermore, analysis of the consistent patterns of responses provided data that were interpreted as reflecting underlying learning processes and as explaining why the groups required different amounts of training. The report also included data relevant to the types of comparisons listed as (1) and (2) above, but these comparisons were not discussed in the report.

Note that when any one of the types of comparisons suggested by Goulet is made, the method of control by equation is implied. None of the comparisons is particularly interesting unless the tasks are equated across age levels. However, when the types of comparisons are combined, the amount of training is systematically varied, and the data of interest become the shapes of the performance curves, rather than their absolute levels. Therefore, the designs described by Goulet are most effective when they are combined, thereby permitting control through systematic variation and avoidance of the problems associated with control by equation.

Validity and Learning to Learn

The occurrence of learning to learn necessarily changes the validity of the repeated task by affecting the efficiency of learning. Hence, in longitudinal learning research, age effects may be confounded with age differences in task validity. This problem is not unique to research on learning—it appears as the repeated-testing effect in any longitudinal research (see Chapter Seventeen)—but, whereas it exists as a possibility in longitudinal research on other kinds of psychological processes, it exists with extremely high probability in longitudinal research on learning when the time span between repetitions of the task is short. However, the problem is *known* to exist only for small time spans; there is no research showing that learning to learn will develop if the repetitions of the task are widely separated in time. Therefore, even though simple longitudinal designs are inappropriate for studying the development of learning over small age ranges (short time spans between repetitions), they may be useful for large age ranges with long periods between repetitions of the task.

The discussion of learning to learn as a confounding factor in short-term research on learning (rather than development) leads to another complicating methodological feature. If research on developmental learning is aimed at explaining the components of development, learning to learn can take on the status of a salient process—not to be controlled but to be studied.

Summary

It is important to distinguish between learning and performance. In developmental learning research, the data of interest are age differences in performance, but the phenomena of interest are age effects on learning processes or age effects on systems that support the learning process. The phenomena, not directly observable, are inferences from the data. How the inferences are made depends on whether you use a multiprocess or a uni-process theory, but the same validity problems arise (although at different points).

The meaning or validity of a learning task can change with age in unexpected ways, and it can change across trials within the task. Thus, possible changes in validity may be confounded with age differences. The age changes in validity could also produce age changes in the reliability of a task, thus also confounding reliability changes with age differences. Another valid-ity problem arises from the necessity of using inference rather than direct observation to yield statements about learning. An inference that the learning process changes with age is invalid if changes in the support systems occur. That is, age differences in performance may not reflect the development of more efficient processes but, rather, may reflect age differences in systems that affect performance without affecting learning itself.

Furthermore, developmental researchers have been concerned about possible floor and ceiling effects. A floor effect means that the task is too difficult for at least one of the age groups, and a ceiling effect means that it is too easy for at least one. The existence of floor or ceiling effects in one of the performance curves makes group differences in the shape or slope of the curve uninterpretable.

In attempting to prevent floor and ceiling effects, some researchers have varied the nature or amount of the material to be learned. The procedure is sometimes used in the hope that it will make the task the ''same'' for all age groups, but this method of control by equation has been criticized. One problem is that this procedure may change the validity or meaning of the task. An alternative procedure is control by systematic variation, in which a variable such as task difficulty or attentiveness is systematically varied within each age group. The data of interest are differences in the shape of the curve relating performance to the various levels of the manipulated variable. If the shapes of the curves are similar across ages, then it can be inferred that the learning process is the same.

Unfortunately, developmental learning researchers have seldom been concerned about possible changes in the validity and reliability of their tasks. Similarly, they have paid less attention to the study of learning as a component of development than to the study of learning as a dependent variable.

The research problems discussed in this chapter also depend to some extent upon whether the design used is cross-sectional or longitudinal. The issues of validity and reliability arise regardless of which design is used. In cross-sectional research on learning, the validity of a task may change with age; in addition, in longitudinal research covering small age ranges, the occurrence of learning to learn adds to this validity problem. Learning to learn refers to improvement in performance over a series of tasks of the same kind, all with different specific materials. It apparently results from the acquisition of more effective learning processes. Age groups may differ in the amount of training required to acquire these processes and in the specific processes finally acquired.

If the repetitions of a task are widely separated in time—perhaps at yearly intervals—learning to learn may not occur and therefore may be of less concern in long-span longitudinal research on learning. Several designs are available for investigating these possibilities and for disentangling the various components involved in learning processes and related developmental differences.

Chapter Twenty-Three

Developmental Research on Learning: Single-Subject Designs

In the preceding chapter, learning was discussed as the most direct way by which psychologists have studied intraindividual change. Interindividual differences in learning are studied by examining age effects in learning. In Chapter Twenty-Two it was also concluded that research aimed at addressing the relationship between learning and development, or using learning as an analogue for development, is often lacking. In that discussion, we considered two kinds of developmental approaches derived from the learning-theory tradition in psychology. One involved the study of different age groups in a relatively unintegrated manner; the other emphasized the analysis of conditions and processes of systematic behavior change.

In this chapter we consider a third approach, based on learning but not derived from the learning-theory tradition. Rather, it is derived from a reaction against that tradition. The approach is *functional analysis*, which has developed out of B. F. Skinner's operant psychology (for example, Bijou & Baer, 1961; Etzel, LeBlanc, & Baer, 1977; Hoyer, 1974; Skinner, 1938). The salient feature of the approach is that it is aimed at the functional relationship between environment and behavior, rather than the relationship between environment and any assumed underlying processes. The functional analysis, in other words, does not deal with unobservable, inferred processes, but rather deals only with observed environmental events and observed behavioral events.

The emphasis in this chapter, in contrast to the preceding chapter, is on details of procedure. We did not feel that procedures needed to be emphasized in the preceding chapter because they are in principle the same as those of the standard developmental designs. Here, however, a new set of procedures is involved.

Also in contrast to the preceding chapter, here we do not discuss the problems of validity and reliability and developmental differences therein. The reason is that these problems are essentially the same in a functional analysis as in the approaches discussed in the preceding chapter, and consequently almost everything said there is applicable here. Similarly, the question of whether learning is identical with development or is a useful analogue applies with equal significance.

Objectives

Baer (1973) has outlined a strategy for the functional or experimental analysis of psychological development (see also Chapter Nineteen on developmental simulation). The first step involves laboratory research that shows that a specified target behavior is operant and can be brought under stimulus control. The second step involves observational research in the natural environment to see whether the required contingencies seem to occur. That is, is the target behavior in its natural setting followed by events that might serve as reinforcers? The final step is manipulative research in the natural environment to see whether or not the naturally occurring contingencies are in fact effective. That is, given that the behavior is operant and can be controlled by contingencies (Step 1), and given that contingencies seem to occur naturally (Step 2), are these contingencies actually functioning as reinforcers (Step 3)?

Successful outcomes in the three steps of the program would imply that the development of the behavior in the natural environment results from the same principles (homology; see Chapter Nineteen) that account for its development in the laboratory—namely, reinforcement contingencies. A slow rate of development in the natural environment would be suspected to result from inefficient programming of the contingencies in the natural environment, and this suspicion could be tested by manipulative research in the natural environment.

Research Designs

For a variety of reasons, operant psychologists generally prefer to use single-subject designs whenever possible. In Baer's program, these designs would be applied in the first and third steps. The rationale of the designs has been succinctly outlined by Risley and Wolf (1973; see also Hersen & Barlow, 1976; Hoyer, 1974), whose analysis is summarized below and in Figures 23-1 and 23-2. In many ways, single-subject designs are a specific form of time-series methods (see Chapter Eighteen).

Reversal Design

The most straightforward single-subject design is the reversal design (Figure 23-1), in which the spontaneous rate of emitting a behavior is assessed (Baseline), and then a treatment (Experimental Condition) is imposed—the first "reversal"—and the rate of the behavior is again assessed, and so on.

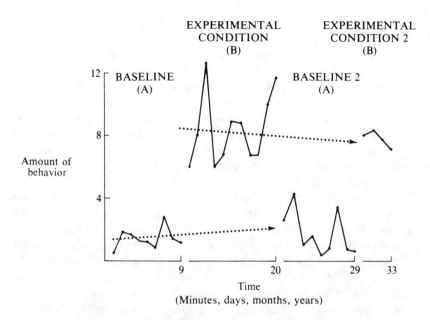

Figure 23-1. Illustration of reversal design. The data in the second A condition support the forecast from the first A condition, and, similarly, the data in the second B condition support the forecast from the first B condition. From "Strategies for Analyzing Behavioral Change over Time," by T. R. Risley and M. M. Wolf. In J. R. Nesselroade and H. W. Reese (Eds.), *Life-Span Developmental Psychology: Methodological Issues*. Copyright 1973 by Academic Press, Inc. Reprinted by permission.

As shown in Figure 23-1, the first assessment yields a baseline, which may reveal a constant amount of behavior or a constant rate of change in the amount of the behavior. It is assumed that the behavior will continue indefinitely in the same quantity (or same rate of change) as long as the environmental setting is unchanged. Consequently, it is possible to predict future amounts or rates by projecting the baseline and comparing it with the outcome obtained when an experimental condition is introduced.

It is possible, however, that the underlying assumption was wrong —that is, that it is not true that the behavior would have continued at the same rate if the environmental conditions were not changed. To check this possibility, the original environmental setting is reimposed (Baseline 2)—the second reversal—and the rate of the behavior is assessed again. If the rate returns to the projected level, then the assumption is confirmed. Further reversals (for example, Experimental Condition 2) may be introduced to increase the credibility of the conclusion that the treatment is effective. Further reversals are needed because there is no widely accepted method of statistical analysis that can be used with this design, and therefore only the "eyeball test" can provide convincing evidence that the treatment had a real effect.

Because it is necessary to project the baseline into the treatment phase, it is necessary to obtain a stable estimate of the rate of the behavior in the baseline phase. If the rate were unstable, there would be no basis for predicting what its rate would be later. However, if the rate of the behavior is unstable, there is a possibility that seems to have been generally overlooked. The projection, in this case, is not a particular rate but rather an assertion that the rate will remain unstable. Then, if the rate is found to stabilize in the treatment phase, and to become unstable again in the reversal to the baseline condition, the projection is confirmed and a convincing argument can be made that the treatment has an effect.

It is important to emphasize that not all behaviors can be studied with the reversal design, because the design requires that the rate of a behavior return to the projected baseline when the baseline condition is reinstated. This is particularly true for research on development, since development is often conceived of as fully or partially irreversible (for example, Lerner, 1976; Wohlwill, 1970a, b). This requirement of reversibility makes the design inapplicable to some treatments and to some behaviors. Some treatments are irreversible, making it impossible to reinstate the baseline condition. An example of such a treatment is brain surgery.

An irreversible treatment, then, is one that cannot be undone; an irreversible behavior is one that is unaffected by reinstating the baseline condition. To deal with these treatments and behaviors, an alternative design can be used.

Multiple-Baseline Designs

The alternative to the reversal design is the multiple-baseline design summarized in Figure 23-2. In this design, at least two independent behaviors (Measure 1, Measure 2) are observed during the initial baseline phase; then the treatment is applied to one of the behaviors (Measure 1 in Figure 23-2) while the other is continued under the baseline condition; then the treatment is applied to the second behavior (Measure 2 in Figure 23-2) while the first behavior continues under the treatment condition or is returned to the baseline condition. Ideally and in principle, the process involves more than two behaviors and continues until enough of the behaviors have been observed to

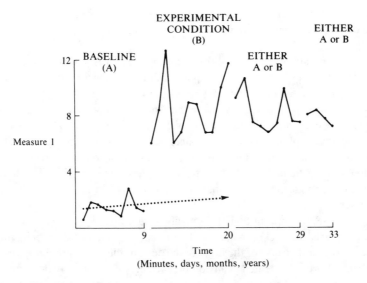

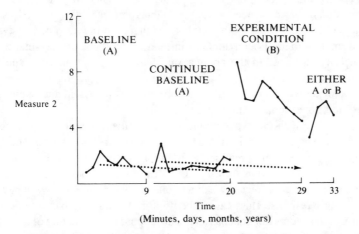

Figure 23-2. Illustration of multiple-baseline design. Two (or more) behavioral measures are recorded simultaneously. Treatments are then introduced sequentially, first for one behavior (1) and then for the second (2). The continuation of Measure 2 from one A Condition baseline to the next—as forecasted—supports the forecast made from the baseline of Measure 1. From "Strategies for Analyzing Behavioral Change over Time," by T. R. Risley and M. M. Wolf. In J. R. Nesselroade and H. W. Reese (Eds.), *Life-Span Developmental Psychology: Methodological Issues.* Copyright 1973 by Academic Press, Inc. Reprinted by permission.

change under the treatment while the untreated behaviors do not change. "Enough" means enough to provide a convincing argument that the treatment is effective.

The rationale for a multiple-baseline design is similar to that of the reversal design in that the baseline phase for a behavior provides a prediction for comparison with the rate of that behavior in the treatment phase. However, there are three differences. One is that the accuracy of the prediction is assessed by comparing the predicted level of the behavior with the concurrent baseline levels of the as yet untreated behaviors. The second is that the behaviors involved are independent, an assumption difficult to accept for a structurally oriented researcher (for example, Lerner, 1976). The third is that it is necessary to assume that all behaviors are influenced by the same treatment.

The assumption that all behaviors are influenced by the same treatment is partially checked when the treatment is applied to each behavior in turn. However, because of the logic of the design, the assumption implies that the behaviors can be treated in any order: each behavior can provide a check on predictions about the others only if the ordering is irrelevant. Risley and Baer (1973) illustrated this point by noting that, if standing, walking, and running were treated in that order, "the continuing zero level of walking and running would lend little support to the prediction of standing, since these behaviors cannot be influenced by any variables until standing is well established" (p. 299). Because of the implication that ordering must be irrelevant, the assumption that all behaviors are influenced by the same treatment cannot be fully checked. In the application of the design to any one subject, there is only one ordering of the behaviors, and consequently there is no way to know whether a different ordering would yield the same data (unless additional subjects are tested).

In line with the expectations of structuralism, it sometimes happens that, when one behavior is treated, other behaviors also change in rate. Operant researchers interpret such a finding as indicating that the behaviors belong to a single "response class." By definition, a response class includes all behaviors that are affected when any one is treated. Obviously, behaviors from a single response class cannot be used in the multiple-baseline design, which requires independent behaviors. But suppose that the nature of the target behavior is such that there are no independent behaviors. Then the multiple-baseline design cannot be used.

There is, however, an analogue to this design, in which different subjects instead of different behaviors are treated in each phase. The logic of the design is the same as that of the multiple-baseline design, but with the assumption that all subjects are affected by the treatment in the same way. This assumption is checked by applying the treatment to each subject in turn. Until a given subject is treated, his or her performance provides a check on the baseline projection of the treated subjects.

A novel feature of this modification of the multiple-baseline design is that the data it provides can be analyzed statistically. For example, the performance of each subject can be divided into two phases, baseline (however long the baseline phase might be) and treatment. By using a subject's mean performance level in these phases as the data, the researcher converts the design into the standard pre-post group design and can use standard methods of statistical analysis.

Reinforcement

Since much of the literature on single-subject methodology is tied to operant psychology, it is desirable to briefly review terminology and procedures used in this branch of psychology. A key concept in operant psychology is *reinforcement*. Reinforcement is the process of increasing the rate of a behavior. It results from making reinforcers contingent upon the occurrence of the behavior.

The contingency can be that the reinforcer is presented following the behavior, or is withdrawn following the behavior. When the presentation of a stimulus following the behavior results in an increase in the rate of the behavior, the stimulus is called a *positive reinforcer*; and when the withdrawal of the stimulus results in an increase in the rate of the behavior, the stimulus is called a *negative reinforcer*. When presenting a stimulus following the behavior results in a reduction in the rate of the behavior, the stimulus is a *punisher*; and when withdrawing a stimulus following the behavior results in a reduction in the rate of the behavior, the stimulus is a *response cost*.

These four categories of stimuli are defined by their effect on behavior when they are presented or withdrawn contingently; therefore, they may be independent categories with little overlap. Nevertheless, positive reinforcers are likely to function also as response costs, and negative reinforcers are likely to function as punishers.

For example, praise from a parent is a stimulus, and if it is presented contingent upon some behavior and the behavior increases in rate of occurrence, then the praise is a positive reinforcer. If continuous praise is terminated following a behavior and the rate of the behavior drops, then the praise is a response cost.

Table 23-1 shows how the four categories of stimuli are related to behavior in the various training contingencies. Table 23-2 shows how these contingencies can be used in the modification of behavior. Note that the change in behavior can be accomplished by applying the contingency directly to the behavior or, alternatively, by applying the contingency to an incompatible behavior that interferes with the occurrence of the target behavior.

Table 23-1.   Training contingencies

Type of Training	Manipulation of Stimulus[a]	Effect on Response Rate	Category of Stimulus[a]
Reinforcement			
Positive	Presented	Increase	Positive reinforcer
Negative	Withdrawn	Increase	Negative reinforcer
Punishment	Presented	Decrease	Punisher
Omission[b]	Withdrawn	Decrease	Response cost
Extinction	Never presented	Change[c]	Any category

[a]Stimulus contingent upon occurrence of response.
[b]Also called response-cost training. It is classified as a punishment contingency.
[c]Direction of change depends upon previous type of training. Following positive or negative reinforcement, extinction results in decrease in response rate; following punishment and omission training, extinction results in increase in response rate.

Procedures

The experimental analysis of behavior has traditionally been based on the procedures of operant learning. The five procedures most relevant for developmental psychology are conditioning, shaping, fading, discrimination, and generalization. All involve ways of applying the contingencies listed in Table 23-1.

Conditioning

Conditioning refers here to changing the strength of an operant response through direct application of any of the contingencies listed in Table 23-1 to the response. It is generally called *operant conditioning* or *instrumental conditioning*.

It is not necessary to apply the contingency to every occurrence of the response; the schedule can be intermittent. Intermittent schedules affect the rate of the response differently from continuous schedules, however, and the details of these differences can influence the choice of schedule to be used in any specific application. (For a discussion of some of the differences, see Siqueland & Ryan, 1970.)

Table 23-2.   Applications of training contingencies

Problem	Alternative Contingencies
Desirable behavior too weak	a. Positive reinforcement of the behavior, by making already available positive reinforcers contingent upon the behavior, or introducing new positive reinforcers contingent upon the behavior
	b. Negative reinforcement of the behavior, by subtracting already present negative reinforcers contingently, or introducing new negative reinforcers and subtracting them contingently
	c. Punishment of incompatible behaviors, by making already available punishers contingent (or withdrawing available response costs contingently), or introducing new punishers contingently (or introducing new response costs and withdrawing them contingently)
	d. Extinction of incompatible behaviors, by removing the reinforcers that are maintaining them
Undesirable behavior too strong	a. Punishment of the behavior
	b. Extinction of the behavior
	c. Positive reinforcement of incompatible behaviors
	d. Negative reinforcement of incompatible behaviors

Adapted from "Behavior Modification: Clinical and Educational Applications," by D. M. Baer and J. A. Sherman. In H. W. Reese and L. P. Lipsitt (Eds.), *Experimental Child Psychology*. Copyright 1970 by Academic Press, Inc. Reprinted by permission.

Shaping

Shaping is a procedure designed to introduce a response into a subject's response repertoire. For example, Siqueland (1968) studied conditioning of head-turning responses in newborn infants. His definition of this response required a rotation of at least ten degrees; but note that, if the infant never turned his head as much as ten degrees, no reinforcers would be given and no conditioning could occur. Siqueland therefore introduced a shaping procedure when any infant failed to give a criterion response during the first minute of the experimental session. Shaping consisted of initially reducing the response requirement, so that any head movement, no matter how small, was reinforced and then requiring progressively larger head movements until full ten-degree turns were being produced. At that point, reinforcers were presented only for turns of at least ten degrees.

In general, shaping always follows this pattern: a very loose response requirement is used initially, then successively closer approximations to the criterion response are required until finally the criterion response itself is required.

The procedure can be used whenever the desired response is not spontaneously emitted by the subject. Even when the subject seems to emit no responses that approximate the desired response, careful analysis will reveal that perhaps remote approximations are being emitted. For example, rats do not spontaneously climb ladders, and they do not even take the first step. However, they do approach food located at ground level, and they can be trained to approach the ladder by means of placing the food at its base. Once the rat has learned to go immediately to the base of the ladder, the food can be placed on the first rung, requiring that the rat stand on its hind legs to reach the food. Once the rat has learned to perform this response reliably, the food can be placed higher, requiring that the rat climb to the first rung. It should be obvious that, as the response requirement is increased, the rat will eventually climb the ladder. In fact, just such a procedure was used to train rats to climb a ladder and do high dives into a net.

Fading

In shaping, the desired response is obtained by manipulating the response requirements. In *fading*, the desired response is obtained by manipulating stimuli. The response is brought under control of an antecedent stimulus, through usual operant-conditioning methods; then the antecedent stimulus is gradually reduced until it can be omitted entirely without affecting the rate of occurrence of the desired response. Alternatively, the antecedent stimulus can be gradually changed to approximate more and more closely any other stimulus that is desired to control the response.

Examples of shaping-fading sequences can be seen in several studies of language development in mute children (see Risley & Baer, 1973). The problem was to teach the child a rudimentary vocabulary. The first step was to teach the child to imitate vocalizations by the experimenter. This step was accomplished by the use of a shaping procedure. At first any vocal response by the child, following the experimenter's vocalization, was reinforced; then successively closer approximations to the experimenter's vocalization were required.

After the child had learned to imitate the experimenter's vocalizations reliably, the child was shown a series of objects, one at a time. The experimenter named each one, and the child was required to imitate each name. Then, continuing to present the same objects, the experimenter changed his vocalizations to a whisper, but required the child to say the appropriate names aloud. Next, still with the same objects, the experimenter changed from whispers to voiceless mouthings of the names, and required the child to say the names aloud. Finally, the experimenter presented the objects with no cues and the child said the names aloud. Thus, the child had learned to emit the names of the objects through fading of the cues supplied by the experimenter. Subsequently, the child would name new objects spontaneously after hearing the experimenter name them only once.

Discrimination

Discrimination means that a response occurs in the presence of some stimuli and not in the presence of others, as a consequence of the history of reinforcement of the response in the presence of the stimuli (or in the presence of similar stimuli).

When no reinforcement history is required for the occurrence of a response in the presence of a particular stimulus, discrimination is not involved. For example, a knee jerk will immediately follow a tap on the patellar tendon, and it will not follow a tap on the sole of the foot (in the absence of relevant training). However, to borrow an example from Risley and Baer (1973), offering money to a merchant for service and not similarly offering it to a boyfriend or girlfriend requires training, and therefore involves discrimination.

The stimuli involved in discrimination are called discriminative stimuli, and the responses controlled by the discriminative stimuli are called discriminated responses, or responses under stimulus control. After stimulus control has been established, the response is reliably emitted in the presence of one set of discriminative stimuli and is reliably omitted in the presence of the other set of discriminative stimuli. An example is crossing the street on the green signal and not crossing on the red signal.

To establish a discrimination, the response is reinforced in the presence of one stimulus (or set of stimuli) and is either punished or simply not reinforced (*extinguished*) in the presence of the other stimuli.

Generalization

Generalization refers to the occurrence of behavior in settings other than the one in which training was given. For example, if a behavior is trained in the classroom and subsequently occurs spontaneously on the playground, generalization has occurred. Similarly, if a response is brought under control of one discriminative stimulus—say, a red light—and subsequently occurs spontaneously in the presence of a similar stimulus—another shade of red, for example—generalization is demonstrated. If generalization is desired, however, contingent reinforcers may need to be presented in the generalized setting, because if the generalized setting does not contain contingencies to maintain the behavior, it may extinguish (Risley & Baer, 1973).

Developmental Applications

As mentioned before, developmental learning research of the kinds discussed in this chapter, and in Chapter Twenty-Two, has one or both of two aims. One aim is descriptive and focuses on learning itself; the other is explanatory and deals with development as a learning process.

Thus, research on the development of learning may be intended to identify differences in the nature of learning processes characteristic at different ages, or age differences in the efficiency or rate of learning, or in the systems that support learning. Alternatively, the intent may be to test hypotheses about the effects of these differences on the developmental trends observed in other behavioral domains. In both cases, however, the developmental trends in the learning processes themselves need to be explained. Consequently, the descriptive task is to identify age differences in learning processes, and the explanatory task is to explain these differences and to use them to explain other kinds of age differences or developmental changes.

The way these tasks are conducted depends upon one's conceptualization of development. The simplest conception is that behavioral development results from environmental contingencies, which are poorly programmed in the natural environment but which can be efficiently programmed in an experimental environment to optimize development (for example, Baer, 1970; Bijou & Baer, 1961). According to this conception, behavioral development results from conditioning, shaping, fading, and discrimination and generalization training.

The aim of the "functional" analysis of development is to test the limits of this conception—for example, by means of the three-step research program outlined by Baer (1973) and discussed at the beginning of this chapter. Note that the approach can be used even to deal with the kinds of changes in learning processes discussed in Chapter Twenty-Two. The procedure in this case would be to select a particular inferred process for analysis—sequential rehearsal, for example—then to find some way to make it observable, and finally to determine whether it is subject to the same contingencies that control other types of behavior already analyzed in previous research (see Baer, 1973). The usual internal and external validity problems would arise, of course, and would be dealt with in subsequent research of the types specified for the second and third steps in Baer's (1973) program.

The majority of developmental psychologists have more complex conceptions of development (see Lerner, 1976, for review), but the functional analysis of development is now in its infancy, and, if the projected program is successful, perhaps more developmentalists will take the simpler view.

Summary

The research strategy for the functional or experimental analysis of behavior begins with the assumption that psychological development results primarily from operant conditioning. The first step, then, is to determine in the laboratory whether a target behavior is operant, by determining whether it can be controlled by contingent stimuli. The second step is to determine whether contingent stimuli occur in the natural environment. If they do, then the third step is to determine whether these contingent stimuli are actually functioning as reinforcers.

The methodological problems encountered in the functional analysis of development are in principle the same as those discussed in Chapter Twenty-Two. However, the research design customarily used—the single-subject design—has unique features. The ideal design is the reversal design, in which baseline performance is assessed and compared with performance in a treatment phase. Reversals from treatment back to baseline and back to treatment again are used to verify predictions about performance levels that would be obtained had the treatment not been given. In a variant of this design, the multiple-baseline design, the baseline and treatment conditions are applied separately to different independent behaviors. This design is used when the treatment or the behavior cannot be reversed (precluding use of the reversal design). When there are no independent behaviors for use in the multiple-baseline design, one can use a variant in which different subjects serve as analogues of independent behaviors.

Much of the literature on single-subject designs is tied to operant psychology. A key concept in operant psychology is reinforcement, which involves stimuli contingent upon the occurrence of behavior. The contingent stimuli can be positive reinforcers (presentation increases response rate), negative reinforcers (withdrawal increases response rate), punishers (presentation reduces response rate), or response costs (withdrawal reduces response rate). They can be applied to every occurrence of the target behavior, or they can be applied intermittently.

When the target behavior does not occur spontaneously, it can be shaped by reinforcing behavior that resembles it in some way, then gradually requiring closer and closer approximations to the target behavior. Fading is used when the target behavior is easy to bring under control of some stimulus but hard to bring under control of the stimulus that should control it. After being brought under control of the first stimulus, that stimulus is faded out, leaving the behavior under control of the desired stimulus.

Discrimination training is used when the target behavior should occur in some situations and not in others. The training consists of reinforcing the behavior in the desired situation and either not reinforcing it or punishing it in other situations. Generalization means that the behavior occurs in situations other than the one in which training was given. If the generalization is undesirable, discrimination training is given. If it is desirable but does not occur, then it can be trained by reinforcing the behavior in a variety of settings, continuing the procedure until the behavior generalizes as widely as desired.

These procedures—conditioning, shaping, fading, discrimination, and generalization—are believed to account for development in the natural environment, in which development is slow, presumably because of inefficient programming of the contingent stimuli.

Chapter Twenty-Four

Structural Models: The Continuing Search for Causes

Throughout this introductory book, the uniqueness of developmental research has been emphasized in terms of its joint focus on change in antecedents and consequents and its concern with long-term historical linkages. Some of the related issues were discussed in detail; others, because of various constraints, received only cursory attention. We have attempted to foster recognition of the ultimate value of systematically developing research within a general orientation—as is provided, for example, by a focus on historical-developmental paradigms or the mechanistic and organismic models of humankind.

It has been noted that tightly controlled experimental research, highly desirable from the standpoint of internal validity, may suffer an unfortunate lack of generalizability, or external validity. Many vital and interesting research questions dealing with the description and explanation of development cannot be studied easily—some not at all—within the rigorous but restrictive experimental laboratory. Moreover, we have seen that, for some intriguing problems, an appropriate method is often not available within the field of developmental psychology, and that it is desirable to search outside the field—in other disciplines concerned with the study of change—for potentially useful alternatives (see Chapter One). This final chapter is written to illustrate how familiarity with parallel or separate developments in other disciplines (in this case, economics and sociology) might assist the developmental psychologist in reaching a new level of competency. In this sense, the chapter aims to bridge disciplines and to suggest one of many largely unexplored alternatives in research methodology.

In this chapter, a general approach to explanatory research will be discussed that has not been widely used by developmental psychologists—or by psychologists in general, for that matter. However, as has been the case in other social and behavioral sciences, we believe that these approaches will become more and more prevalent in developmental-research practice. The chapter is focused primarily on the topic of modeling and testing causal explanations in other than manipulative-experimental settings. We do not intend to downgrade classical approaches to experimentation and research design in developmental psychology but, rather, to sketch out an alternative, perhaps more general methodological approach to the construction of explanations of developmental change.

We realize that this chapter is in some ways repetitive and not so explicit as the reader might like it to be. At the same time, we feel that refocusing on the objective of identifying causes of development and leaving the reader with a set of uncompleted tasks and questions might be a good reflection of where we find ourselves in developmental research methodology at present. We hope, however, that our presentation is rich enough to whet the reader's appetite for more; and more can be found, largely in economics and sociology (for example, Duncan, 1975; Goldberger & Duncan, 1973), but also, more recently, in the psychological literature (Jöreskog, in press; Rogosa, in press).

The Significance of Causal Relationships

In Chapter Four we briefly showed why the establishment of causal relationships among variables is a fundamental aspect of the scientific enterprise. The concerns of developmentalists in regard to determining cause-and-effect relationships range over a vast domain of variables and across both short and long intervals of time. Let's consider a couple of examples and, in so doing, attend to the limitations one must deal with in trying to produce convincing evidence of causality in a network of variables.

How will adults differ in level of conscientiousness if they are exposed to quite different amounts of physical punishment by their parents during the period of growing up? In contemporary society, the problem so defined cannot be studied using powerful experimental procedures such as random assignment of subjects to treatment groups. The dilemma is that, whereas on the one hand it is desirable to firmly establish the nature of relationships among particular variables that permit explanation and prediction, on the other hand the kinds of variables and questions of most interest to a particular researcher may preclude the use of traditional experimental tactics, which involve measuring effects while holding some variables constant and manipulating others.

To take another example, how does a researcher study in the laboratory the impact of massive social experiments such as busing to achieve equal educational opportunity? At stake here, of course, is the specification of causal relationships. Without the capability of manipulating and controlling the presence or intensity of one set of variables so that the effects upon another set can be clearly studied, it becomes difficult if not impossible to argue for causal linkages among variables within the narrow definition of causality. In relation to internal validity of design, for instance, many other social changes, such as widespread unemployment or teachers' strikes, may coincide with busing programs, and the effect of each could not be separately established. Moreover, in this context the focus might reasonably be on the more general question of whether social concern leads to events such as busing, whether events such as busing lead to social concern, or, of course, whether some other causal agent is responsible for both.

Evidence of Causal Relationships

If important problems are defined so that strict, manipulative experimentation is difficult or impossible to conduct (see also Chapter Nineteen on simulation), can alternative procedures be used to establish causal explanations? Some researchers have argued forcefully that acceptable cause-effect evidence rests solely upon applications of experimental method (see also Chapter Four). Others have responded with the assertion that there are several kinds of causes, appropriate in different contexts (Overton & Reese, 1973). Glass, Willson, and Gottman (1972) stated that the only way causal relationships can be established is to specify the possible causal interrelationships and then systematically proceed to eliminate all of them save one. The logic is not unlike that used by the school principal who, after establishing that Johnny, Jimmy, or Jerry is the culprit who broke the window, upon ascertaining that the window could not possibly have been broken by Jimmy or Jerry, points the finger of guilt in Johnny's direction with no further hesitation.

It does seem fair to say that the developmentalist's search for powerful explanatory principles has, to date, been less than totally satisfactory. One can both admire experimentalists for the zeal and energy with which they have undertaken the task of explaining systematic behavior changes and continue to recognize the need to attend to other kinds of research strategies, data, and evaluative criteria. However, it is clear that if, in addition to experimental findings, nonexperimental data are to be exploited in the construction of causal explanations of long-term developmental phenomena, systematic procedures and safeguards for dissecting the fragile tissue of causality must be observed. The very nature of historical-developmental paradigms (see Chapters One and Two) makes the search for causality a complicated task.

The Representation of Causal Relationships:
Structural Models

The ability to make at least some inferences and generalizations about causal relationships in situations that preclude manipulative experiments has long been highly desired by social and behavioral scientists. After all, astronomers, for example, have been doing it for decades, seemingly with great success.

Some developmentalists have simply proceeded to make untested (often untestable) assertions about causes and effects. Others, faced with the inability to draw conclusions about causal relationships, have amassed descriptive information. Researchers in various disciplines have plunged forward with the development of techniques for the mathematical specification and testing of hypothesized causal schemes. What has emerged is a set of procedures, generally called *structural-equation models*, that appears to be widely applicable for the purpose of systematically evaluating the fit between data and hypothesized causal networks of variables. From a historical point of view, contemporary writers credit a geneticist named Sewall Wright (1934), who developed *path analysis* to study genetic influences in families, with performing the "spade work" in developing structural models. Many extensions of path analysis may be found in the sociological literature; a few are found in the psychometric literature.

Before considering the main aspects of structural-equation models, the reader should be aware of a qualification concerning the interpretation of outcomes generated in using them. Structural-equation models are not intended to be used as a way to search through nonexperimental data until a plausible causal ordering of variables is found. Duncan (1975), for example, pointed out that any set of empirical correlations among variables will be consistent with any causal ordering of those variables. Structural-equation models are intended for the testing of empirical relationships among variables, given explicit, well-articulated statements about the hypothesized causal ordering.

The fundamental ingredient for the proper use of structural-equation models is a clear, precise, and explicit model or conception of the network of causal relationships among variables, which can be further expressed as a set of mathematical equations. One cannot proceed with a set of ambiguous, ill-defined relationships. The advantages to having such an explicit account, as noted by Duncan (1975), are: (1) arguments, especially long-winded ones, do not suffer from changes in premises and assumptions; (2) more precise conclusions can be reached; and (3) conclusions are susceptible to empirical refutation. Armed with an explicit model, one should address three general points in employing the structural-equations approach. We will consider them basically in the order an investigator using the procedure would, although in practice some repetition and backtracking may be required.

Specification of the Model

The actual structural equations—and they are essentially ordinary mathematical equations—are statements about the dependency of one variable upon one or more others preceding it in the causal chain as hypothesized. Specification of the model involves writing these equations and any other definitions, constraints, assumptions, and so forth made by the investigator. One may assume, for example, that certain variables are uncorrelated with other ones in the model. All of this information is part of the specification of the model, and, as one might expect, it is possible to make errors in specifying a model. Sometimes one can test for and evaluate the effects of "specification errors," but a discussion of that process is well beyond the purview of this chapter.

Identification of the Model

Not every system of equations in a set of unknowns has a solution, as the reader knows. For example, one may have more unknowns than equations—a situation that yields no solutions. There may be more equations than unknowns—a situation often resulting in inconsistencies. Or, one may have exactly the same number of equations and unknowns and obtain a unique solution to a set of equations.

In using structural equations to model a causal chain, one is interested, of course, in solving for the unknown parameters of the model; but the issue of number of unknowns and number of equations must be faced. Some model specifications may result in a number of equations insufficient to provide solutions to some of the unknown parameters of the model. Such parameters are said to be *underidentified*. Parameters that are uniquely resolved due to the right number of equations are said to be *just identified*, and those for which there are more equations than needed are *overidentified*. In the last case, many different solutions tend to be available, so estimation techniques are often employed to provide a particular solution. The point is that, after the model is specified, the issue of identification must be confronted. Underidentified models cannot be tested, regardless of how provocative and appealing the underlying theoretical model of causality may be.

Estimation and Testing

An identified or overidentified model can be solved. The solution can then be used in the evaluation of a given set of empirical data presumed to have been generated by that causal model. The techniques and procedures of estimating the values of parameters and testing the goodness of fit of one or more models are well beyond the scope of this discussion. Extensive discussions and computer programs for these purposes are available, however (see, for example, Goldberger & Duncan, 1973).

Uses of Structural Models

In this section we will take a brief look at some examples of structural-model applications. Our purpose is not to prepare you to actually construct and solve such models but merely to acquaint you with the basic notions and to help you judge their relevance for future developmental investigation. Keep in mind that any explanatory power gained from using structural models is as much a function of having a well-articulated theory of causality as it is of using sophisticated mathematical and statistical techniques.

In specifying a structural-equation model one may discriminate among several kinds of variables. Broadly speaking, there are the variables we wish to account for and the variables by which we expect to account for them. Of course, in a causal chain, intermediate variables may be both effects of prior variables and causes of subsequent ones. In addition, we may distinguish between explicitly identified causal variables and those that are not explicitly identified but are, nevertheless, hypothesized to be involved in the network of interrelationships. The latter type of variables are often referred to as *disturbances*; the psychologically oriented reader may be more comfortable thinking about them as *sources of error variance*. In any case, they are a conglomerate of all those influences that are not given a more explicit representation in the structural model.

Evaluating Consistency between Data and Postulated Structural Models

A very simple model is presented in Figure 24-1 to illustrate this particular approach to explanatory developmental research. Represented in Figure 24-1 is the hypothesis that a person's score on the personality trait *dominance* is dependent upon the dominance scores of the person's mother and father. Of course, other influences would be causally involved and are allowed for, but they remain without precise specification.

Writing the information depicted in Figure 24-1 as an equation gives:

$$Y = a + b_1 X_1 + b_2 X_2 + u,$$

which may be read: "A person's score on dominance at age 20 (the variable Y) is equal to some constant (a) plus some amount (b_1) of the father's dominance score (X_1) plus some amount (b_2) of the mother's dominance score (X_2) plus a contribution from various other sources (u)." Given sufficient data, one could proceed to estimate the unknown values of a, b_1, and b_2, for example, to see if the data suggest that b_1 and b_2 are actually different from zero and, if they are, just how well the two together account for the offspring's dominance scores.

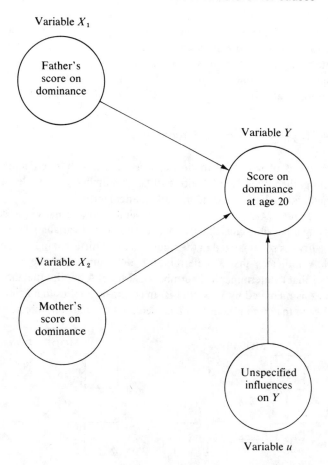

Figure 24-1.   Representation of a structural model specifying that dominance is a function of a person's mother's and father's dominance levels.

Imagine, for example, that the estimates of the values of b_1 and b_2 are not different from zero. From an explanatory viewpoint the equation would then reduce to: $Y = a + u$, or, in verbal terms, "A person's score on dominance at age 20 (Y) is equal to a constant (a) plus a contribution from other sources (u)." With that result, the hypothetical explanation that dominance scores at age 20 are dependent upon the person's mother's and father's dominance scores is not given empirical support, and the researcher is left with a very impoverished, uninformative account of what "causes" Y—other sources. The reasonable conclusion to be reached from such an attempt is that the data are not consistent with the hypothesized causal ordering. If the data used in an analysis of this type are reliable, the outcome amounts to a refutation of the hypothesized causal ordering.

If, on the contrary, the parameters b_1 and b_2 turn out to be different from zero, the plausibility of the causal model is sustained, and one can at least estimate how powerful the two causal variables (X_1 and X_2) are in relation to how much of the variability in Y is still explained by the unidentified causal factors represented by u.

Testing Competing Structural Models

Tests of structural models can be used to help one decide between competing theoretical explanations of a phenomenon, provided that both explanations can be formalized in mathematical terms.

Figure 24-2, for instance, represents two alternative models, each expressing a possible causal network among selected variables. The direction of causality, as schematized in the figure, is quite different in the two models. Model A indicates that X determines Y determines Z, whereas Model B indicates that Y determines X determines Z. Model A implies that the influence of X on Z is mediated by Y. Model B, in contrast, implies that X influences Z directly and that Y's influence on Z is mediated through variable X.

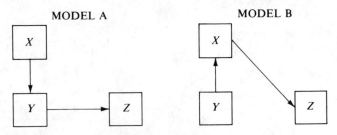

MODEL A   MODEL B

Figure 24-2. Two structural models offering competing representations of the X, Y, and Z interrelationships.

Duncan (1975) showed that the plausibility of Model A hinged upon the correlation (population parameters) of X and Z being equal to the product of the correlation of X and Y times the correlation of Y and Z, and that the plausibility of Model B depended upon the correlation of Y and Z being equal to the product of the correlation of X and Y times that of X and Z. The population values can only be estimated from the value of correlations in the sample, but the estimated values may provide a case for rejecting at least one of the two competing causal explanations.

Of course, the example just given is only a very simple one, used to illustrate the logic of eliminating competing alternative explanations. The texts by Duncan (1975) and Goldberger and Duncan (1973) provide much more thorough displays of technical possibilities.

To gain some additional familiarity with the concepts and rationale of the structural-equation-models approach, consider briefly what has been termed analysis of *cross-lagged panel correlations* (Kenny, 1973; Pelz & Andrews, 1964; Rozelle & Campbell, 1969). The technique was developed quite independently of the principal work on structural-equation models, for the purpose of exploiting information about the temporal ordering of observations in searching for causal relationships in nonexperimental, repeated-measures data. The minimum data set for a cross-lagged panel analysis consists of measurements on each of two variables repeated on the same units at each of two time points. Given the premise that effects do not precede their causes in time, the correlations among the variables, both within and across occasions, can be evaluated for their consistency with hypotheses about causal relationships between the measured variables.

The potential usefulness of cross-lagged panel correlations to developmental researchers is obvious, and the technique has, in fact, been used by them to some extent. Clarke-Stewart (1973), for example, presented data on certain aspects of social and psychological interactions between mothers and their children.

The nature of some of Clarke-Stewart's data is indicated in Figure 24-3. The numbers shown in the figure are correlation coefficients between the indicated measures. Notice, especially, that the correlation between attachment at time one (Y_1) and attention at time two (X_2) is substantially higher than the correlation between attention at time one (X_1) and attachment at time two (Y_2). But the nature of the disparity between correlations reverses from time two to time three.

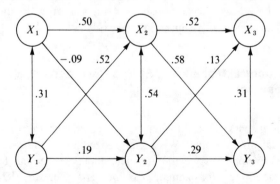

Figure 24-3. Pattern of intercorrelations between attention and attachment, measured at each of three time points. X_1, X_2, X_3 represent attention paid to child by mother at times one, two, and three, respectively. Y_1, Y_2, Y_3 represent attachment of child to mother at times one, two, and three, respectively. Adapted from Clarke-Stewart (1973).

Oversimplifying our summary a bit, the logic of causality led Clarke-Stewart to conclude that, over time, first one and then the other variable is the causal agent, as mother and child try to achieve a balanced interaction. Our aim here is not to question Clarke-Stewart's conclusions but simply to illustrate briefly the concept behind cross-lagged panel correlation and to indicate that it can be represented as a structural-equation model and evaluated and tested within that framework (see, for example, Goldberger, 1971; Kenny, 1973). Clarke-Stewart's data and use of cross-lagged panel analysis have been examined in a useful introduction to structural models by Rogosa (in press).

Revising Causal Models

At the grave risk of capitalizing on chance, the structural-equations approach may also be used to reshape and tidy one's initial notion of a causal-relationship network in relation to empirical findings. It may be, for example, that the postulated representation of a causal chain specifies a certain degree of association between variables X and Y.

When the appropriate structural representation is specified and solved, the researcher may find that there is simply no statistical support for the viability of that particular relationship. Such an outcome suggests, from a causal point of view, that the relationship in question can be eliminated from the model. Obviously, such cleaning up or trimming of applications of structural models is useful in the elaboration and refinement of theory, but conclusions reached should be regarded with a healthy skepticism that should be allowed to diminish only in proportion to the amount of additional data consistently supporting the explanation.

Structural Models and Future Developmental Research

The discussion in this chapter has dealt with the very simplest of structural-analysis concepts. We reemphasize that social scientists, especially, have developed very elaborate and complex procedures for estimating structural models (see, for example, Goldberger & Duncan, 1973), whereas, up to the present time, structural models have hardly been used at all in developmental research.

The application of structural models in developmental research has been suggested recently (Jöreskog, in press; Labouvie, 1974; Rogosa, in press; Werts & Linn, 1970), however, and will no doubt be tried as more researchers become familiar with the possibilities and as appropriate data are generated. But, as was emphasized earlier, use of structural models is not a substitute for theory; rather, it is dependent upon a theory about the causal nature of the system, as well as upon measures of the concepts involved (see also Chapter Nineteen for parallels to the strategy of developmental simulation). Thus, close attention must be given to the development and testing of theory if nonexperimental data are to be exploited in the search for explanations of developmental changes. Simply forcing clear and concise specification of possible causal networks so that they can be given mathematical expression may prove to be the great virtue of the structural-models approach. By bringing about a closer relationship between theorizing and data collection and analysis, the structural-models emphasis may help to promote an attitude of more careful scrutiny of diverse sources of data, including the reasoned use of experimental techniques. After all, within a carefully specified causal system the fruits of isolated and narrow but highly internally valid research designs are likely to be even more fully enjoyed.

One thing is sure: developmentalists urgently need to produce theoretical accounts of the nature of developmental change so that explanatory work can be programmatic and explicit. Such theoretical accounts, however, must not only be empirically testable; they must also be subjected to continual empirical scrutiny and must prove to provide a better explanation for natural events than any alternative theories. Given the very real limitations of traditional experimental research, we believe that the formulation and application of structural models represent a potentially useful ally in the quest for explanatory developmental principles, particularly for the study of complex and long-term developmental phenomena. In this sense, this book closes on an optimistic note. We hope that our optimism will help you, the reader, in dealing with the many methodological cautions expressed and with the lacunae identified throughout the book.

Summary

The use of structural models—of which path analysis is a special case—is a set of strategies for explanatory research that, so far, has found little application in developmental psychology but is widely used in economics and sociology. When experimental manipulation of the variables of interest is undesirable, difficult, or impossible, yet the interest is in explanatory research, the methods of path analysis and structural models can sometimes be used. These methods allow one to systematically generate support for causal statements on the basis of data without requiring experimental manipulations of the putative causal variables. Since much of developmental research deals with variables (such as age, cohort) that are not directly manipulable, structural models hold high promise for future explanatory-analytic work in the field.

Structural models require that a theory expressible in mathematical equations (to represent hypothesized relationships among variables) be available before data can be collected and the fit between the theory and the data can be assessed. Predictions from competing theories can also be tested in essentially the same way, and the results can be used as a basis for modifying one or both of the theories.

These research methods have been used only very rarely in developmental research, perhaps because most of the available theories are insufficiently precise to yield quantitative predictions expressible as prediction equations. However, the availability of the methods as substitutes for experimental-manipulative methods might stimulate attempts to develop theories of the required kind. It is argued that future research on the explanation of complex, long-term developmental phenomena may benefit from the inclusion of the structural-model approach in the developmentalist's array of research designs and data-analytic strategies. Structural models may provide the link whereby nonexperimental data can be involved more directly in the effort to specify and construct explanations of developmental change.

References

Ahammer, I. M. Social-learning theory as a framework for the study of adult personality development. In P. B. Baltes & K. W. Schaie (Eds.), *Life-span developmental psychology: Personality and socialization.* New York: Academic Press, 1973.

American Psychological Association (Ed.). *Ethical standards for research with human subjects.* Washington, D. C.: American Psychological Association, 1973. (a)

American Psychological Association (Ed.). *Standards for development and use of educational and psychological tests.* Washington, D. C.: American Psychological Association, 1973. (b)

Amick, D. J., & Walberg, H. J. (Eds.). *Introductory multivariate analysis for educational, psychological and social research.* Berkeley, Calif.: McCutchan, 1975.

Anastasi, A. Heredity, environment, and the question "How?" *Psychological Review*, 1958, *65*, 197–208.

Anastasi, A. *Psychological testing* (3rd ed.). New York: Macmillan, 1968.

Anderson, J. E., & Cohen, J. T. The effect of including incomplete series in the statistical analysis of longitudinal measurements of children's dental arches. *Child Development*, 1939, *10*, 145–149.

Arenberg, D. A longitudinal study of problem solving in adults. *Journal of Gerontology*, 1974, *29*, 650–658.

Baer, D. M. An age-irrelevant concept of development. *Merrill-Palmer Quarterly*, 1970, *16*, 238–245.

Baer, D. M. The control of developmental process: Why wait? In J. R. Nesselroade & H. W. Reese (Eds.), *Life-span developmental psychology: Methodological issues.* New York: Academic Press, 1973.

Baer, D. M., & Sherman, J. A. Behavior modification: Clinical and educational applications. In H. W. Reese & L. P. Lipsitt (Eds.), *Experimental child psychology.* New York: Academic Press, 1970.

Bakwin, H. The secular change in growth and development. *Acta Paediatrica*, 1964, *53*, 79–89.

249

Baldwin, J. M. *Mental development in the child and the race*. New York: Macmillan, 1906.

Baltes, P. B. *Langsschnitt- und Querschnittsequenzen zur Erfassung von Alters- und Generationseffekten*. Unpublished doctoral dissertation, University of Saar, Saarbrücken, 1967. (a)

Baltes, P. B. Sequenzmodelle zum Studium von Altersprozessen: Querschnitt- und Längsschnittsequenzen. In F. Merz (Ed.), *Bericht über den 25. Kongress der Deutschen Gesellschaft für Psychologie in Münster 1966*. Göttingen: Hogrefe, 1967. (b)

Baltes, P. B. Longitudinal and cross-sectional sequences in the study of age and generation effects. *Human Development*, 1968, *11*, 145–171.

Baltes, P. B. Prototypical paradigms and questions in life-span research on development and aging. *Gerontologist*, 1973, *13*, 458–467.

Baltes, P. B., Baltes, M. M., & Reinert, G. The relationship between time of measurement and age in cognitive development of children. *Human Development*, 1970, *13*, 258–268.

Baltes, P. B., & Cornelius, S. W. Some critical observations on dialectics in developmental psychology: Theoretical orientation vs. scientific method. In N. Datan & H. W. Reese (Eds.), *Life-span developmental psychology: Dialectical perspectives on experimental research*. New York: Academic Press, in press.

Baltes, P. B., Cornelius, S. W., & Nesselroade, J. R. Cohort effects in behavioral development: Theoretical and methodological perspectives. In W. A. Collins (Ed.), *Minnesota Symposium on Child Psychology* (Vol. 11). New York: Crowell, in press.

Baltes, P. B., Eyferth, K., & Schaie, K. W. Intra- and intercultural factor structures of social desirability ratings by American and German college students. *Multivariate Behavioral Research*, 1969, *4*, 67–78.

Baltes, P. B., & Goulet, L. R. Status and issues of a life-span developmental psychology. In L. R. Goulet & P. B. Baltes (Eds.), *Life-span developmental psychology: Research and theory*. New York: Academic Press, 1970.

Baltes, P. B., & Goulet, L. R. Exploration of developmental variables by simulation and manipulation of age differences in behavior. *Human Development*, 1971, *14*, 149–170.

Baltes, P. B., & Labouvie, G. V. Adult development of intellectual performance: Description, explanation, modification. In C. Eisdorfer & M. P. Lawton (Eds.), *The psychology of adult development and aging*. Washington, D. C.: American Psychological Association, 1973.

Baltes, P. B., & Nesselroade, J. R. Multivariate longitudinal and cross-sectional sequences for analyzing ontogenetic and generational change: A methodological note. *Developmental Psychology*, 1970, *2*, 163–168.

Baltes, P. B., & Nesselroade, J. R. The developmental analysis of individual differences on multiple measures. In J. R. Nesselroade & H. W. Reese (Eds.), *Life-span developmental psychology: Methodological issues*. New York: Academic Press, 1973.

Baltes, P. B., & Nesselroade, J. R. *A developmentalist's view of regression toward the mean: A largely irrelevant issue in the study of developmental change?* Unpublished manuscript, The Pennsylvania State University, 1976.

Baltes, P. B., Nesselroade, J. R., & Cornelius, S. Multivariate structural change in development and environmental influence patterns. *Multivariate Behavioral Research*, in press.

Baltes, P. B., Nesselroade, J. R., Schaie, K. W., & Labouvie, E. W. On the dilemma of regression effects in examining ability-level-related differentials in ontogenetic patterns of intelligence. *Developmental Psychology*, 1972, *6*, 78–84.

Baltes, P. B., & Reinert, G. Cohort effects in cognitive development of children as revealed by cross-sectional sequences. *Developmental Psychology*, 1969, *1*, 169–177.

Baltes, P. B., & Schaie, K. W. On life-span developmental research paradigms: Retrospects and prospects. In P. B. Baltes & K. W. Schaie (Eds.), *Life-span developmental psychology: Personality and socialization*. New York: Academic Press, 1973.

Baltes, P. B., & Schaie, K. W. On the plasticity of intelligence in adulthood and old age: Where Horn and Donaldson fail. *American Psychologist*, 1976, *31*, 720–725.

Baltes, P. B., Schaie, K. W., & Nardi, A. N. Age and experimental mortality in a seven-year longitudinal study of cognitive behavior. *Developmental Psychology*, 1971, *5*, 18–26.

Baltes, P. B., & Willis, S. L. Toward psychological theories of aging and development. In J. E. Birren & K. W. Schaie (Eds.), *Handbook of the psychology of aging*. New York: Van Nostrand Reinhold, 1977.

Barber, T. X. Hypnotic age regression: A critical review. *Psychosomatic Medicine*, 1962, *24*, 286–299.

Bath, K. E., Daly, D. L., & Nesselroade, J. R. Replicability of factors derived from individual P-technique analyses. *Multivariate Behavioral Research*, 1976, *11*, 147–156.

Bechtoldt, H. P. Construct validity: A critique. *American Psychologist*, 1959, *14*, 619–629.

Becker, W. C. Consequences of different kinds of parental discipline. In M. L. Hoffman & L. W. Hoffman (Eds.), *Review of child development research* (Vol. 1). New York: Russell Sage Foundation, 1964.

Beilin, H. Constructing cognitive operations linguistically. In H. W. Reese (Ed.), *Advances in child development and behavior* (Vol. 11). New York: Academic Press, 1976.

Bell, R. Q. Convergence: An accelerated longitudinal approach. *Child Development*, 1953, *24*, 145–152.

Bell, R. Q. An experimental test of the accelerated longitudinal approach. *Child Development*, 1954, *25*, 281–286.

Bell, R. Q., & Hertz, T. W. Toward more comparability and generalizability of developmental research. *Child Development*, 1976, *47*, 6–13.

Belmont, J. M., & Butterfield, E. C. The relations of short-term memory to development and intelligence. In L. P. Lipsitt & H. W. Reese (Eds.), *Advances in child development and behavior* (Vol. 4). New York: Academic Press, 1969.

Benedict, R. Continuities and discontinuities in cultural conditioning. *Psychiatry*, 1938, *1*, 161–167.

Bengtson, V. L., & Cutler, N. E. Generations and intergenerational relations: Perspectives on age groups and social change. In R. Binstock & E. Shanas (Eds.), *Handbook of aging and the social sciences*. New York: Van Nostrand Reinhold, 1976.

Bentler, P. M. Assessment of developmental factor change at the individual and group level. In J. R. Nesselroade & H. W. Reese (Eds.), *Life-span developmental psychology: Methodological issues*. New York: Academic Press, 1973.

Bereiter, C. Some persisting dilemmas in the measurement of change. In C. W. Harris (Ed.), *Problems in measuring change*. Madison: University of Wisconsin Press, 1963.

Bergmann, G. *Philosophy of science*. Madison: University of Wisconsin Press, 1957.

Bertalanffy, L. von. *General system theory*. New York: George Braziller, 1968.

Bijou, S. W., & Baer, D. M. *Child development: A systematic and empirical theory* (Vol. 1). New York: Appleton-Century-Crofts, 1961.

Birren, J. E. Principles of research on aging. In J. E. Birren (Ed.), *Handbook of aging and the individual*. Chicago: University of Chicago Press, 1959.

Bitterman, M. E. Toward a comparative psychology of learning. *American Psychologist*, 1960, *15*, 704–712.

Blalock, H. M. Aggregation and measurement error. *Social Forces*, 1971, *50*, 151–165.

Blalock, H. M., & Blalock, A. B. (Eds.). *Methodology in social research*. New York: McGraw-Hill, 1968.

Bloom, B. S. *Stability and change in human characteristics*. New York: Wiley, 1964.

Boesch, E. E., & Eckensberger, L. Methodische Probleme des interkulturellen Vergleichs. In C. F. Graumann (Ed.), *Handbuch der Sozialpsychologie*. Göttingen: Hogrefe, 1969.

Bohrnstedt, G. W. *Structural equations and the analysis of change*. Unpublished manuscript, Institute of Social Research, Indiana University, 1975.

Box, G. E. P., & Jenkins, G. M. *Time series analysis forecasting and control*. San Francisco: Holden-Day, 1970.

Brackbill, Y., & Fitzgerald, H. E. Development of the sensory analyzers during infancy. In L. P. Lipsitt & H. W. Reese (Eds.), *Advances in child development and behavior* (Vol. 4). New York: Academic Press, 1969.

Brand, D. H. Games theory, decision processes, and man-machine interaction. In R. B. Cattell (Ed.), *Handbook of multivariate experimental psychology*. Chicago: Rand McNally, 1966.

Braun, P. H. Finding optimal age groups for investigating age-related variables. *Human Development*, 1973, *16*, 293–303.

Bronfenbrenner, U. B. *External validity in the study of human development*. Unpublished manuscript, Department of Human Development and Family Studies, Cornell University, 1976.

Brown, A. L. The development of memory: Knowing, knowing about knowing, and knowing how to know. In H. W. Reese (Ed.), *Advances in child development and behavior* (Vol. 10). New York: Academic Press, 1975.

Bühler, C. *Der menschliche Lebenslauf als psychologisches Problem* (1st ed.). Leipzig: Hirzel, 1933. (2nd ed.) Göttingen: Verlag für Psychologie, 1959.

Bunge, M. *Causality: The place of the causal principle in modern science*. Cleveland: World, 1963.

Buss, A. R. An extension of developmental models that separate ontogenetic changes and cohort differences. *Psychological Bulletin*, 1973, *80*, 466–479.

Buss, A. R. A general developmental model for interindividual differences, intraindividual differences, and intraindividual changes. *Developmental Psychology*, 1974, *10*, 70–78.

Campbell, D. T. Reforms as experiments. *American Psychologist*, 1969, *24*, 409–429.

Campbell, D. T., & Fiske, D. W. Convergent and discriminant validation by the multitrait-multimethod matrix. *Psychological Bulletin*, 1959, *56*, 81–105.

Campbell, D. T., & Stanley, J. C. Experimental and quasi-experimental designs for research on teaching. In N. L. Gage (Ed.), *Handbook for research on teaching*. Chicago: Rand McNally, 1963.

Campbell, D. T., & Stanley, J. C. *Experimental and quasi-experimental designs for research*. Chicago: Rand McNally, 1966.

Carver, R. P. Two dimensions of tests: Psychometric and edumetric. *American Psychologist*, 1974, *29*, 512–518.

Cattell, R. B. *The description and measurement of personality.* New York: World Book, 1946.

Cattell, R. B. *Personality and motivation structure and measurement.* New York: World, 1957.

Cattell, R. B. Validity and reliability: A proposed more basic set of concepts. *Journal of Educational Psychology,* 1964, *55;* 1–22.

Cattell, R. B. (Ed.). *Handbook of multivariate experimental psychology.* Chicago: Rand McNally, 1966.

Cattell, R. B. Separating endogenous, exogenous, ecogenic, and epogenic component curves in developmental data. *Developmental Psychology,* 1970, *3,* 151–162.

Cattell, R. B. Unravelling maturational and learning development by the comparative MAVA and structured learning approaches. In J. R. Nesselroade & H. W. Reese (Eds.), *Life-span developmental psychology: Methodological issues.* New York: Academic Press, 1973.

Child, I. L. Personality in culture. In E. F. Borgatta & W. W. Lambert (Eds.), *Handbook of personality theory and research.* Chicago: Rand McNally, 1968.

Clarke-Stewart, K. A. Interactions between mothers and their young children: Characteristics and consequences. *Monographs of the Society for Research in Child Development,* 1973, *38,* (6–7, Serial No. 153).

Coan, R. W. Basic forms of covariation and concomitance designs. *Psychological Bulletin,* 1961, *25,* 317–324.

Coan, R. W. Child personality and developmental psychology. In R. B. Cattell (Ed.), *Handbook of multivariate experimental psychology.* Chicago: Rand McNally, 1966.

Cook, T. C., & Campbell, D. T. The design and conduct of quasi-experiments and true experiments in field settings. In M. D. Dunnette (Ed.), *Handbook of industrial and organizational research.* Chicago: Rand McNally, 1975.

Corballis, M. C., & Traub, R. E. Longitudinal factor analysis. *Psychometrika,* 1970, *35,* 79–98.

Cronbach, L. J. The two disciplines of scientific psychology. *American Psychologist,* 1957, *12,* 671–684.

Cronbach, L. J. Beyond the two disciplines of scientific psychology. *American Psychologist,* 1975, *30,* 116–127.

Cronbach, L. J., & Furby, L. How should we measure "change"—or should we? *Psychological Bulletin,* 1970, *74,* 68–80.

Cronbach, L. J., Gleser, G. C., Nanda, H., & Rajaratnam, N. *The dependability of behavioral measurements: Theory of generalizability for scores and profiles.* New York: Wiley, 1972.

Cutler, N. E., & Harootyan, R. A. Demography of the aged. In D. S. Woodruff & J. E. Birren (Eds.), *Aging: Scientific perspectives and social issues.* New York: Van Nostrand Reinhold, 1975.

Danish, S. J. Human development and human services: A marriage proposal. In I. Iscoe, B. L. Bloom, & C. D. Spielberger (Eds.), *Community psychology in transition.* New York: Haworth Press, in press.

Datan, N., & Reese, H. W. (Eds.). *Life-span developmental psychology: Dialectical perspectives on experimental research.* New York: Academic Press, in press.

Davies, D. F. Mortality and morbidity statistics. I: Limitations of approaches to rates of aging. *Journal of Gerontology,* 1954, *9,* 186–195.

Dawes, R. M. A note on base rates and psychometric efficiency. *Journal of Consulting Psychology,* 1962, *26,* 422–424.

Denenberg, V. H., Karas, G. G., Rosenberg, F. M., & Schell, S. F. Programming life histories: An experimental design and initial results. *Developmental Psychobiology*, 1968, *1*, 3–9.

Denney, N. Personal communication, July 1975.

Dohrenwend, B. S., & Dohrenwend, B. P. (Eds.). *Stressful life events: Their nature and effects*. New York: Wiley, 1974.

Droege, R. C. Effectiveness of follow-up techniques in large-scale longitudinal research. *Developmental Psychology*, 1971, *5*, 27–31.

Duncan, O. D. *Introduction to structural equation models*. New York: Academic Press, 1975.

Eckensberger, L. H. Methodological issues of cross-cultural research in developmental psychology. In J. R. Nesselroade & H. W. Reese (Eds.), *Life-span developmental psychology: Methodological issues*. New York: Academic Press, 1973.

Eisdorfer, C., Nowlin, J., & Wilkie, F. Improvement of learning in the aged by modification of autonomic nervous system activity. *Science*, 1970, *170*, 1327–1329.

Elder, G. H., Jr. Age differentiation and the life course. *Annual Review of Sociology*, 1975, *1*, 165–190.

Elkind, D. Cognitive development. In H. W. Reese & L. P. Lipsitt (Eds.), *Experimental child psychology*. New York: Academic Press, 1970.

Emmerich, W. Personality development and concepts of structure. *Child Development*, 1968, *39*, 671–690.

Erlenmeyer-Kimling, L., & Jarvik, L. F. Genetics and intelligence: A review. *Science*, 1963, *142*, 1447–1478.

Ervin, S. M. Language and TAT content in bilinguals. *Journal of Abnormal and Social Psychology*, 1964, *68*, 500–507.

Etzel, B. C., LeBlanc, J. M., & Baer, D. M. (Eds.). *New developments in behavioral research*. Hillsdale, N. J.: L. Erlbaum Associates, 1977.

Fahrenberg, J. Aufgaben und Methoden der psychologischen Verlaufsanalyse (Zeit-reihenanalyse). In K. J. Groffmann & K. H. Wewetzer (Eds.), *Person als Prozess*. Bern: Huber, 1968.

Feigl, H. Naturalism *and* humanism. *American Quarterly*, 1949, *1*, 135–148.

Feigl, H. Notes on causality. In H. Feigl & M. Brodbeck (Eds.), *Readings in the philosophy of science*. New York: Appleton-Century-Crofts, 1953.

Feigl, H., & Brodbeck, M. (Eds.). *Readings in the philosophy of science*. New York: Appleton-Century-Crofts, 1953.

Ferguson, G. A. On learning and human ability. *Canadian Journal of Psychology*, 1954, *8*, 95–112.

Ferguson, G. A. On transfer and the abilities of man. *Canadian Journal of Psychology*, 1956, *10*, 121–131.

Fiske, D. W., & Rice, L. Intra-individual response variability. *Psychological Bulletin*, 1955, *52*, 217–250.

Fitzgerald, H. E., & Brackbill, Y. Classical conditioning in infancy: Development and constraints. *Psychological Bulletin*, 1976, *83*, 353–376.

Frederiksen, N. Toward a taxonomy of situations. *American Psychologist*, 1972, *27*, 114–123.

Frijda, N., & Jahoda, G. On the scope and methods of cross-cultural research. *International Journal of Psychology*, 1966, *1*, 109–127.

Furby, L. A theoretical analysis of cross-cultural research in cognitive development: Piaget's conservation task. *Journal of Cross-Cultural Psychology*, 1971, *2*, 241–255.

Furby, L. Interpreting regression toward the mean in developmental research. *Developmental Psychology*, 1973, *8*, 172–179.

Furry, C. A., & Baltes, P. B. The effect of ability-extraneous performance variables on the assessment of intelligence in children, adults, and the elderly. *Journal of Gerontology*, 1973, *28*, 73–80.

Furth, H. G. Piaget, IQ and the nature-nurture controversy. *Human Development*, 1973, *16*, 61–73.

Gagné, R. M. *Essentials of learning for instruction*. Hinsdale, Ill.: Dryden, 1974.

Gesell, A., & Thompson, H. Learning and growth in identical infant twins: An experimental study by the method of co-twin control. *Genetic Psychology Monographs*, 1929, *6*, 1–124.

Glass, G. V., Willson, V. L., & Gottman, J. M. *Design and analysis of time-series experiments*. Boulder, Colo.: Laboratory of Educational Research Report, University of Colorado, 1972.

Goldberger, A. S. Econometrics and psychometrics: A survey of commonalities. *Psychometrika*, 1971, *36*, 83–107.

Goldberger, A. S., & Duncan, O. D. *Structural equation models in the social sciences*. New York: Seminar Press, 1973.

Gottman, J. M., McFall, R. M., & Barnett, J. T. Design and analysis of research using time series. *Psychological Bulletin*, 1969, *72*, 299–306.

Goulet, L. R. Verbal learning in children: Implications for developmental research. *Psychological Bulletin*, 1968, *69*, 359–376.

Goulet, L. R. Training, transfer, and the development of complex behavior. *Human Development*, 1970, *13*, 213–240.

Goulet, L. R. The interfaces of acquisition: Models and methods for studying the active, developing organism. In J. R. Nesselroade & H. W. Reese (Eds.), *Life-span developmental psychology: Methodological issues*. New York: Academic Press, 1973.

Goulet, L. R. Longitudinal and time-lag designs in educational research: An alternative sampling model. *Review of Educational Research*, 1975, *45*, 505–523.

Goulet, L. R., & Baltes, P. B. (Eds.). *Life-span developmental psychology: Research and theory*. New York: Academic Press, 1970.

Goulet, L. R., Hay, C. M., & Barclay, C. R. Sequential analysis and developmental research: Descriptions of cyclical phenomena. *Psychological Bulletin*, 1974, *81*, 517–521.

Gribbons, W. D., Halperin, S., & Lohnes, P. R. Applications of stochastic models in research on career development. *Journal of Counseling Psychology*, 1966, *13*, 403–408.

Gulliksen, H. *Theory of mental tests*. New York: Wiley, 1950.

Hagen, J. W., Jongeward, R. H., & Kail, R. V. Cognitive perspectives on the development of memory. In H. W. Reese (Ed.), *Advances in child development and behavior* (Vol. 10). New York: Academic Press, 1975.

Hall, C. S., & Lindzey, G. *Theories of personality*. New York: Wiley, 1970.

Harris, D. B. (Ed.). *The concept of development*. Minneapolis: University of Minnesota Press, 1957.

Hebb, D. O. A return to Jensen and his social science critics. *American Psychologist*, 1970, *25*, 568.

Hebb, D. O. Whose confusion? *American Psychologist*, 1971, *26*, 736.

Hersen, M., & Barlow, D. H. *Single case experimental designs: Strategies for studying behavior change*. New York: Pergamon Press, 1976.

Hess, E. H., & Petrovich, S. B. The early development of parent-young interaction in nature. In J. R. Nesselroade & H. W. Reese (Eds.), *Life-span developmental psychology: Methodological issues*. New York: Academic Press, 1973.

Hirschman, R., & Katkin, E. S. Psychophysiological functioning, arousal, attention, and learning during the first year of life. In H. W. Reese (Ed.), *Advances in child development and behavior* (Vol. 9). New York: Academic Press, 1974.

Hook, S. *Dialectical materialism and scientific method.* New York: Committee on Science and Freedom, 1957.

Hooper, F. H. Cognitive assessment across the life-span: Methodological implications of the organismic approach. In J. R. Nesselroade & H. W. Reese (Eds.), *Life-span developmental psychology: Methodological issues.* New York: Academic Press, 1973.

Hooper, F. H., Fitzgerald, J., & Papalia, D. Piagetian theory and the aging process: Extensions and speculations. *Aging and Human Development,* 1971, *2,* 3–20.

Horn, J. Organization of data on life-span development of human abilities. In L. R. Goulet & P. B. Baltes (Eds.), *Life-span developmental psychology: Research and theory.* New York: Academic Press, 1970.

Horn, J. L. Human abilities: A review of research and theory in the early 1970's. *Annual Review of Psychology,* 1976, *27,* 437–485.

Hoyer, W. J. Aging as intraindividual change. *Developmental Psychology,* 1974, *10,* 821–826.

Hoyer, W. J., Labouvie, G. V., & Baltes, P. B. Modification of response speed deficits and intellectual performance in the elderly. *Human Development,* 1973, *16,* 233–242.

Hultsch, D. F. Learning to learn in adulthood. *Journal of Gerontology,* 1974, *29,* 302–308.

Hultsch, D. F., & Hickey, T. External validity in the study of human development. Unpublished manuscript, College of Human Development, The Pennsylvania State University, 1976.

Hultsch, D. F., Nesselroade, J. R., & Plemons, J. K. Learning-ability relations in adulthood. *Human Development,* 1976, *19,* 234–247.

Hultsch, D. F., & Plemons, J. K. Life events and life-span development. In P. B. Baltes (Ed.), *Life-span development and behavior* (Vol. 2). New York: Academic Press, in press.

Huston-Stein, A., & Baltes, P. B. Theory and method in life-span developmental psychology: Implications for child development. In H. W. Reese (Ed.), *Advances in child development and behavior* (Vol. 11). New York: Academic Press, 1976.

Hutt, S. J., Lenard, H. G., & Prechtl, H. F. R. Psychophysiological studies in newborn infants. In L. P. Lipsitt & H. W. Reese (Eds.), *Advances in child development and behavior* (Vol. 4). New York: Academic Press, 1969.

Jarvik, L. F. Thoughts on the psychobiology of aging. *American Psychologist,* 1975, *30,* 576–583.

Jarvik, L. F., Blum, J. E., & Varma, A. O. Genetic components and intellectual functioning during senescence: A 20-year study of aging twins. *Behavior Genetics,* 1972, *2,* 159–171.

Jarvik, L. F., & Falek, A. Intellectual stability and survival in the aged. *Journal of Gerontology,* 1963, *18,* 173–176.

Jensen, A. R. How much can we boost IQ and scholastic achievement? *Harvard Educational Review,* 1969, *39,* 1–123.

Jones, H. E. The environment and mental development. In L. Carmichael (Ed.), *Manual of child psychology* (2nd ed.). New York: Wiley, 1954.

Jöreskog, K. G. Statistical estimation of structural models in longitudinal-developmental investigations. In J. R. Nesselroade & P. B. Baltes (Eds.),

Longitudinal research in the behavioral sciences: Design and analysis. New York: Academic Press, in press.

Kagan, J. The three faces of continuity in human development. In D. A. Goslin (Ed.), *Handbook of socialization theory and research.* Chicago: Rand McNally, 1969.

Kagan, J., & Klein, R. E. Cross-cultural perspectives on early development. *American Psychologist*, 1973, *28*, 947–961.

Kagan, J., & Moss, H. A. *Birth to maturity: A study in psychological development.* New York: Wiley, 1962.

Kalish, R. A. *Late adulthood: Perspectives on human development.* Monterey, Calif.: Brooks/Cole, 1975.

Kausler, D. H. Retention-forgetting as a nomological network for developmental research. In L. R. Goulet & P. B. Baltes (Eds.), *Life-span developmental psychology: Research and theory.* New York: Academic Press, 1970.

Kendler, H. H., & Kendler, T. S. Vertical and horizontal processes in problem solving. *Psychological Review*, 1962, *69*, 1–16.

Keniston, K. Psychological development and historical change. *Journal of Interdisciplinary History*, 1971, *2*, 330–345.

Kenny, D. A. Cross-lagged and synchronous common factors in panel data. In A. S. Goldberger & O. D. Duncan (Eds.), *Statistical equation models in the social sciences.* New York: Seminar Press, 1973.

Kerlinger, F. N. *Foundations of behavioral research.* New York: Holt, Rinehart & Winston, 1964.

Kessen, W. Research design in the study of developmental problems. In P. Mussen (Ed.), *Handbook of research methods in child development.* New York: Wiley, 1960.

Kimble, G. A. *Hilgard and Marquis' conditioning and learning* (2nd ed.). New York: Appleton-Century-Crofts, 1961.

Kowalski, C. J., & Guire, K. E. Longitudinal data analysis. *Growth*, 1974, *38*, 131–169.

Krantz, D. H., Luce, R. D., Suppes, P., & Tversky, A. *Foundations of measurement* (Vol. 1). New York: Academic Press, 1971.

Krasnogorski, N. I. [The formation of artificial conditioned reflexes in young children.] *Russkii Vrach*, 1907, *36*, 1245–1246. (Translated and republished in Y. Brackbill & G. G. Thompson (Eds.), *Behavior in infancy and early childhood: A book of readings.* New York: Free Press, 1967.)

Kuhlen, R. G. Age and intelligence: The significance of cultural change in longitudinal vs. cross-sectional findings. *Vita Humana*, 1963, *6*, 113–124.

Kuhn, D. Inducing development experimentally: Comments on a research paradigm. *Developmental Psychology*, 1974, *10*, 590–600.

Kuhn, T. S. *The structure of scientific revolutions.* Chicago: University of Chicago Press, 1962.

Labouvie, E. W. Developmental causal structures of organism-environment interactions. *Human Development*, 1974, *17*, 444–452.

Labouvie, E. W. The dialectical nature of measurement activities in the behavioral sciences. *Human Development*, 1975, *18*, 396–403. (a)

Labouvie, E. W. An extension of developmental models: Reply to Buss. *Psychological Bulletin*, 1975, *82*, 165–169. (b)

Labouvie, E. W., Bartsch, T. W., Nesselroade, J. R., & Baltes, P. B. On the internal and external validity of simple longitudinal designs: Drop-out and retest effects. *Child Development*, 1974, *45*, 282–290.

Labouvie, G. V., Frohring, W., Baltes, P. B., & Goulet, L. R. Changing relationship between recall performance and abilities as a function of stage of learning and timing of recall. *Journal of Educational Psychology*, 1973, *64*, 191–198.

Labouvie-Vief, G. V., Hoyer, W. F., Baltes, M. M., & Baltes, P. B. An operant analysis of intelligence in old age. *Human Development*, 1974, *17*, 259–272.

Lawton, M. P., & Nahemow. L. Ecology and the aging process. In C. Eisdorfer & M. P. Lawton (Eds.), *The psychology of adult development and aging*. Washington, D. C.: American Psychological Association, 1973.

Lerner, R. M. *Concepts and theories of human development*. Reading, Mass.: Addison-Wesley, 1976.

Lerner, R. M., & Ryff, C. D. Implementation of the life-span view of human development: The sample case of attachment. In P. B. Baltes (Ed.), *Life-span development and behavior* (Vol. 1). New York: Academic Press, in press.

Le Vine, R. A. Cross-cultural study in child psychology. In P. H. Mussen (Ed.), *Carmichael's manual of child psychology* (3rd ed.). New York: Wiley, 1970.

Levinson, B., & Reese, H. W. Patterns of discrimination learning set in preschool children, fifth-graders, college freshmen, and the aged. *Monographs of the Society for Research in Child Development*, 1967, *32*(7, Whole No. 115).

Lipsitt, L. P. The experiential origins of human behavior. In L. R. Goulet & P. B. Baltes (Eds.), *Life-span developmental psychology: Research and theory*. New York: Academic Press, 1970.

Lockard, R. B. Reflections on the fall of comparative psychology: Is there a message for us all? *American Psychologist*, 1971, *26*, 168–179.

Lohnes, P. R. Research frontier: Markov models for human development research. *Journal of Counseling Psychology*, 1965, *12*, 322–327.

Longstreth, L. E. *Psychological development of the child*. New York: Ronald Press, 1968.

Looft, W. R. Socialization and personality throughout the life span: An examination of contemporary psychological approaches. In P. B. Baltes & K. W. Schaie (Eds.), *Life-span developmental psychology: Personality and socialization*. New York: Academic Press, 1973.

Lord, F. M. Elementary models for measuring change. In C. W. Harris (Ed.), *Problems in measuring change*. Madison: University of Wisconsin Press, 1963.

Lord, F. M., & Novick, M. R. *Statistical theories of mental test scores*. Reading, Mass.: Addison-Wesley, 1968.

Luborsky, L., & Mintz, J. The contribution of P-technique to personality, psychotherapy and psychosomatic research. In R. M. Dreger (Ed.), *Multivariate personality research: Contributions to the understanding of personality in honor of Raymond B. Cattell*. Baton Rouge, La.: Claitor's Publishing Division, 1972.

Marriott, F. H. C. *The interpretations of multiple observations*. London: Academic Press, 1974.

Mason, K. O., Mason, W. M., Winsborough, H. H., & Poole, W. K. Some methodological issues in cohort analysis of archival data. *American Sociological Review*, 1973, *38*, 242–258.

McCall, R. B. The use of multivariate procedures in developmental psychology. In P. H. Mussen (Ed.), *Carmichael's manual of child psychology* (3rd ed.). New York: Wiley, 1970.

McCandless, B. R., & Spiker, C. C. Experimental research in child psychology. *Child Development*, 1956, *27*. 75–80.

McClearn, G. E. Genetic influences on behavior and development. In P. H. Mussen (Ed.), *Carmichael's manual of child psychology* (3rd ed.). New York: Wiley, 1970.

McFarland, R. A. The sensory and perceptual processes in aging. In K. W. Schaie (Ed.), *Theory and methods of research on aging*. Morgantown: West Virginia University Press, 1968.

McGraw, M. B. Neural maturation as exemplified by the achievement of bladder control. *Journal of Pediatrics*, 1940, *16*, 580–590.

Mead, M. *Coming of age in Samoa*. New York: Morrow, 1928.

Mead, M. *Growing up in New Guinea*. New York: Morrow, 1930.

Meehl, P. E., & Rosen, A. Antecedent probability and the efficiency of psychometric signs, patterns, or cutting scores. *Psychological Bulletin*, 1955, *52*, 194–216.

Meredith, H. V. A descriptive concept of physical development. In D. B. Harris (Ed.), *The concept of development*. Minneapolis: University of Minnesota Press, 1957.

Meredith, H. V. Change in the stature and body weight of North American boys during the last 80 years. In L. P. Lipsitt & C. C. Spiker (Eds.), *Advances in child development and behavior* (Vol. 1). New York: Academic Press, 1963.

Milgram, N. A. Verbal context versus visual compound in paired-associate learning by children. *Journal of Experimental Child Psychology*, 1967, *5*, 597–603.

Mitteness, L. S., & Nesselroade, J. R. *Attachment in adulthood: Factor analytic investigations of mother-daughter affective interdependencies*. Unpublished manuscript, College of Human Development, The Pennsylvania State University, 1976.

Morgan, C. L. An introduction to comparative psychology (Rev. ed.). London: Walter Scott, 1903.

Munn, N. L. *The evolution and growth of human behavior* (2nd ed.). Boston: Houghton Mifflin, 1965.

Murphy, L., & Murphy, G. Perspectives in cross-cultural research. *Journal of Cross-Cultural Psychology*, 1970, *1*, 1–4.

Nagel, E. Determinism and development. In D. B. Harris (Ed.), *The concept of development*. Minneapolis: University of Minnesota Press, 1957.

Nesselroade, J. R. Application of multivariate strategies to problems of measuring and structuring long-term change. In L. R. Goulet & P. B. Baltes (Eds.), *Life-span developmental psychology: Research and theory*. New York: Academic Press, 1970.

Nesselroade, J. R., & Baltes, P. B. Adolescent personality development and historical change: 1970-72. *Monographs of the Society for Research in Child Development*, 1974, *39* (1, Whole No. 154).

Nesselroade, J. R., & Bartsch, T. W. Multivariate experimental perspectives on the construct validity of the trait-state distinction. In R. B. Cattell & R. M. Dreger (Eds.), *Handbook of modern personality theory*. New York: Hemisphere, 1976.

Nesselroade, J. R., & Reese, H. W. (Eds.). *Life-span developmental psychology: Methodological issues*. New York: Academic Press, 1973.

Nesselroade, J. R., Schaie, K. W., & Baltes, P. B. Ontogenetic and generational components of structural and quantitative change in adult behavior. *Journal of Gerontology*, 1972, *27*, 222–228.

Neugarten, B. L., & Datan, N. Sociological perspectives on the life cycle. In P. B. Baltes & K. W. Schaie (Eds.), *Life-span developmental psychology: Personality and socialization*. New York: Academic Press, 1973.

Newman, H. H., Freeman, F. N., & Holzinger, K. J. *Twins: A study of heredity and environment.* Chicago: University of Chicago Press, 1937.

Nunnally, J. C. *Psychometric theory.* New York: McGraw-Hill, 1967.

Nunnally, J. C. *Introduction to psychological measurement.* New York: McGraw-Hill, 1970.

Nunnally, J. C. Research strategies and measurement methods for investigating human development. In J. R. Nesselroade & H. W. Reese (Eds.), *Life-span developmental psychology: Methodological issues.* New York: Academic Press, 1973.

O'Connor, E. F., Jr. Extending classical test theory to the measurement of change. *Review of Educational Research*, 1972, *42*, 73–97.

Overton, W. F. On the assumptive base of the nature-nurture controversy: Additive versus interactive conceptions. *Human Development*, 1973, *16*, 74–89.

Overton, W. F., & Reese, H. W. Models of development: Methodological implications. In J. R. Nesselroade & H. W. Reese (Eds.), *Life-span developmental psychology: Methodological issues.* New York: Academic Press, 1973.

Palermo, D. S., & Howe, H. E. An experimental analogy to the learning of past tense inflection rules. *Journal of Verbal Learning and Verbal Behavior*, 1970, *9*, 410–416.

Parrish, M., Lundy, R. M., & Leibowitz, H. W. Hypnotic age-regression and magnitudes of the Ponzo and Poggendorff illusions. *Science*, 1968, *159*, 1375–1376.

Pastalan, L. A. *The simulation of age related sensory losses: A new approach to the study of environmental barriers.* Unpublished manuscript, Department of Architecture, University of Michigan, 1971.

Pavlov, I. P. [*Conditioned reflexes*] (G. V. Anrep, trans.). London: Oxford University Press, 1927.

Pelz, D. C., & Andrews, F. M. Detecting causal priorities in panel study data. *American Sociological Review*, 1964, *29*, 836–847.

Pepper, S. C. *World hypotheses: A study in evidence.* Berkeley: University of California Press, 1942.

Porges, S. W. Ontogenetic comparisons. *International Journal of Psychology*, in press.

Pressey, S. L., & Kuhlen, R. G. *Psychological development through the life span.* New York: Harper & Row, 1957.

Raser, J. *Simulation and society.* Boston: Allyn & Bacon, 1969.

Reese, H. W. The scope of experimental child psychology. In H. W. Reese & L. P. Lipsitt (Eds.), *Experimental child psychology.* New York: Academic Press, 1970.

Reese, H. W. Life-span models of memory. In P. B. Baltes (Ed.), Life-span models of psychological aging: A white elephant? *Gerontologist*, 1973, *13*, 472–478.

Reese, H. W. The development of memory: Life-span perspectives. In H. W. Reese (Ed.), *Advances in child development and behavior* (Vol. 11). New York: Academic Press, 1976.

Reese, H. W., & Lipsitt, L. P. (Eds.). *Experimental child psychology.* New York: Academic Press, 1970.

Reese, H. W., & Overton, W. F. Models of development and theories of development. In L. R. Goulet & P. B. Baltes (Eds.), *Life-span developmental psychology: Research and theory.* New York: Academic Press, 1970.

Reinert, G. Comparative factor analytic studies of intelligence throughout the human life span. In L. R. Goulet & P. B. Baltes (Eds.), *Life-span developmental psychology: Research and theory.* New York: Academic Press, 1970.

Riegel, K. F. Developmental psychology and society: Some historical and ethical considerations. In J. R. Nesselroade & H. W. Reese (Eds.), *Life-span developmental psychology: Methodological issues.* New York: Academic Press, 1973. (a)

Riegel, K. F. An epitaph for a paradigm: Introduction for a symposium. *Human Development,* 1973, *16,* 1–7. (b)

Riegel, K. F. (Ed.). The development of dialectical operations. *Human Development,* 1975, *18* (No. 1–3).

Riegel, K. F. The dialectics of human development. *American Psychologist,* 1976, *31,* 689–700.

Riegel, K. F. The dialectics of time. In N. Datan & H. W. Reese (Eds.), *Life-span developmental psychology: Dialectical perspectives on experimental research.* New York: Academic Press, in press.

Riegel, K. F., & Riegel, R. M. Development, drop, and death. *Developmental Psychology,* 1972, *6,* 306–319.

Riegel, K. F., Riegel, R. M., & Meyer, G. Sociopsychological factors of aging: A cohort-sequential analysis. *Human Development,* 1967, *10,* 27–56.

Riley, M. W. Aging and cohort succession: Interpretations and misinterpretations. *Public Opinion Quarterly,* 1973, *37,* 35–49.

Riley, M. W. Age strata in social systems. In E. Shanas & R. Binstock (Eds.), *Handbook of aging and the social sciences.* New York: Van Nostrand Reinhold, 1976.

Riley, M. W., Johnson, W., & Foner, A. (Eds.). *Aging and society* (Vol. 3): *A sociology of age stratification.* New York: Russell Sage Foundation, 1972.

Risley, T. R., & Baer, D. M. Operant behavior modification: The deliberate development of behavior. In B. M. Caldwell & H. N. Ricciuti (Eds.), *Review of child development research* (Vol. 3). Chicago: University of Chicago Press, 1973.

Risley, T. R., & Wolf, M. M. Strategies for analyzing behavioral change over time. In J. R. Nesselroade & H. W. Reese (Eds.), *Life-span developmental psychology: Methodological issues.* New York: Academic Press, 1973.

Rogosa, D. Causal models in longitudinal research. In J. R. Nesselroade & P. B. Baltes (Eds.), *Longitudinal research in the behavioral sciences: Design and analysis.* New York: Academic Press, in press.

Rohwer, W. D., Ammon, P. R., & Cramer, P. *Understanding intellectual development: Three approaches to theory and practice.* Hinsdale, Ill.: Dryden Press, 1974.

Rosen, S., Bergman, M., Plester, D., El-Mofty, A., & Satti, M. H. Presbycusis study of a relatively noise-free population in the Sudan. *Annals of Otology, Rhinology and Laryngology,* 1962, *71,* 727–743.

Rosen, S., Plester, D., El-Mofty, A., & Rosen, H. V. High frequency audiometry in presbycusis: A comparative study of the Mabaan tribe in the Sudan with urban populations. *Archives of Otolaryngology,* 1964, *79,* 18–32.

Rozelle, R. M., & Campbell, D. T. More plausible rival hypotheses in the cross-lagged panel correlation technique. *Psychological Bulletin,* 1969, *71,* 74–80.

Russell, B. On the notion of cause, with applications to the free-will problem. In H. Feigl & M. Brodbeck (Eds.), *Readings in the philosophy of science.* New York: Appleton-Century-Crofts, 1953.

Ryan, T. J. Discrete-trial instrumental conditioning in children. In H. W. Reese & L. P. Lipsitt (Eds.), *Experimental child psychology.* New York: Academic Press, 1970.

Ryder, N. B. The cohort as a concept in the study of social change. *American Sociological Review,* 1965, *30,* 843–861.

Sadovsky, V. N. General systems theory: Its tasks and methods of construction. *General Systems*, 1972, *17*, 171–179.

Scarr-Salapatek, S. Unknowns in the IQ equation. *Science*, 1971, *174*, 1223–1228.

Schaie, K. W. Cross-sectional methods in the study of psychological aspects of aging. *Journal of Gerontology*, 1959, *14*, 208–215.

Schaie, K. W A general model for the study of developmental problems. *Psychological Bulletin*, 1965, *64*, 92–107.

Schaie, K. W. Age changes and age differences. *The Gerontologist*, 1967, *7*, 128–132.

Schaie, K. W. A reinterpretation of age-related changes in cognitive structure and functioning. In L. R. Goulet & P. B. Baltes (Eds.), *Life-span developmental psychology: Research and theory*. New York: Academic Press, 1970.

Schaie, K. W. Limitations on the generalizability of growth curves of intelligence: A reanalysis of some data from the Harvard Growth Study. *Human Development*, 1972, *15*, 141–152.

Schaie, K. W. Methodological problems in descriptive developmental research on adulthood and aging. In J. R. Nesselroade & H. W. Reese (Eds.), *Life-span developmental psychology: Methodological issues*. New York: Academic Press, 1973.

Schaie, K. W. Quasi-experimental research designs. In J. E. Birren & K. W. Schaie (Eds.), *Handbook of the psychology of aging*. New York: Van Nostrand Reinhold, 1976.

Schaie, K. W., Anderson, V. E., McClearn, G., & Money, J. (Eds.). *Developmental human behavior genetics: Nature-nurture redefined*. Lexington, Mass.: Heath-Lexington, 1975.

Schaie, K. W., & Baltes, P. B. On sequential strategies in developmental research and the Schaie-Baltes controversy: Description or explanation? *Human Development*, 1975, *18*, 384–390.

Schaie, K. W., Labouvie, G. V., & Buech, B. V. Generational and cohort-specific differences in adult cognitive functioning: A fourteen-year study of independent samples. *Developmental Psychology*, 1973, *9*, 151–166.

Schaie, K. W., & Strother, C. R. A cross-sequential study of age changes in cognitive behavior. *Psychological Bulletin*, 1968, *70*, 671–680. (a)

Schaie, K. W., & Strother, C. R. The effects of time and cohort differences on the interpretation of age changes in cognitive behavior. *Multivariate Behavioral Research*, 1968, *3*, 259–294. (b)

Selltiz, C., Wrightsman, L. W., & Cook, S. W. *Research methods in social relations* (3rd ed.). New York: Holt, Rinehart & Winston, 1976.

Siqueland, E. R. Reinforcement patterns and extinction in human newborns. *Journal of Experimental Child Psychology*, 1968, *6*, 431–442.

Siqueland, E. R. Instrumental conditioning in infants. In H. W. Reese & L. P. Lipsitt (Eds.), *Experimental child psychology*. New York: Academic Press, 1970.

Siqueland, E. R., & Ryan, T. J. Basic learning processes: II. Instrumental conditioning. (Editorial merger of separate contributions by the authors.) In H. W. Reese & L. P. Lipsitt (Eds.), *Experimental child psychology*. New York: Academic Press, 1970.

Sjostrom, K. P., & Pollack, R. H. The effect of simulated receptor aging on two types of visual illusions. *Psychonomic Science*, 1971, *23*, 147–148.

Skinner, B. F. *The behavior of organisms*. New York: Appleton-Century-Crofts, 1938.

Smith, J. E. K. Analysis of qualitative data. *Annual Review of Psychology*, 1976, *27*, 487–499.

Solzhenitsyn, A. I. *The Gulag Archipelago*. New York: Harper & Row, 1973.

Sontag, L. W. The history of longitudinal research: Implications for the future. *Child Development*, 1971, *42*, 987–1002.

Spence, J. T. Learning theory and personality. In J. M. Wepman & R. W. Heine (Eds.), *Concepts of personality*. Chicago: Aldine, 1963.

Spence, K. W. *Behavior theory and conditioning*. New Haven, Conn.: Yale University Press, 1956.

Spilerman, S. The analysis of mobility processes by the introduction of independent variables into a Markov chain. *American Sociological Review*, 1972, *37*, 277–294.

Spilerman, S. Forecasting social events. In K. C. Land & S. Spilerman (Eds.), *Social indicator models*. New York: Russell Sage Foundation, 1975.

Staats, A. *Child learning, intelligence, and personality: Principles of a behavioral interaction approach*. New York: Harper & Row, 1971.

Süssmilch, J. P. *Die göttliche Ordnung in den Veränderungen des menschlichen Geschlechtes, aus der Geburt, dem Tod und der Fortpflanzung desselben erwiesen*. Berlin: Realschulbuchhandlung, 1741.

Sutton-Smith, B. Developmental laws and the experimentalist's ontology. *Merrill-Palmer Quarterly*, 1970, *16*, 253–259.

Tanner, J. M. *Growth at adolescence*. Oxford: Blackwell Publications, 1962.

Thorndike, R. L. Regression fallacies in the matched groups experiment. *Psychometrika*, 1942, *7*, 85–102.

Torgerson, W. J. *Theory and methods of scaling*. New York: Wiley, 1958.

Toulmin, S. *The philosophy of science: An introduction*. London: Hutchinson, 1962.

Tucker, L. R. Learning theory and multivariate experiment: Illustration by determination of generalized learning curves. In R. B. Cattell (Ed.), *Handbook of multivariate experimental psychology*. Chicago: Rand McNally, 1966.

Tucker, L. R., Damarin, F., & Messick, S. A base-free measure of change. *Psychometrika*, 1966, *31*, 457–473.

Underwood, B. J. *Psychological research*. New York: Appleton-Century-Crofts, 1957.

United Nations (Ed.). *World population prospects as assessed in 1968*. (Population Studies, No. 53.) New York: United Nations, Department of Economic and Social Affairs, 1973.

U. S. Bureau of the Census. *Current population reports: Population estimates and projections*. Washington, D. C.: U. S. Government Printing Office, 1970, Series P-25, No. 441.

U. S. Bureau of the Census. *Current population reports: Trends and prospects, 1950–1990*. Washington, D. C.: U. S. Government Printing Office, 1974, Series P-23, No. 49.

U. S. Bureau of the Census. *Current population reports: Projections of the population of the U. S., 1975–2050*. Washington, D. C.: U. S. Government Printing Office, 1975, Series P-25, No. 601.

Urban, H. B. *Issues in human development intervention*. Unpublished manuscript, The Pennsylvania State University, 1975.

Urban, H. B. The concept of development from a systems perspective. In P. B. Baltes (Ed.), *Life-span development and behavior* (Vol. 1). New York: Academic Press, in press.

Vandenberg, S. G. Contributions of twin research to psychology. *Psychological Bulletin*, 1966, *66*, 327–352.

Vernon, P. E. Practice and coaching effects in intelligence tests. *Educational Forum*, 1954, *18*, 269–280.

Waring, J. M. Social replenishment and social change: The problem of disordered cohort flow. *American Behavioral Scientist*, 1975, *19*, 237–256.

Webb, E. J., Campbell, D. T., Schwartz, R. D., & Sechrest, L. *Unobtrusive measures*. Chicago: Rand McNally, 1966.

Weber, M. Die "Objektivität" sozialwissenschaftlicher und sozialpolitischer Erkenntnis. In M. Weber (Ed.), *Methodologische Schriften*. Frankfurt, West Germany: Fischer, 1968.

Werner, H. *Einführung in die Entwicklungspsychologie*. Leipzig: Barth, 1926.

Werner, H. Process and achievement—A basic problem of education and developmental psychology. *Harvard Educational Review*, 1937, *7*, 353–368.

Werner, H. *Comparative psychology of mental development*. New York: International Universities Press, 1948.

Werner, H. The concept of development from a comparative and organismic point of view. In D. B. Harris (Ed.), *The concept of development*. Minneapolis: University of Minnesota Press, 1957.

Werts, C. E., & Linn, R. L. Path analysis: Psychological examples. *Psychological Bulletin*, 1970, *74*, 193–222.

Westoff, C. F. The populations of the developed countries. *Scientific American*, 1974, *231*, 109–120.

Wheeler, L. R. A comparative study of the intelligence of East Tennessee mountain children. *Journal of Educational Psychology*, 1942, *33*, 321–334.

Whelpton, P. K. *Cohort fertility: Native white women in the United States*. Princeton, N. J.: Princeton University Press, 1954.

Whimbey, A. E., & Denenberg, V. H. Experimental programming of life histories: The factor structure underlying experimentally created individual differences. *Behaviour*, 1967, *28*, 296–314.

White, S. H. Evidence for a hierarchical arrangement of learning processes. In L. P. Lipsitt & C. C. Spiker (Eds.), *Advances in child development and behavior* (Vol. 2). New York: Academic Press, 1965.

Windle, C. Test-retest effect on personality questionnaires. *Educational and Psychological Measurement*, 1954, *14*, 617–633.

Wohlwill, J. F. The age variable in psychological research. *Psychological Review*, 1970, *77*, 49–64. (a)

Wohlwill, J. F. Methodology and research strategy in the study of developmental change. In L. R. Goulet & P. B. Baltes (Eds.), *Life-span developmental psychology: Research and theory*. New York: Academic Press, 1970. (b)

Wohlwill, J. F. *The study of behavioral development*. New York: Academic Press, 1973.

Woodruff, D. S., & Birren, J. E. Age changes and cohort differences in personality. *Developmental Psychology*, 1972, *6*, 252–259.

Wozniak, R. H. Dialecticism and structuralism: The philosophical foundations of Soviet psychology and Piagetian cognitive developmental theory. In K. F. Riegel & G. Rosenwald (Eds.), *Structure and transformation: Developmental aspects*. New York: Wiley, 1975.

Wright, S. Correlation and causation. *Journal of Agricultural Research*, 1921, *20*, 557–585.

Wright, S. The method of path coefficients. *Annals of Mathematical Statistics*, 1934, *5*, 161–215.

Wundt, W. *Probleme der Völkerpsychologie.* Leipzig: Wiegandt, 1911.

Yerkes, R. M. Comparative psychology: A question of definitions. *Journal of Philosophy, Psychology, and Scientific Methods*, 1913, *10*, 580–582.

Zeaman, D., & House, B. J. The role of attention in retardate discrimination learning. In N. R. Ellis (Ed.), *Handbook of mental deficiency.* New York: McGraw-Hill, 1963.

Name Index

Subject Index